THE MIDRANGE THEORY

Basketball's Evolution in the Age of Analytics

Seth Partnow

TRIUMPH
BOOKS

To the searchers.
You know it's about the journey.

First Triumph Books paperback edition 2022

The Library of Congress has catalogued the previous edition as follows:

Names: Partnow, Seth, author.
Title: The midrange theory : basketball's evolution in the age of analytics
  / Seth Partnow ; [foreword by Tim Bontemps].
Description: Chicago, Illinois : Triumph Books LLC, [2021] | Summary: "From
  one of basketball's foremost experts in the field of analytics, a
  fascinating new perspective on how to watch and think about the game"—
  Provided by publisher.
Identifiers: LCCN 2021045271 (print) | LCCN 2021045272 (ebook) | ISBN
  9781629379210 (Hardcover) | ISBN 9781641256971 (ePub) | ISBN
  9781641256988 (mobi) | ISBN 9781641256995 (PDF)
Subjects: LCSH: Basketball—Statistics. | Basketball—Statistical methods.
  | Quantitative research.
Classification: LCC GV885.55 .P37 2021 (print) | LCC GV885.55 (ebook) |
  DDC 796.323002/1—dc23/eng/20211106
LC record available at https://lccn.loc.gov/2021045271
LC ebook record available at https://lccn.loc.gov/2021045272

This book is available in quantity at special discounts for your group or organization. For further information, contact:
  Triumph Books LLC
  814 North Franklin Street
  Chicago, Illinois 60610
  (312) 337-0747
  www.triumphbooks.com

Printed in U.S.A.
ISBN: 978-1-63727-096-7
Design by Patricia Frey

Contents

Foreword

The moment I realized how much the influx of data had changed the game of basketball didn't come in an NBA arena, or even a college one.

Instead, it happened in the Randolph Central School gymnasium in January 2020.

I was back in my hometown of Randolph, New York, to watch my high school team play on a rare off night during the NBA season (it helped that I had to be in Toronto, about three hours north, for a game the following evening). As the game began and the teams started going up and down the court, my jaw hit the floor.

Why? Because, in this high school gym in the middle of nowhere, I saw my high school coach running the same offense I generally see teams run in the NBA on a nightly basis. Two players would sprint the court and run to the corners, from where they would not move. Two more would be at the top of the key and would alternate running pick-and-rolls with the team's center.

Whether the starters or backups were in the game, the offense was the same. There were two shot-clock violations on the night, because kids panicked and tried to dribble back to the three-point line rather than shoot a midrange jumper before the shot clock expired.

When I was in high school, playing for the same coach, not only would I have not been encouraged to shoot a three-pointer, I would've been instantly benched if I'd tried.

That night, though, crystallized for me what I already knew: thanks to the influx of data into basketball, the sport had irrevocably changed.

My time covering the sport at the NBA level over the past decade had already shown me how things had changed at its highest level.

Ironically, when I first started covering the NBA, in the summer of 2011, there was no actual basketball to write about. Instead, I spent the first several months of my time covering The Association waiting in various hotel ballrooms, and standing on various sidewalks outside of said hotels, around New York City during the summer and fall of that year, as the NBA and the National Basketball Players Association went through a lockout before, ultimately, agreeing to a new labor deal at about 5:00 AM on the Saturday of Thanksgiving weekend.

Less than a month later, the 2011–12 season began on Christmas Day, a 66-game sprint of a regular season that featured teams playing back-to-back-to-back sets of games, five games in six days, and generally running everyone—including the people like me trying to cover it—into the ground to finish the season on time.

Looking back on it now, just 10 years later, it's incomprehensible that those things happened. Can you imagine how such a season would play out in today's environment? If your answer was you can't, you'd be right—because it wouldn't. And, frankly, it shouldn't. Thanks to advancements in injury management and prevention, both teams and players would never sign up for enduring such an endeavor.

That is just one small way that, in the 10 years I have lived and breathed this business, the use of data has changed the way the game is played. There are countless others. For example, when I first began covering the league, writing about the Brooklyn Nets for the *New York Post* (the only sports section anyone should read in The World's Greatest City, I will add), no one used offensive and defensive ratings in stories. Instead, everyone used points per game to measure how teams did on offense and defense.

I can actually remember the first time I started using offensive and defensive ratings to describe how the Nets were playing in games. At first, I got a little pushback from my editors. But once I explained what I was doing, and why it was important, they relented. Now, just a handful of years later, it's basically impossible to find anyone talking about gauging teams offensively and defensively in a way *other* than offensive and defensive rating.

The point in retelling these stories about my life and career, aside from making myself feel old, is to show that, beyond the way it has impacted how teams view the sport, the rise of data and "analytics" in basketball has had a profound impact on how the conversation around the sport has grown and evolved over the past decade.

And I'm here to tell you: that's a great thing!

For a basketball fan today, there has never been more information available at your fingertips to learn about your favorite players and teams, and there has never been more great content to consume—be it in written, audio, or televised form—about what makes the league, its teams, and its players tick. All of that is possible, in part, because we have more ways to measure what is happening on the court—and off of it—than we ever have before.

And, as you begin this book, you're about to get a front row seat to as good of a description of not only how that evolution has taken place, but also why it matters, as one could possibly hope for.

It is that second part—why it matters—that often gets lost when any discussion of "analytics" comes up. I'm not a fan of that word and how it is used, though I fall victim to using it as shorthand as much as anyone else in my world does. The reason it bothers me is because it is used to dismiss a conversation that, if that word never came up, would likely sound basically the same as it would if it did.

One of the joys of this job is getting the chance to talk about basketball with some of the legends who have been around it for generations. That goes for players, like Jerry West and Walt Frazier, and journalists, like Bob Ryan, Peter Vecsey, and Michael Wilbon. All of them have been playing and watching this sport for longer than I've been alive. All of them have a wealth of knowledge about the game.

And all of them, in the right moment, might scoff at the influx of data into the sport.

But ask any of them about the things that matter when it comes to winning basketball games, and they're going to say the same things: spacing and sharing the ball on offense; teamwork and connectivity on defense. Making your offense work until it gets a quality, open shot, and using your defense to make their offense take contested, difficult ones.

These are universal axioms—and aren't things that data, or "analytics," would argue with. Instead, all that analytics is, at its core, is a way to show how the things that people have been searching for in players and teams for decades can be distilled into statistics.

That is what made, for me, reading the book you're about to dive into so enjoyable. The beauty of Seth's work in putting this project together is that each chapter is its own story—all used to explain, in totality, both the impact of data science on the sport of basketball and how those using it in the sport go about their day-to-day lives.

In that way, it's a book that anyone—be it my uncle in his late 50s who is a casual sports fan, or someone in college hoping to follow in Seth's footsteps and work for a team in its analytics department—can enjoy. The trick is in the examples he uses to explain what he's doing (none of which I will spoil now; otherwise, what would be the point in going any further?).

It's also a conversation that I wish we could have on a wider scale. As I said, over the past decade there's been a flood of information into the sport that we all are only beginning to understand. And while teams are way ahead of the general public in that regard, it's still amazing to me how quickly many of these things have been adopted.

Still, I do at times worry that those changes are turning off a number of fans that otherwise would want to embrace today's NBA, with its free-flowing offenses and featuring fantastic talents from all across the globe. The frustrating part for me is that those fans are being turned off not because of data coming into the sport, but because of the perception of what that data coming into the sport is doing to it.

As you'll read in this book, however, all the data is doing is augmenting the conversations that were already going on across the sport. The greatest coaches of yesteryear—men like Red Auerbach and Dean Smith—were looking decades ago at things in similar ways we are now. It's only recently that the rest of the basketball world caught up with them.

We're doing the same thing now with how we talk about the game. Again, think back to where the discourse around the sport was 10 years ago, when I first began covering it, and how much it has changed. Imagine how different it will be a decade from now?

That, to me, is exciting. As someone who eats, sleeps, and lives basketball the vast majority of my waking moments (to the dismay of my beautiful and lovely wife), data has given me another way to tell stories about what is happening, and to find ways to describe what is happening, and what is about to happen.

Take the 2021 NBA Finals, for example, which I'm covering as I write this. In Game 1, the Phoenix Suns took 26 free throws, and the Milwaukee Bucks only took 16. Given the Suns were the team with the lowest free-throw attempt rate in the playoffs, and the second lowest in the NBA this season, it was unlikely that trend would continue as the series progressed.

(Narrator: It did not.)

That doesn't mean stories using data are the only ones anyone wants to read. It doesn't replace the ability to talk to the players and coaches who step onto that court every night about what happened, and why it happened, and what makes them get out of bed and do their job every morning.

But what it does do is give me another way to explain to fans how and why things are happening—or, through a different lens, how and why a team should do something differently moving forward.

Just as it is for teams, it is another tool in my toolbox to help me do my job to the best of my abilities. It isn't replacing anything; it's augmenting *everything*.

And that, too often, is the part of the conversation that gets lost.

Here's the other part: just because there's data doesn't mean it only tells one story.

As Seth and I have gotten to know each other over the past several years, we have agreed on many things. Just as often, however, we have disagreed on things (including some of the topics touched upon in this book). And that's okay! In fact, it's better than okay. It's exactly how things are supposed to be.

I believe there is a mistaken belief that the data revolution in basketball has led to everyone thinking about things in the exact same way. That is most certainly not the case. While, yes, shooting more threes and fewer midrange shots is a pretty universally held truism at this point, there are still endless arguments about all sorts of different parts of the game, and the players and teams that play it.

And it's those arguments that are both the lifeblood of what I do, and what makes it so fun to follow the sport. Data just gives us another thing to argue about.

Ultimately, the influx of data into basketball has helped the sport in so many more ways than some believe it may have hurt it. And while things may not be perfect—for example, I'm now ready to shoot the whole concept of replay review to Jupiter and never look back—basketball is in as good a place as it has ever been.

You can now spend the next 300 pages or so reading why that is the case.

Tim Bontemps is an NBA writer at ESPN. He previously covered the league for The Washington Post *and the* New York Post. *Follow him on Twitter* @TimBontemps.

Introduction

Perhaps the greatest frustration in writing a book like this is that at any reasonable length, the discussion is still incomplete. I've had to pick and choose what to talk about, and so over the course of the pages that follow, I've focused almost completely on what might be called the Fantasy GM aspects of basketball analytics. Evaluating and picking players. Assessing game strategy. Observing trends.

But that focus shouldn't be taken as an argument that those are the *only* things. They are just the areas I'm most competent to talk about which also happen to string together to reach book length. But I would be remiss to not at least touch on two others before we start.

I didn't come to love basketball because of an elegant player value model or the lure of the game's statistical record. It was the speed, power, intensity, and artistry. And I do worry that inundation of the game with numbers and theorems might take away from that experience. I don't think the game is close to being *solved*. However, even if it is not, the perception of a solution could serve to remove the mystery and suspense. Everything could become, in a word, boring.

Basketball, at least at the level of production value which makes all of my fancy data feeds possible, is showbiz. As such, aesthetics isn't just a thing, it is ultimately *the* thing. If millions of people no longer enjoy watching the games, there are no more games, at least not at this scale. Taking seriously complaints that fans don't find the "analytically indicated" style pleasing isn't just being neighborly, it's imperative.

If we accept at face value the complaint that there was something from the early 2000s version of the game people are longing for, it behooves those working in and around the game to examine that complaint and see if there exists a problem worth fixing. If the issue is as simple as some fans missing the post-up game, I'm not sure there is much to be done. As I'll describe in detail later, the conditions which produced that style are gone and are not coming back.

According to Evan Wasch, the NBA's Executive Vice President of Basketball Strategy & Analytics, the league's extensive research on the subject found that "fans love fast breaks and dunks and plays at the basket and long three-point shots. They don't particularly like slow-down, grind-it-out action." Unfortunately for lovers of the back-to-the-basket game, the environment needed to bring that back as a central part of the game isn't something most consumers seem to want.

While I've done my best to explain the development of the modern style of play from a statistical standpoint, and how the history, rules, and strategic imperatives have shaped where we are today, I didn't spend much time trying to prove why the game is "better" today than it was then. From a narrowly technocratic standpoint, proving the median team in 2021 would boatrace all but the best teams from the golden years of the early '90s is trivial. But that's using the wrong definition of "better." The competitive aspects are only relevant insofar as they service the aesthetic and entertainment aspects.

As baseball struggles with sustaining fan interest in a "three true outcomes" environment, we have to acknowledge there is no particular reason why a more competitively advantageous strategy necessarily coincides with a better viewing experience.

This isn't a new concern. Stalling tactics such as the "four corners" offense did serve to increase the likelihood that a heavy underdog might win a game. In statistical terms, it is easier to defy the odds for 20 possessions than it would be for 100. But watching a team hold the ball and run dribble weaves out near half court for minutes on end *sucked*. On aggregate, it sucked more than the occasional huge upset was cool. So, a shot clock was instituted, dramatically limiting the degree to which a team can slow down the pace of a game.

Which is how it should work. If the strategic equilibrium of the game is in a bad place from the standpoint of fan enjoyment, the proper response isn't finger (and chin) wagging about the purity of the game, it's to change the rules. Give teams and players the proper incentives to do better, more entertaining things.

There is no magic formula here. It's a hard call, or series of hard calls as to how to best steward the game through a minefield of changing viewership and consumption habits, a rapidly shifting media landscape, and an increasingly empowered and assertive[1] player group. Detailed study of data might inform those choices, but the issues are too complex to be reached in "perfectly objective" fashion.

Speaking of difficulties, what of ethics? Not just in terms of the medical ethics of wearable technologies or detailed scanning techniques. Viewing the participants of a sport from afar tends to turn them into two-dimensional caricatures. Tracking data, the most recent large-scale advance in statistical analysis of the sport, literally collapses them even further, down to the level of moving dots on a screen.

Some degree of commodification is inescapable. In a competition between two parties, only one can win. At least in that confrontation, whether a single possession or an NBA Finals series, one belligerent is proven superior to the other. Against that backdrop, how could we not compare and seek to know who is better and who is best? But there are limits, and while we try not to think about it too much, there is more than a vague unease which arises from discussing players as "assets."

No small part of this discomfort comes from the obvious differences in demographics between who is doing the valuing and who is being valued. As of this writing, only one of 30 NBA teams has a Black head of analytics, at least on a day-to-day basis. As of mid-2020, full-time analytics professionals in the NBA were around 75% Caucasian and over 90% male. Much

---

1. And I mean this in the most positive way. In any industry, nobody cares more about your career or life away from it than you do yourself, so I applaud the players for taking control as equal partners in the endeavor.

of this imbalance reflects the similar dynamics within the upper levels of STEM education in the U.S. But that is an insufficient explanation.

It is frequently argued that the field of analytics represents yet another conduit for the traditional haves to take a greater stake in the game at the expense of the have-nots. The rise of the value of statistical thinking—some might say management consultant techniques—has largely outpaced the ability of those within front office career tracks to adapt. The addition of this new requirement serves to disadvantage the so-called basketball lifer, and in particular the ex-player.

Anyone who has experienced that most diabolical of board games *Chutes and Ladders* will know the feeling of unfairness whereby landing on the wrong space returns a player to square one as others race ahead. So, you can empathize with those who feel they have been skipped over by an unlucky roll of the die.

From my perspective, the facts don't support the charge that analytics has *caused* the dynamic mentioned above. Both things are happening, but the number of true "metrics guys"[2] in the upper echelons of decision-making for NBA teams is comfortably in single digits.

However, winning the point is largely irrelevant; as long as the demographics of the field are what they are today, it doesn't matter. If a discipline which is supposed to be about unlocking secrets and broadening understanding is instead seen as exclusionary, there is much work to be done.

While balancing fairness and inclusivity is a challenge as the world becomes inexorably more data driven, nowhere is this more vital than in sports. An endeavor meant to spread joy and bring communities together can't lose sight of those things even as the methods of competition change.

It is not merely a question of fairness or equity, though both are worthy enough goals on their own. A narrowly drawn field is not as *effective* as it could be. If the training and background of the discipline is homogenized, so largely are the ranges of experience and strengths, but also critically the gaps and weaknesses. If we all know the same things, we also *don't* know

---

2. And at that level it remains overwhelmingly bordering on exclusively guys. Still.

the same things. Worse, we don't know what we don't know. A range of perspectives can provide protection against at least a portion of the lapses.

In the end the questions of equity and effectiveness are hopelessly intertwined anyway. Analytics is at heart about asking the right questions. The focus on fighting only the most extremely straw-manned descriptions of what the discipline is or how it works keeps us from having the needed conversations. Stupid analytics arguments make for stupid arguers.

These discussions are not just about how best to compete, but how the game should look. Without trust that everyone involved ultimately does in fact want what's best, these talks simply won't be productive. Building that trust in an environment of suspicion and opposition is unlikely at best.

I hope it is not too self-aggrandizing a note to end on to offer my contribution as a way to help dispel some of that suspicion insofar as it arises from misperception and misunderstanding. On a multisport panel at the 2018 Sloan Sports Analytics Conference, longtime researcher Voros McCracken said, "My job is not statistics or technology or analytics. My job is baseball."

If I've done one thing successfully over the ensuing pages, I would like to think I've shown that all of this is just basketball. That's all it is, so let's talk some hoops, and we'll all learn something new.

An Introductory Note on Data and Context

If there is "one rule to rule them all" in sports analytics, it is that context is everything. I'm told that one of the largest challenges in writing a "current" sports book is that sports keep happening, meaning by the time you have read this, it will already be somewhat outdated. In the world of 2020 and 2021, these factors combine to present both a difficulty and a solution.

The context in which the 2020–21 basketball season was played was completely unique. While every season is different, even without all the off-court considerations imposed by the COVID-19 pandemic, 2020–21 was *different*. Whereas some of the changes will probably turn out to be part of the normal strategic and technical evolution of the game, others will end up being products of the environment or even the sorts of statistical artifact which emerge within any large collection of data.

All of which is to say, I expect the play on the floor in the 2021–22 season to look more like the 2019-to-March-2020 version of the NBA than the 2020–21 version. In fact, the season itself could easily resemble 2018–19 more than the subsequent two. For this reason, I am relying most heavily on 2018–19 as the most recent "full" season for purposes of many of the demonstrations and analysis herein.

This is certainly a convenient position to take for the purposes of writing this book; it's easier to not worry about being overtaken by events if I have already decided that those events are sui generis.

Nor should this be taken as an argument that anything which occurred in the 2020 bubble or throughout the 2020–21 season somehow does not count. We're just not far enough past the events to know *how* they should be compared to everything which has come before.

I can't promise there will be no math and an absence of equations. But the equations will be nothing more complicated than multiplication or division, and the higher-level math or statistics will be described rather than performed. For the consumer of analytics information, the technique employed only matters insofar as it can help inform on what a metric or conclusion *isn't* capturing and *can't* tell us.

The entire purpose of these techniques is to simplify. As Rajiv Maheswaran, CEO of Second Spectrum, recounts in Chapter 2, all of the machine learning and algorithmic processing employed in the study of player and ball tracking data is not done to produce numbers. Rather the goal is a distillation of basketball concepts from what can at first glance appear to be a jumble of data.

My hope is that this book is the same. There is some statistics and some math. I would have to hand in my analytics union card if there were not plenty of charts and graphs. But in the end, it's just basketball.

Chapter 1

What Basketball Analytics Is Not

"There is a way of being wrong which
is also sometimes necessarily right."
—**Author and environmentalist Edward Abbey**

This is a book about analytics. I hate analytics.

Not the discipline mind you, but the word. The word has become hopelessly poisoned, reduced, confused, and misapplied. But we're stuck with the word so we might as well define it properly. Before we do so, there are plenty of misconceptions to cast aside. So, here is what *won't* be in this book: one neat trick to solve basketball.

Basketball analytics is often portrayed as a realm of hubris, unearned certitude, and disrespect for knowledge gleaned without the aid of a calculator. Of trying to reduce the game's artistry to spreadsheets and graphs. I have to admit, these charges aren't made from whole cloth; it is not difficult to find real world examples of each. But those missteps are not "analytics," they are "analytics done poorly." No true Scotsman[1] could think otherwise.

---

1. More technically known as an appeal to purity, the "No True Scotsman" fallacy is the attempt to insulate a group from criticism based on the actions of a member of the group by asserting that no one who would do such a thing could be a member. No *real* analyst would ever speak dismissively and with outsized assuredness about the understanding of the less technically advanced. It sucks to discover there are in fact no *real* analysts around.

1

Done well, analytics is the realm of constant curiosity. The hard-won expertise of experienced professionals is vital to the process, even if the lessons drawn from that expertise are occasionally challenged. While many techniques do require some flattening of events for easier calculation and comparison, this is not the aim unto itself, rather in service of creating a deeper and more nuanced understanding and even aesthetic appreciation of the game.

Analytics exist at the intersections of math, statistics, and computer science. However, those are merely the tools rather than the field itself. They might even be the primary tools as applied to basketball and other sports. However, the tools aren't the thing. Rather, it is a mode of thought seeking to reduce the impact of the cognitive biases we all suffer from. In a world wrought with imperfect information and uncertain outcomes, it is about putting oneself in a position to be less wrong. Or if you're an optimist, to be correct more often than the competition, and by doing so winning big.

For as much backward-revised narrative as there can be describing why certain drafted players "make it" and others bust, we're talking about the degree to which you can know what an 18-year-old will be when he's 24. Such projection is incredibly difficult and inexact. On players, you do the best you can, make the pick, and take your chances. These wagers can have better or worse odds of success, but the lens of hindsight won't always help separate out good bets from wild-assed gambles that happened to come in.

Anyone who has been buffeted by the winds of macroeconomic trends in their first job out of college[2] understands the degree to which things are often out of one's control. My own first job was at an e-commerce startup, which basically failed around 18 months after I joined. Could I have done more to prevent this? Sure, but I don't think slightly better merchandising choices by a 23-year-old business analyst was the difference between riches and ruins. For me, it was wrong place, wrong time.

And so it is with young players. Some will become long-term NBA stalwarts, a few even All-Stars and MVPs. Most won't.

---

2. Which is to say, all of us who entered the job market upon graduation.

Sometimes these outcomes were easily predictable. For others, the invisible forces of the basketball universe aligned against them. They ended up with the wrong team, the wrong coach, in the wrong city. Picked the wrong agent or business manager. The wrong trainer. Got injured. Got sick. Developed the wrong skills for the direction in which the league or his team was moving. Sometimes, shit happens even to the most "can't miss" of prospects. Greg Oden was in parts unlucky and doomed by his own physiology[3] even though when he was able to be on the court, he was every bit as dominant as the evaluation which had him as the consensus top pick over Kevin Durant would have suggested.

Even for established players changing teams, fit can vary from perfect to abysmal. When I was in the Milwaukee Bucks front office, we signed Brook Lopez to a one-year deal for the biannual exception. As the name implies, this "BAE" provides a mechanism, usable once every two seasons, for a team to exceed the amount otherwise allowed by the salary cap[4] to sign a player.

Sounds impressive, but the BAE is the second-smallest exception available under the league's collective bargaining agreement. It allows for a player to be paid an amount for which you are happy to find a decent seventh or eighth man. Not a starter and certainly not a high-impact player.

It was a good get for us. We upgraded our center position without having to give up any long-term assets or trade chips.

By reputation, Lopez had been an excellent scorer but mediocre defender for much of his career. As he hit free agency in the summer of 2018, he had become known as much for the bloated contract that had just run out as for his play on the floor. That previous deal, signed just before the "traditional" center was hit by the asteroid that was the Golden State Warriors, made him appear to be an overpaid dinosaur rather than a difference-making acquisition.

---

3. It was discovered at some point early in Oden's NBA career that one leg was significantly longer than the other, an imbalance which could have contributed to the string of lower-body injuries which wrecked the career of perhaps the best defensive prospect since Tim Duncan.

4. Without at least a solid understanding of the NBA's complex salary cap system, a solid chunk—perhaps even a majority—of the personnel moves which occur are all but incomprehensible. In Chapter 7, we'll explicitly look at how "The Cap" influences the manner in which teams are put together.

Signing Lopez was a low-cost, reasonable-upside play, addressing what had been a weakness[5] by adding a proven player who had developed the three-point shooting desired for the offensive system we wanted to play.

Brook immediately became the linchpin of the defense which graded as the best in the league for the next two years.[6] He had the perfect combination of size, surprising agility, thorough understanding of the NBA's illegal defense rules, and willingness to get physical in rebounding battles that we needed.

So did we make a brilliant signing of a player the rest of the league dramatically undervalued, or did we just get lucky? In short, both.

I would imagine the overlap between people reading this and those who are passingly familiar with the work of behavioral economists such as Daniel Kahneman and Amos Tversky to be considerable.[7] That in mind, I'm not going to go through the proofs of all the ways in which our minds routinely trick us into short-circuiting rational decision-making.[8] Suffice it to say that our brains are bad at avoiding those traps absent attentive care and feeding.

Meanwhile concepts like probabilistic thinking and understanding the practical implications of variance and expectation are incredibly useful for comprehending what's going on in basketball.

I'll get back to this later, but "useful for comprehending" is not "necessary for enjoying" or even "required for understanding." Over a lifetime spent in basketball, people who can't distinguish a linear regression from retrograde motion have experienced and observed enough things enough times, have gotten the reps,[9] to have developed pretty sharp opinions ("heuristics" to be slightly technical about it) about what works and what doesn't.

---

5. None of the centers who appeared for the 2017–18 Bucks were even on an NBA roster by the start of Lopez's third year with the team in 2020 despite all of them being 30 years old or younger.

6. Not to mention that Lopez was a key cog for the Bucks as they won the 2021 NBA title.

7. For those unfamiliar with the work of the pair, Kahneman's *Thinking Fast and Slow* is one of the seminal works in the area, but Michael Lewis' *The Undoing Project* is a more accessible accounting of both their findings and how they came to reach their theories and conclusions.

8. At least not until we get to Chapter 13 on the NBA draft.

9. "Reps" have become something of a cliché in sports, but the importance of sufficient, regular, *quality* reps in any aspect of basketball, whether player evaluation or jump shot form, cannot be overstated.

Similarly, is "understanding" a requirement for enjoyment from the standpoint of fandom? For me it is, but that's my individual taste.

If it were up to me there would be no in-arena music or sound effects during live play, we'd be using the Elam Ending,[10] and for god's sake there would be no fucking T-shirt cannons.

But NBA teams are reasonably efficient profit-maximizing engines, and they pump up the jams and develop larger and larger gatling-gun-style apparel distribution machines. We have to assume *somebody* likes those things enough that it affects their decision to attend games and spend money.

And that's fine.

Just like it's fine to not really care about the hows or whys of defending a spread pick-and-roll attack, worry over definitions and measurements of shot quality, or care about the intricacies of predraft modeling and projection of college players. There is nothing at all wrong with preferring to take in the spectacle and leave it at that. I'm just not wired that way.

I have always wanted to take things apart and see which buttons are pushed to reach specific outcomes. What happens if you pull on this string and not that one? And the more you do this with basketball, the more you come to realize shit happens. Not necessarily negative shit. All kinds of shit. The full range of shit that could happen probably has happened before and done so many times. The trick is figuring out which shit happens most often and using that shit to your advantage.

There is a large degree of randomness inherent in sports. Or at least things that are random seeming to our capacity for perception. A shot in flight will go where it is going to go, the path determined by the Newtonian laws which govern our physical universe. As observers, heck as *shooters*, we

---

10. The Elam Ending is perhaps most familiar to NBA fans for its use in the 2020 All-Star Game. Named for its creator, Dr. Nick Elam of Ball State University, the Elam Ending is an attempt to solve the interminability of close games where intentional fouling and excessive timeout-ing can stretch the last 60 seconds of game action to encompass nearly 20 minutes of real time. Under the Elam Ending, a game is played on a normal clock until a set time remaining, perhaps three minutes. After the next stoppage of play under 3:00, the game clock is turned off and instead of the game concluding at the expiration of time, a set number—seven points in the most common formulation of the Ending—is added to the total currently on the board for the team in the lead, and the first team to hit "top score + 7" wins.

cannot perceive the microscopic differences between one shot motion and the next, which can mean the inch's worth of difference between a perfect "BRAD"—back rim and down—and a brick off the back iron. From our standpoint, it's a make or miss league. Even after technological advancements have allowed us to better understand and predict the likelihood of a jumper going in, at the moment of release it is still a roll of the dice governed by that expectancy.

Back to Lopez. Were some of the signs of Brook's excellence-to-come there when we decided to bet on his fit and value? Sure.

We believed the perception of him as a player around the league was overly negative, more about his previous contract than his current contributions. More importantly, we had reasons to believe that his defensive shortcomings were overstated. His poor reputation in that area was largely due to both his poor individual rebounding totals and his inability to function in the aggressive defensive schemes in vogue around the league for much of his career.

In terms of rebounding, Lopez was a nearly perfect example of the difference between individual and team stats. He might not have grabbed many rebounds himself, but his team always ended up corralling the bulk of opponent misses while he was on the floor.

Among the 100 centers[11] who played at least 2,500 minutes over the five seasons prior to his arrival in Milwaukee, Lopez ranked 94th in defensive rebounding percentage. Over the same period he was rated as the *sixth-most-positive impactful player* on his team's defensive rebounding, according to Regularized Adjusted Plus/Minus techniques.[12] In terms of *team* success, is it more important for the center to accumulate defensive rebounds or for the team to "finish" defensive possessions by virtue of *someone* grabbing the board? To ask the question is to answer it, and over his

---

11. Give or take. Positional designations have always been at least somewhat squishy in the NBA. That fuzziness has only increased as the strictures of traditional roles become more relaxed with big men shooting threes, guards rebounding, and big wings taking on the sorts of offense initiation duties usually reserved to point guards.

12. Much more on RAPM and RAPM-derived metrics in Chapter 6.

career Lopez had proven himself elite at the truly important bit of helping his team gain possession of the ball.[13]

We also suspected that the defensive scheme we wanted to play would better fit Lopez's ability than what had been the trend for most of his career to that point. With the success of first Boston (Kevin Garnett) and then Chicago (Joakim Noah) in using an agile center to "hedge" on ball screens in the late 2000s and early 2010s—Garnett would frequently chase a point guard nearly to half court!—many teams adopted this brand of coverage. While Lopez is quick and very agile for his size, "for his size" is still 7'1" and 280-ish pounds. Cue the hippo ballet from *Fantasia.*

Though he was never going to win a race with the league's point guards at the top of the floor, Brook had shown a consistent ability to defend at the rim. According to the NBA's player tracking data, over the same five seasons in which he had been such an impactful rebounding presence, opponents had only managed to score on 53.7% of shots in the restricted area with Lopez within five feet of the shooter as the closest defender, 87th percentile among all players and just a tick behind Anthony Davis. In the conservative defensive strategy our coaching staff planned to employ, Lopez would be asked to protect the rim first, second, and third, relying upon our guards to chase and harry opposing ballhandlers.

Given these statistical and schematic arguments, we were fairly confident he'd be a perfectly solid defender for us. Had we (or anyone) thought he would make an All-Defense team, he wouldn't have been available as such a bargain signing. After all, he had received a grand total of zero (0) votes for All-Defense honors to that point. Ever. This isn't to say he never made the First or Second Teams. He hadn't shown up on a single ballot. Even by accident. And every year a few truly *wretched* defenders garner stray All-Defense votes.

---

13. Interestingly, Brook's twin brother, Robin, had much the same profile, ranking 42nd in rebounding impact (among the 831 players who appeared) despite ranking 98th of 100 centers in DRB%. I'm still not completely sure whether it should have or not, but the fact that both twins appeared to have this attribute gave us more confidence that it was a real skill and not some sort of statistical anomaly.

So, while we made an astute signing, correctly predicting that Lopez would outperform his reputation, we also got really lucky.[14]

You don't often hear about the signings and moves which ended up doing really well as being products of good fortune. There are fairly strong incentives for everyone involved to claim, "I meant that," much like a jump shooter holding his follow-through after a banked-in three from the top of the key. But just as bad breaks can upend the best-laid plans (literally in the case of freak injuries), fortune can fall in your lap.

Which gets us back to our own cognitive bias. If one ascribes all the wins to skill and all the losses to bad luck, improvement is borderline impossible. Why examine past decisions if everything you've done has either been a perfect masterstroke or beset by unforeseeable misfortune?

Systematically examining decision-making processes is hard, even in retrospect. It is a humbling and often painful exercise, even when considering things that went well. Being right for the wrong reasons is better than the reverse, but it's not exactly a great sign for getting decisions right in the future.

Being swayed by the eventual outcome of a decision is only natural. The frequency with which the commentary on the wisdom of a shot attempt will turn on whether it was made—"good aggressive play by LeBron James"—or missed—"I don't like that shot"—is considerable. But in many cases, process better predicts future results than do past results. Tomes have been written about the general fallacy of "the Hot Hand theory" by which many a selfishly jacked-up jumper is rationalized by "But I made the last one, Coach!"[15]

Analytics are frequently described as bringing "objective analysis" to the examination of future decisions and reexamination of those made in the past. But I don't think that's right. While many of the tools and techniques

---

14. An additional bit of good fortune is that Lopez was willing to sign with us. It is often forgotten by critics of a front office that a deal in free agency is an *agreement* in which the player is an equal party with absolute veto power over any given destination.

15. In fact, more recent research has shown that there may be something to the Hot Hand, in that players can "get hot." Unfortunately, the increase in shooting ability is offset by a willingness to increase shot difficulty. So the net effect tends to be vanishingly small.

used can *reduce* the likelihood of poor choices, they don't wholly eliminate the possibility.

Kahneman himself has described sources of error in decision-making as arising from two main sources: bias and noise.

"Bias" is irrationality in the process of coming to a decision. Playing favorites. Ignoring contrary indicators. Paying attention to the wrong evidence. Outright hostility to certain groups or backgrounds. "Noise" is the effect of the unknowable or at least the unknown. Pure randomness falls in here, but so do things we can't measure, at least not yet or not reliably.

Atmospheric conditions in the arena affect the flight of the ball and do so in defined ways. Which is neat to know but doesn't really help if we can't take the exact conditions into account when evaluating the shot. From a practical standpoint, there is an upper bound on what a team can know about the traits which get lumped under the heading of "character and background" of any one player, let alone what they can learn about the entire universe of players from which they have to choose for any given personnel decision.

The tools of analytics can help in both areas.

More in-depth data collection and the application of advanced statistical techniques can chip away at the noise element. Prior to the advent of player tracking data, what is now formally defined as "shot quality" was understood qualitatively. The battle to get "good shots" and avoid bad ones has been a key strategic and coaching point practically since the game was invented. Now, with the use of objective data, the difference between the two can be more easily determined.

But it cannot be *precisely* determined in many cases. There are a few absolutes. An uncontested dunk is always a good shot, while a backcourt heave with plenty of time remaining on the game and shot clock is universally terrible. Beyond that, it depends. Is a long three-pointer at the end of the game a good shot or a bad shot?

Consider Damian Lillard's step-back 36-foot buzzer-beating three to eliminate Oklahoma City from the 2019 playoffs. According to Second Spectrum[16] estimates, that shot would be made by an average player around

---

16. The league's provider of player and ball tracking data. *Much* more to be said about Second Spectrum in the coming chapters.

22% of the time. At the same time, Lillard is one of the very best in the world at shooting very, extremely, ridiculously long shots, hitting just over 34% of his nearly 300 attempts from beyond 30 feet between 2017–18 and 2019–20. The closest Thunder defender, Paul George, got a hand up and was close enough to require Lillard to step backward toward his right shoulder,[17] so that's nice for the defense. On the other hand the shot was in the air with 0:00 on the clock, something of an imperative when getting the last shot in a tied game.

So while quantifying shot quality doesn't directly tell us whether it was a good shot or not, it is a useful tool in discussing and debating the issue. The application of technology and data science reduces the fog of uncertainty without lifting it completely. There is still going to be some noise. While "shot quality" is a concept that occurs along a continuum of every possibility from the open dunk to the unnecessary heave, the result of the shot is binary. Either it goes in or it doesn't. Make or miss league. There's really nothing to be done to control for that element of randomness.

That very element of randomness is what allows for the other source of poor evaluation and decision-making: bias. If what "should" happen always did, making correct choices would end up being straightforward. Mistakes might still be made, though they would be easy to learn from and correct for. Judging process by end results would be just fine. The feedback loop of decision-outcome would be an almost perfect game of *Operation*, with a buzzer sounding and a shock applied for any misstep.

But it doesn't work that way. To paraphrase William H. Munny in *Unforgiven*, sometimes deserve's got nothing to do with it. You can do everything right and the ball rims out, while a series of poor decisions can still turn out well.

The temptation will always be there to say, "See, it worked" after positive outcomes no matter how that outcome came to be. That sort of results-oriented thinking is the most common form of bias to fight against. Good

---

17. Most shooters find it more difficult to shoot stepping back toward their shooting hand. It is a reasonably common scouting note to find that a right-handed perimeter scorer tends to try to get all the way to the basket when driving right, whereas they are much more likely to shoot a pull-up or step-back jumper when going left.

decisions will sometimes go poorly, while ludicrous decisions will work out just fine at times because the universe has a dark sense of humor.

That will never change. Good process and analysis can serve to tilt the odds in one's favor. Basketball analytics isn't always about having the answers, it's about asking the right questions so that you can be on the right side of those odds often enough to come out ahead in the long run.

Keep this admonition in mind as you read the following chapters. No matter how grounded in evidence and statistical fact the conclusions I reach and arguments I make will be, they are on some level just my opinion, man. We're going to take a tour through what I suspect, what I know, and what I think I can prove[18] about a range of topics, from shot selection to the NBA draft to measuring defensive impact to what innovation is coming next.

So with that in mind, let's get to it.

---

18. Putting precise values on the relative degree of confidence in an opinion has always struck me as foolish, so these more categorical terms hopefully provide useful signpost estimates.

Chapter 2

Speaking the Dialect: Basketball Stats as Language

"'Meow' means 'woof' in cat."

—George Carlin

The Miami Heat's Bam Adebayo and the New Orleans Pelicans' Steven Adams crouch down in the center circle, their right hands inches apart. Referee John Goble tosses the ball up into the air. Adebayo, perhaps touching the ball prior to it reaching the apex of its flight, tips the ball to Meyers Leonard. Leonard drops a bounce pass to Tyler Herro standing at the top of the arc in the backcourt. Shadowed but not really pressured by Lonzo Ball, Herro crosses over right-to-left between his legs, then moves up the court with a left-hand dribble. While Leonard, Adebayo, and Duncan Robinson array themselves around the right elbow and corner areas, Jimmy Butler posts up and receives a bounce pass from Herro around 27 feet from the basket on the left wing, forced out that far by Brandon Ingram's pressure.

As Herro cuts through the left elbow on his way to the left corner, Leonard and Adebayo set up staggered pindown screens for Robinson coming out of the right corner. Eric Bledsoe beats Robinson to the spot above Meyers' screen, so instead of continuing on toward Adebayo, Robinson sharply changes direction and cuts directly toward the basket, closely shadowed by Bledsoe. As Robinson cuts, Adebayo sets the same screen initially intended for Robinson for Leonard. As Leonard saunters to an area just above the free-throw line, Robinson reverses his cut and screens Adams, who is still attached to Adebayo at the hip, from the basket side.

Adebayo cuts behind this back pick toward the basket, and Bledsoe sinks into the paint for just a moment to protect against the lob from Butler to the athletic Adebayo. Unfortunately, this is part of the play's design, with Leonard now perfectly positioned to screen for Robinson to roll to the top of the arc with considerable space between himself and Bledsoe. As the ball is in the air from Butler to Robinson, now curling across the three-point line, Leonard's defender Zion Williamson recognizes that Robinson is about to catch the ball behind the arc with no defender in close proximity. This is an "oh shit" moment for a defense, given Robinson's status as one of the most elite movement shooters[1] in the world.

Williamson lunges toward Robinson, but it is much too late. The third-year player out of Michigan by way of Williams College[2] catches in perfect shooting rhythm and rises up for a clean look. For the average NBA player, this shot would be expected to go in around 37% of the time, despite the distance and the fact that Robinson is moving to his left and thus somewhat "away" from the basket as a right-hand shooter.[3]

And that's before we factor in that it's Robinson shooting rather than Average Man. Heading into the 2020–21 season, Robinson was seventh in accuracy since 2013–14[4] on catch-and-shoot threes off of movement, suggesting he would make this shot well over 40% of the time even with Williamson's despairing lunge.

---

1. Both a qualitative *and* quantitative assessment. More on the quantification to come later.

2. Shoutout to my sister Alix, Williams class of 2002.

3. Especially on longer-range shots, for most players it is easier to maintain proper shooting form when a player's shooting hand is "outside" as they rotate toward the basket (a right-handed player pivoting into a shot with their left shoulder starting closer to the hoop).

4. AKA the tracking data era.

The shot splashes through, gently kissing the back rim on its way down, putting Miami up 3–0. The official play-by-play log of the game records the sequence as:

> 12:00: Jump Ball Adebayo vs. Adams: Tip to Leonard
> **11:43: Robinson 26' 3PT Jump Shot (3 PTS) (Butler 1 AST)**

According to the algorithms processing the actions of all 10 players in .04-second increments, the play featured six dribbles, five off-ball screens, four passes, three points scored, two defensive switches, and, since this was the opening play of the first game on Christmas Day 2020, a partridge in a pear tree.

Which of those three descriptions—the narrative, the game log, or the incremental totals—is is most accurate?

We understand what happens in a game in large part by how the story gets told. To tell the story with statistics, those stats can't just be numbers. The numbers must take on the properties of conversational language.

Bill James, one of the titans in the history of sports statistics and analysis, once wrote, "Baseball statistics, unlike the statistics in any other area, have acquired the power of language."[5] While James' apparent intent was to observe that certain baseball statistical thresholds had entered into the common vernacular of and even outside of the sport,[6] the idea behind it is equally applicable to any attempt at statistical communication.

Numerical and probabilistic information is hard for the human mind to take in and process in that form. However, if those numbers or percentages can be tied back to a more familiar concept, the information is much more easily understood.

Much as chess masters can nearly instantly recall the position of the pieces from game play but are no better than the novice at recalling the arrangement of pieces placed at random, "the numbers" must be attached to a familiar narrative to stick. When analytics professionals are advised on the need to speak the language of basketball, which they are frequently, this is what is meant.

---

5. From the 1985 edition of James' annual Baseball Abstract series.
6. "Batting .400" became a well-understood description of extreme excellence regardless of field.

At the same time, the words used help shape the story as much as the reverse. The language with which we describe basketball can't help but influence the way we think about the game.[7] Or maybe the way we think about the game influences the language. More likely some of both.

The familiar box score stats are the perfect example. Any game recap will use these stats to illustrate the story of that game: "Led by 33 points from Stephen Curry, the Warriors..." and so forth. At the same time, those numbers shape our view as to what matters.

Stats are incredibly useful in describing and recording the game. But they are not themselves the game. Not exactly. Even those familiar columns in the box score, which through longstanding use now appear to be some sort of natural basketball law, are abstractions.

We know this intuitively. Even as averages of points, rebounds, and assists is shorthand for a player's production, we recognize that "production," "impact," and "talent" are three different things. "Good stats on a bad team" is not an invention of the analytics movement. Identifying players who have greatly expanded opportunities to rack up counting stats has been an important consideration for fantasy league players since Tony Campbell put up 20 a game for the expansion Timberwolves or the ridiculous pace of the Paul Westhead–era Nuggets turned a journeyman named Blair Rasmussen into a double-double machine.

Those things happened, and the stats are accurate as descriptions. But those numbers don't tell the whole story, so we continue to search for better statistical words which will.

Tradition

Back to the opening of that Christmas Day tilt.

Certainly, the first description is the most precise. However, using that as the standard at which to analyze games is untenable. I used 604 words to describe 17 seconds of game play. At that rate, one game would take over 100,000 words to describe.[8]

---

7. In Chapter 9, I'll argue that a major factor in why we struggle to evaluate and quantify defense is that we lack the vocabulary to do so.

8. Longer even than this book!

Though the future of the NBA schedule is somewhat in flux,[9] if the league returns to an 82-game schedule, it would take us around 125 *million* words to get through a single campaign. The sheer scale renders such detailed recording completely unwieldy.

Even beyond the lack of parsimony, that level of detail still contains all sorts of assumptions and value judgments about what has occurred. We would never try to verbalize the description of the actions of all 10 players[10] at the 25-frames-per-second rate of tracking data, so we've already mentally simplified into concepts like "dribbles," "passes," "cuts," and "picks."

In some cases, those concepts flow inevitably from the rules of the game. Herro was required to bounce the ball every few steps he moved and had to do so with only one hand at a time. Though the name "dribble" is arbitrary, the action being described is not, at least within the context of the game's laws.

Other concepts derive naturally from the ruleset as well. The ball must be thrown into play following a stoppage, transferring from a player standing out of bounds to a teammate within the playable area. This requires the concept of the "pass" to exist. Though there are some differences between inbounding the ball and moving it between players during play, it's not a huge leap to equate the two as both being "passes."

That the words used to identify and separate one basketball concept from another represent a sensible taxonomy does not mean that they are the only set of vocabulary that is or would have been possible. If we were starting from scratch today, the language would probably not match the vocabulary which has been passed down.

---

9. Eighty-two games are demonstrably more than is needed from a competitive standpoint, as the same teams end up in the 16 playoff spots in approximately the right order after around 65 games anyway. Teams have begun behaving accordingly, which puts the league in a spot of balancing the potential degradation of the product from having games perceived to be extraneous by everyone involved with the revenue generated by those games. While as of this writing we're likely moving back to an 82-game schedule for 2021–22 for both ease of administration and financial reasons, the league, led by commissioner Adam Silver, has clearly signaled the willingness to examine and experiment with changes to the schedule, possibly in the form of an in-season tournament or other sort of FA Cup–style alternative/secondary competition.

10. And the ball.

For example, with a modern understanding of the game we would catalog shot attempts completely differently than the method we have inherited. Back in the days of peach baskets and short shorts, all field goals were worth two points. Tallying the location of every shot was not practical, not to mention the impossibility of transmitting, maintaining, and storing that information.

The jump shot had yet to be invented, and people took running hook shots from what look like outlandish distances to the modern eye. In that environment, a shot is a shot is a shot, and from a record-keeping standpoint, one was probably happy just to know who shot how many times.[11]

Fast forward to today. All shots are no longer equal, literally, with some spots on the floor generating a 50% bonus. More than a decade before optical tracking data was widespread, technology was introduced to capture reasonably accurate locations for every shot taken in the NBA.[12] With that data in hand, basic analysis[13] reveals that "shots" can and probably should be divided into two broad categories: attempts at the rim in one group, and jumpers in another.

As three-pointers have replaced two-point jumpers to a degree, the bifurcation between the two types of shots has become a little more apparent, but shots are all lumped together under the label "field goal attempts." Which leads to the bizarre outcome that players who can't reliably "shoot" past the length of their arms are the most accurate "shooters" in NBA history (minimum 2,000 attempts):

1. DeAndre Jordan
2. Rudy Gobert
3. Clint Capela

---

11. The box scores of my high school games didn't even include field goal attempts, just made shots. Also, they spelled my name wrong at that one tournament in San Diego, which wouldn't be a big deal, but I went for my career high down there as, and I'm not making this up, "Sepk Parthenon."

12. League-tracked "chartable" shot data assigning an X and Y coordinate to each attempt first came online for the 1996–97 season. While the data quality was insufficient to support a lot of modern analysis, those kinks got worked out in relatively short order, and I would consider "shot chart detail" information collected from around the 2000–01 season on to be sufficiently accurate and reliable to be used as an input for most purposes.

13. This analysis and much more in Chapter 8 on the three-point evolution of the NBA.

4. Montrezl Harrell

5. Brandan Wright

These five, all centers in today's game, combined to go 6-of-82 from three-point range and hit 63.3% of their free throws entering the 2020–21 season. But they know their limitations as shooters—nothing wrong with that—so stick mostly to dunks and layups. With that mix of attempts, they do tend to make a lot. So, as measured on the stat sheet, they are "great shooters" even though on the scouting report they are listed as "non-shooters."

Another oddity in the recording of shot attempts is the treatment of fouls. Since time immemorial a shooting foul only counts as a shot attempt if the shot goes in. If it doesn't, it's recorded in the box score as a…nothing. Sure there are two (occasionally three) free throws awarded, but they aren't distinguished as coming via shooting fouls, as opposed to fouls on the floor in the bonus, freebies awarded after technical fouls, or Hack-a-Shaq/DeAndre Jordan/Andre Drummond situations.

The original rationale was sound; getting fouled in the act is good but renders making the shot far more difficult.[14] It wouldn't be fair for a player's percentage to be reduced by these "misses." If we were redesigning the system from scratch, I would record these "scoring attempts" alongside the "layups" and "jumpers" we would already be collating.

The inertia of historical continuity is tremendously powerful. Though the names and descriptions in modern statistical taxonomy result from the kinds of historical accidents just described, "tradition" operates as a statistical Liberty Valance Effect.[15] That very tradition is what gives them power as language. Points, rebounds, and assists don't require a lot of explication or definition.

---

14. According to play-by-play logs from the 2019–20 season, players drawing shooting fouls ended up making the shot for an "and one" just under a quarter of the time.

15. "When the legend becomes fact, print the legend."

New Tech, New Words

For stats and metrics with less historical precedent behind them, finding the right words to capture and communicate their meaning is the first and perhaps most important step. This is even more the case in highly jargonized and technical spaces such as the basketball world. As I've frequently said to co-workers when discussing the importance of mutually agreed upon terms, "It doesn't matter what I know, it matters what we know." Without the proper words, helping you know what I know becomes a challenge.

We'll talk about impact metrics from the Adjusted Plus/Minus family in detail later,[16] but the linguistic challenge of communicating the meaning of stats output by these models was perhaps the largest reason "one-number" valuation metrics struggled to gain acceptance within the league. An RAPM model might suggest that Nick Collison was enormously impactful for the Oklahoma City Thunder during the Durant/Westbrook years.[17] Unfortunately, that model couldn't do much more than say, "Nick Collison? He's really good."

No disrespect to Collison, but he averaged 4.1 points per game between 2011–12 and 2015–16 in a mostly reserve role. One would justifiably need a bit more than "my model said so" to convince a coach or general manager that Collison was having an All-Star-level impact on a per possession basis. The metric and methodology do not provide the tools, the *vocabulary*, to say "See! That! That's a RAPM-enhancing play! That's what Nick Collison does!"

Perhaps the point about the importance of language is best illustrated by way of contrast with the language of another sport. The company currently responsible for the NBA's player and ball tracking is known as Second

---

16. See Chapter 6.

17. According to the version of Regularized Adjusted Plus/Minus found at NBAShotCharts.com, Collison was the 22nd-most impactful of the 814 NBA players to appear between the 2011–12 and 2015–16 seasons, four slots ahead of—but really a statistically meaningless distance from—James Harden. Though the 2011–12 to 2015–16 period is the earliest for which the five-year version of RAPM is available from that site, one suspects he might have shown up as even more impactful if the period was shifted even a year earlier, as the Thunder performed 10.8 points better per 100 possessions with Collison on the floor in 2010–11, a career-best mark for one of the earliest "hidden stars"—tongue most definitely in cheek—of the APM era.

Spectrum. The Los Angeles–based company has over recent years expanded into the world of soccer, providing tracking data for leagues such as the English Premier League and Major League Soccer. Speaking on the differences between how data can tell the story of each game, company CEO Rajiv Maheswaran says:

> Soccer is really interesting. They don't have as many words as they do in basketball because there aren't really "plays" in the same way. But soccer is different in the sense that it is a very geometric game. So all the language of the sport isn't about events, it's about geometry. It's been very interesting to learn the language of sport that is fundamentally different. It's not about a particular play or a particular defensive stat. It's all about formations and lines and angles and space. Soccer has their own language but it's more dynamic and geometric because it's a continuous game with all these pieces that flow throughout the field for 90 minutes. Soccer has its own vocabulary because it's a lot *fuzzier* because the game is more geometric.

For all the experience Second Spectrum has on the technical side, to capture locations of players and identify their movement patterns they not only had to develop a new vocabulary but learn a new language with different grammatical rules to generate useful information for soccer teams.

But Second Spectrum's first language was basketball, where the introduction of player tracking data acted as a nitrous-oxide-like accelerant to the adoption of analytics within the league.

Liftoff was not immediate. Tracking was not immediately seen as revolutionary to the degree it is now recognized to be. Tracking data, perhaps better conceptualized as 11 dots moving on a court representing the players and the ball, does not come pre-packaged with intrinsic meaning. Without a reference point of the activity being tracked—in this case, basketball—a moving dot is just a moving dot.

Simple geometry can help pull some information from those dots. Assuming each one is identifiable as a specific individual, the movement of each player (or the ball) can be viewed and measured over time at a rate of 25 frames per second, a sort of Claymation basketball special. Basic geometry and physics can be used to derive things like distance traveled, speed, and acceleration vectors.

Divorced from useful context, these flightpath-like tracings didn't do much.

"Of what possible use is that information?" was the reaction of longtime NBA head coach Stan Van Gundy at the 2014 Sloan Sports Analytics Conference upon learning that then-Pacers forward Paul George had run almost 130 miles to that point in the season, the highest such figure in the league. Of course, Van Gundy was correct. Perhaps if George were competing in a cross-country meet, miles traveled would be a useful data point. But basketball players aren't measured in miles, they are measured in buckets. And, as it turns out, plenty of other things.

Enter the data people, including but not limited to Second Spectrum.

"When people talk about their problems, they talk about it in words," Maheswaran says. "Words are how they describe strategy or understand the game or help to develop a player. People use words to describe what they want to know and what they want to happen."

What Van Gundy and other coaches wanted to know were basketball strategic questions, such as, how well do certain teams and players defend the pick-and-roll, and if they are successful in defending the play, how did they do so?

According to Maheswaran, "A lot of advanced computer vision and machine learning is basically just 'fancy counting.' The fancy counting has to have a purpose; you don't do counting for counting's sake. The fancy counting enables a machine to understand sports in words."

By first teaching a computer to recognize the basketball action known as the pick-and-roll, the computer can then count all the pick-and-rolls which have occurred in the library of games at hand. Not only can each pick-and-roll be counted, but a wide range of variables and attributes can be cataloged. The identity of the ballhandler. Which player set the screen. The primary defender for both ballhandler and screener. The area on the floor or even the exact location where the screen was set.

By combining the computer's view of the movement of several players, more complex questions could be answered. How did the defense attempt to contain the play? What series of actions did the offense take? And, perhaps most importantly, what was the ultimate outcome of the sequence? This can then be combined and compared with other comparable instances, and now we're cooking.

Suddenly, there is an incredibly rich vocabulary from which to describe this humblest staple of NBA offense. Repeat the exercise with enough basketball concepts and there is now a taxonomy of statistical words correlating precisely to those concepts.

Analytics uses this vocabulary as units of measure. Calling back to Duncan Robinson's Christmas Day Adventure, the third description I offered of the play was "…six dribbles, five off-ball screens, four passes, three points scored, and two defensive switches." Of the three, I think it encompasses the best aspects of the first two: the precision and detail of the short story version along with the conciseness of the play-by-play log.

An irony which arises as we dig deeply into this statistical vocabulary is the notion that there is some firm dichotomy between the qualitative and quantitative approaches to basketball—the "eye test" vs. "the numbers." Even a supposedly qualitative assessment represents a numerical comparison. Opining that Immanuel Quickley was a better shooter than Tyrese Maxey on the eve of the 2020 draft (or vice versa) was a judgment that the former would be able to make more shots more frequently than the latter.

On the other side of the coin, a whole host of qualitative choices have gone into producing "the numbers" which we then analyze. With any luck those choices represent accurate or at least *adequate* judgments about how best to understand the play on the floor. But it should never be forgotten that those choices were made, lest we unconsciously launder our point of view[18] through the lens of mathematics into a sort of assumed objectivity.

Maheswaran notes, "Before it was only about numbers. Big piles of numbers that were scary and only for data people." And for the numbers to have any real meaning, to tell stories, they have to be put into words,

---

18. Our "bias," to put it in more pejorative terms.

concepts which can be combined, shared, and easily understood. And that's my goal for the rest of this book; not to hit you in the face with a bunch of numbers and stats, but to tell you some tales about basketball and how to better understand and explain it.

Chapter 3

Credit Where It's Due

"It is an interesting paradox that the more you surrender the credit for something you've done, the more memorable you become, and the more you actually end up receiving credit."

—Dale Carnegie, *How to Win Friends and Influence People*

Basketball is not baseball, and it's a problem.

Writing about statistical analysis of sports, it is nearly impossible to not at least reference baseball. Baseball "going first," initially through the writing of Bill James and then the Moneyball era, has been a blessing to basketball analytics. It's also been a curse.

On one hand, James popularized the mode of thinking which makes this all possible. We also have the benefit of the early trials and errors to avoid certain mistakes in both analysis and presentation. Many of the questions asked by early baseball research carry over quite well to basketball.

Voros McCracken is the baseball analyst who has had the most influence on my own thinking. McCracken invented the unfortunately acronymic

25

"DIPS"[1]—Defense Independent Pitching Statistics. DIPS was his attempt to solve a problem faced by traditional pitching stats, such as ERA. The issue was that those stats were measuring more than just the pitcher. If his shortstop sucked, he'd look worse, while playing with a fence-climbing, homer-robbing center fielder would make him look better.

This isn't to say that ERA wasn't useful. But for a long time the theory was

ERA = Pitcher Performance

when the more accurate description would be

ERA = Pitcher Performance + Fielding Performance + Variance

McCracken's fundamental insight was the importance that stats evaluating individual performance reflect events the player has control over, and only those events, as much as possible. DIPS was his attempt to subtract out fielding performance to more accurately hone in on pitcher performance.[2] When trying to measure player ability, *looking as directly as possible at that ability* is the goal. While ERA does that to a degree, the train has other stops along the way.

In baseball, addressing this sort of credit apportionment question is straightforward. The combination of the stop-start nature of the game alongside the level at which the detail of events is recorded (and has been for a long time) leads to ease in separating out various components. Additionally, these credit assignment problems are mostly edge cases. The pitcher-hitter

---

1. If there was one trend from baseball that I would fire into the sun, it is the creation of these acronyms. While they are often clever in an inside-jokey sort of way—Nate Silver's baseball projection system PECOTA is a tribute to journeyman major leaguer Bill Pecota—that very insiderishness turns them into a sort of exclusionary secret code when attempting to explain concepts to the broader world.

2. Dealing with variance, at least to a degree, would come later with technologies such as StatCast and PitchFX, which could better measure the quality of contact made by the hitter. From the pitcher's standpoint, hard-hit line drives are bad, weaker contact into the ground or higher into the air is good, even though sometimes the former would be hit directly at a fielder, while the latter might be perfectly placed to find gaps.

confrontation at the heart of the game allows for relative ease in assigning responsibility for the outcome.[3]

For a dynamic, inherently cooperative sport like basketball, credit apportionment is not just A Thing, it is quite often *The* Thing.

As an example, an alley-oop is worth two points. In the box score, those two points go to the dunker. Surely, he is responsible to a degree, as not just anyone can catch and finish a lob in an NBA game.[4] While dunks are easy shots to finish, the same players tend to appear atop the dunk leaderboard every year. Generating those attempts is an indication of player skill as much as finishing them might be.

What about the passer? He had to deliver the ball to a place and at a time where his teammate could reach it and do so without a defender deflecting the ball. He had to beat his man off the dribble or otherwise create a lane to the basket to draw enough help for his high-flying friend to have the proper cutting lane. He had to anticipate and see the passing angles develop.

Zooming out even further, perhaps the penetration resulted from a pick-and-roll or dribble hand-off, or maybe the eventual lob-tosser was able to blow by a defender closing out to him on the perimeter after that defender had to himself give help on penetration elsewhere in the defensive scheme.

If that sounds like a tangled web, it is. In the end, the dunker gets the two points, the passer gets an assist, and we go on with our lives.

Except, what if our lives are devoted to the evaluation of the players involved? Even the most old-school, numbers-are-for-nerds, eye-test-is-the-only-thing acolyte[5] needs to make a mental determination about how to value the passer and the dunker (as well as the potential screeners and spacers) in our lob example.

---

3. We'll get into this more in Chapter 9 discussing defense, but the degree to which credit to hitter and blame to pitcher are equal, opposite, and counted using similar metrics does not apply to basketball at all, and has led to a few fundamental misunderstandings about how to even conceive of measuring defense.

4. For the record, I dunked. Once. In high school. With a volleyball. The rim might have been about 9'10". Still counts.

5. A vanishingly rare breed in the wilds of professional basketball, in my experience. Anyone studying players uses statistics on some level. Most professional evaluators are at least advanced-stat curious. It's just that many place a high burden of proof on the purveyor of statistical wisdom to convince them.

It's not hard to tell if a team is performing well or poorly. Even if the standings can sometimes deceive,[6] Offensive and Defensive Ratings are solid estimates of how well a team has executed on either end of the floor. The Four Factors of Winning which we are about to discuss can further tell us why a team is performing at that level, at least to a degree.

A team with an abnormally high turnover rate might be wasting efficient shooting and find themselves with a mediocre offense, while many a poor defensive club struggles to finish off possessions with a defensive rebound. The explanatory power of these team-level indicators can serve to make the game appear overly solved.

However, as illustrated in the alley-oop example, *how* these team-level inputs are generated is the hard part. We know taking and making good shots is the most important aspect of offensive basketball. "Go make a basket" is not actionable advice for a team trying to improve in that area. Neither is "Hey, do that alley-oop thing more," as if teams simply choose not to dunk every time down the floor.

Reverse engineering how a positive play came to be, or at least discerning which players were most directly responsible, is a necessary first step toward duplicating that play. From a more macro perspective, when trying to assemble the best group of players possible, who gets the credit for this type of play is a useful thing to know.

Untangling the strands of credit is one of the primary functions of basketball analytics. Close observation of the game with an expert eye might identify most things players do to impact the game. But valuing those things systematically and contextually over the course of a 1,230-game schedule is so far beyond the scope of what any human can do that I'm amazed people

---

6. Over- or underperformance in close games can cause a substantial swing in a team's record over the course of the year. In 2018–19, the most recently completed 82-game season, the Clippers were the team whose final record exceeded what would be expected by a team with their underlying scoring margin. According to Cleaning the Glass, the Clippers' non-garbage-time performance was equivalent to that of a 43 win team, yet they won 48, with a 27–16 record in games which featured a score margin of five points or fewer at some point in the last five minutes. Conversely, the Jazz played like a 58-win team, but ended up only 50–32, going 15–18 in "clutch" games. There are a number of reasons why a team might be better or worse than their baseline in close games, aside from variance. But naturally for a game which reduces to around 10% of the possessions of a full game, variance plays a greater role in clutch than non-clutch records.

claim the ability to do so. Which isn't to say the statistical or algorithmic valuations are perfect by any stretch, but they can at least be consistent at scale.

Rebounding and Stealing

Dean Oliver's[7] Four Factors of Winning describe over 90% of the variation in teams' offensive and defensive ratings. These factors—really eight of them, since there are four for offense and four for defense—include Effective Field Goal Percentage for and against, Offensive and Defensive Rebound Percentages, Turnover Percentages for and against, and Free-Throw Rate for and against. The most important Factor has always been eFG%, which accounts for around 40-45% of offensive or defensive performance.

Though the relative weights of the other Factors have changed somewhat over time, excellence in terms of securing defensive rebounds has been and remains a major component of defensive efficiency, and thus winning games. As the coaching saying goes, defense doesn't end until you finish the play by grabbing the rebound.

But a rebound isn't always a rebound. Or rather, a player grabbing a rebound does not always bring the same value to a team. Consider everything that happens to enable a team to grab a defensive rebound.

First, there is the initial defense; no rebounds are awarded for taking the ball out of the net. While the make or miss nature of the NBA means that sound defensive process doesn't perfectly correlate with defensive efficiency, the more consistently good that process is, the fewer baskets the opponent makes. On top of that, some of the same things that affect shot quality also influence the likelihood of an offensive rebound.

A contested, off-the-dribble midrange attempt where the defense has not had to help the primary defender is going to result in an offensive rebound far less frequently than a missed layup after a driver blows by a closeout, completely collapsing the defense.

---

7. Oliver is now an assistant coach with the Washington Wizards and is rightly considered one of the godfathers of basketball analytics.

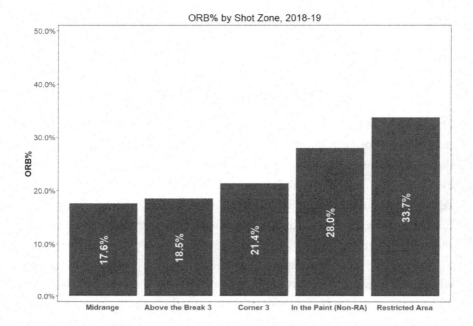

ORB% by Shot Zone, 2018-19

Even once the opponent has been induced into missing a shot, multiple players assist the defense in securing the rebound by either blocking out or simply occupying real estate around the basket. Eventually, someone ends up with the ball.

On the team level, the rebound is the sum of the value of all those things.[8] In an alternating possession game, it's saying, "You're done. I award you no points. My turn now." The proper division of credit for each of those contributions to the rebound doesn't really matter, because from the team standpoint, the value is the same no matter which player did what.

However, put that rebound in the column of a player and tell me how much the *defensive rebounder himself* contributed. Whatever the correct answer turns out to be, it will be less than the total value accruing to the team.

---

8. Though if we want to be really picky, we would note the need to be careful of double counting the value of the pre-shot defense, since those things will show up in terms of opponent eFG% and even opponent free-throw rate to a degree, in that the good defense avoids the bad defensive outcome of committing a foul.

Let's say the defensive rebound is 20% pre-shot defense, 30% "ball in the air" activity, and 50% actually securing the ball. Those percentages are completely made up, and whatever those percentages are change depending on various characteristics of the shot. The relative importance of pre-shot positioning probably decreases as compared to reacting to the ball in the air as shot distance increases; the ball is in the air longer, giving potential rebounders more time to work.

Now, suppose the value of pre-shot defense is equally creditable to all five defenders, while the credit for moving, jostling, and boxing out while the shot is in flight is equally divisible into the three players closest to the basket. After getting full "credit" for winding up with the ball, the rebounder has "produced" just under two-thirds of the value the team gains from *someone* grabbing the board. That other third of the credit pie the rebounder doesn't get to eat, even in allocating him what intuitively feels like a generous helping.

According to the definition of contested rebounds available on NBA.com, between 55% and 60% of all rebounds off of missed field goals are "uncontested defensive rebounds." That is, instances where the offense puts up the shot and largely concedes possession in the event of a miss. On many shots, modern offenses completely abandon any attempt to rebound, instead prioritizing transition defense.[9]

So, on *over half of the rebounds available*, the identity of the defender who ends up with possession after a missed shot doesn't tell us much at all about who deserves credit for the "stop."

This ties into another important aspect of evaluating individual players: the concept of marginal gain.

Depending on leaguewide pace and offensive environment, the worst team in the NBA starts every game with around 80 points, 25 rebounds, and 10 assists. Those stats must still be accumulated and awarded over the course of the game. But across the hundred or so possessions in an average

---

9. In part because of the increases in three-point shooting, smallball lineups, and jump shooting bigs, offensive rebounding is at an all-time low in the NBA right now. Exacerbating this trend has been the repeated demonstration of a tradeoff between offensive rebounding aggressiveness and vulnerability to giving up fast breaks if the opposition does manage to get the rebound. More on this in Chapter 10.

contest, a team with five even vaguely plausible NBA players is going to make some shots and get some stops. These stats are basically the door prize for showing up to play.

A player's production should be thought of less in terms of the share of these free numbers he accumulates, but rather the amount he *adds* to the starting pile. From the standpoint of a defensive player, these uncontested defensive rebounds are much more an allocation of the existing statistical stash than additions to it.

Defensive rebounding percentage can be split into two components, "contested rebound percentage" and "uncontested defensive rebound percentage."[10] In terms of impact on *team* defensive rebounding, contested rebounding is around twice as impactful as uncontested. This ratio carries over to a player's impact on overall defensive efficiency as well.

Recalling the discussion of Brook Lopez's rebounding impact in Chapter 1, Lopez's modest individual rebounding totals historically undersell his ability to help a team rebound. A major reason is that a higher share of Lopez's defensive rebounds are contested rebounds than for most other centers in league. He might not garner a ton of them, but when Lopez grabs a rebound, he's adding something new to the pile, seldom just picking up a rebound that was already there.

This isn't to say rebounding totals are a worthless indicator. But sometimes we have to look a little deeper to see who is actually helping the team and who is just picking up scraps.

The Playmaking of Linsanity

Another facet of the game where credit is easily misallocated is playmaking. The primary metrics for assessing playmaking (Assist Percentage or AST%) and ballhandling (Turnover Percentage or TOV%) tell those stories imperfectly. The calculation of both produces a subtle (or not-so-subtle) pro-chucker bias.

---

10. Each as a percentage of rebounds available, so that DRB% = Contested DRB% + Uncontested DRB%.

Consider the formulae for AST%:

ASSISTS / TEAMMATE FGM WHILE ON FLOOR

and TOV%:

TURNOVERS / (FGA + .44 * FTA[11] + TURNOVERS)

The formulae have one thing in common: a player can "improve" by shooting more. In the case of turnover percentage, the effect is direct. Adding more shots increases the denominator, improving the ratio of turnovers to scoring attempts. The effect on assist percentage is a bit more attenuated, but the player taking more shots means fewer attempts and fewer makes for teammates, which improves the ratio of assists to those makes.

Does it make much sense for shooting more to improve a measure of passing ability? On the ballhandling front, tying a player's turnover rate to their offensive involvement makes some sense, but shooting isn't the only facet of offensive involvement; passing is missing. However, in the established method of accounting, there is nothing a passer can do to improve their standing; they can only avoid the negative of turning the ball over.

---

11. For purposes of "chances used" by a player, the chances taken up by trips to the free-throw line are usually estimated. Play-by-play data makes precise counts possible, but at the NBA level, one scoring attempt for every 2.27 or so free throws provides a close enough estimate that digging into the play-by-play is a lot of extra work for a minor gain in precision. This same estimate is used in calculating both True Shooting Percentage (**PTS / (FGA + .44 FTA**) and usage rate ((**FGA + .44*FTA + TOV) / Chances**).

The list of the 10 highest turnover rates in the 2018–19 season illustrates the point:

Highest TOV%
2018-19

Player	TOV%	Usage
Draymond Green	26.8%	13.1
DeAndre Jordan	21.4%	15.0
Ben Simmons	19.3%	22.1
Mason Plumlee	19.2%	16.2
Evan Turner	18.9%	15.9
Joe Ingles	18.4%	17.5
Kyle Lowry	18.1%	19.6
Ricky Rubio	17.8%	22.7
Dennis Smith Jr.	17.6%	24.8
Trae Young	17.6%	28.4

Aside from Jordan, Plumlee, and possibly Smith Jr., these are excellent ballhandlers and playmakers, so describing them as the players most profligate with the ball is missing something.

I first became aware of this oddity during the height of Linsanity.

Let me preface what follows by saying that Jeremy Lin's run of games in February 2012 was among the most thrilling and inexplicable stretches of basketball in my lifetime. Leaving aside the cultural significance of the first recognizably Asian American star in the modern era of the NBA, this was an undrafted second-year player from *Harvard*[12] emerging from the depths

---

12. I can't speak to the quality of the Ivy League in the late aughts, but in the late teens there was very good basketball played in the conference. Perhaps my favorite scouting trip during my tenure with the Bucks was to New Haven to catch the Ivy League tournament, where the level of play and frankly possible pro talent was a notch above most of the mid-major conference tourneys I was sometimes assigned. The *perception* of Ivy League play around that time was low. Not since Penn's backcourt of Jerome Allen and Matt Maloney combined for 412 NBA appearances over the late 1990s had any Ivy product played in more than 21 NBA games until Lin.

of the Knicks bench[13] to become the most unstoppable player in the league for two weeks. Certainly, the Gotham aspect of it all played into the hype. I'm not sure there would have been the same reaction had Lin come to the rescue of the Charlotte then-Bobcats.[14]

The tenor and fervor of the discussion around Lin suggested the Knicks had found a future Hall of Famer, or at least a multiple- time All-Star. Not only was Lin scoring in bushels, he was playmaking at MVP—Steve Nash levels. And sure, he was turning the ball over a lot, *but so did Nash.*

Linsanity and Nashty
via Basketball-Reference.com

Player Run	Games	AST%	TOV%
Linsanity	7	0.473	0.200
Nash MVPs	154	0.467	0.196

Now, ignoring for a moment the whole seven vs. 154 games thing, this seemed to me less proof that Nash was a good comp for Lin and more than AST% and TOV% were broken, or at least *incomplete* measures of what they purported to record.

Over those two MVP seasons, Nash averaged 15.7 assists/100—leading the league in both total and per game assists—against 4.9 turnovers. Over his magical run, Lin dished out 12.3 assists/100—still an excellent rate—but turned the ball over a mammoth 7.1 times per 100 possessions. According to Basketball-Reference.com, only two minutes-qualified players have ever exceeded that turnover rate for a season.[15] It's a lot.

---

13. Prior to his breakout performance against the Nets on February 4, Lin had only seen the floor in nine of New York's first 23 games.

14. The 2011–12 Bobcats might be the worst team in NBA history, finishing 7–59 in the post-lockout 66-game schedule. They had the distinction of finishing 30th in *both* offensive and defensive rating. The only other team to finish last in both was the 2017–18 Suns, who managed to finish 21–61. Even that Charlotte team averaged 87 points, 39 rebounds, and 20 assists per game.

15. James Harden (7.7 TO/100) and Russell Westbrook (7.6 TO/100), both in 2016–17. Much more on Westbrook's 2016–17 season in Chapter 4.

The reason the established metrics viewed the players similarly despite these differences was the gap usage. Lin used 31.5% of New York's chances while he was on the floor over those seven games. In his MVP seasons, Nash's usage rate was 22%.

With a few years of tracking data to study,[16] we can now estimate that each carried a similar overall share of their team's offense. But despite Nash both setting up teammates and taking care of the ball better than Lin did, the players appeared equivalent in AST% and TOV%.

If the point of rate-based stats is to compare players across roles in different aspects of play, this is a big fat failure. A failure benefiting scoring at the expense of passing and playmaking. Scorers don't need that kind of help to secure credit![17]

So, how can we properly reward playmakers on the same scale as we do scorers? In 2012, there was not an obvious answer. The introduction of tracking data two seasons later provided the needed tools.

In addition to the occasionally inconsistent award of assists,[18] a passer is at the mercy of his shooters to convert the attempts he sets up. Just as a groundball pitcher's ERA reflected the infielders behind him to a degree, a player's assist totals reflected a combination of passing skill and teammates' shooting ability. Tracking data allowed for the collection of "potential assists"; passes leading to a shot where an assist would have been awarded on a make.[19] This serves as a decent playmaking analog to FGA, an "assists attempted" stat.

---

16. According to tracking data, passers realize one assist for every 1.9-2.0 "potential assists." Based on this we can estimate a player's share of his team's offense as (FGA + .44 FTA + TOV + 2 *AST) / Chances, or if we already have advanced stats handy, Usage + AST / 100 plays * 2.

17. As "Yay Points!" wins Sixth Man of the Year for the 20th consecutive year.

18. With the home team tending to get a more generous stroke of the scorekeeping pen.

19. Or at least would be highly likely to have one awarded. The definition of "potential assist" used in both publicly available tracking data and as the default for the more granular stats available to teams is a shot where the player receiving a pass from a teammate shoots within two seconds of that catch and takes fewer than two dribbles. Nearly every made shot which satisfies this definition is accompanied by an assist, as well as a few shots which do not. Past research has in fact indicated these assists tend to be awarded to players on the home team. Potential assists include makes *and* misses. Much as shots are expressed as "Makes-Attempts" in a box score, passing can be described as "Assists-Potential Assists."

Passing could now be put on the same scale as traditional usage. My preferred calculation of this "Playmaking Usage" rate is:

PMU = (Potential Assists + Free-Throw Assists[20]) /
Team Offensive Chances

Calculating this metric for the whole league, unsurprisingly playmaking usage is heavily weighted toward *playmakers*. These players are generally point guards, but playmaking has become more positionally diffuse with the influx of versatile, multi-skilled players who also happen to be very large:

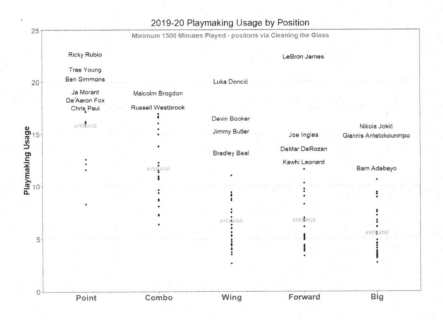

20. In the publicly available suite of stats derived from tracking data, there are two other playmaking actions captured alongside potential assists. One is free-throw assists, which use the same definition as potential assists—under two seconds and two dribbles—but lead to a missed shot on which the shooter was fouled and makes at least one free throw. The other metric tracked is secondary or "hockey" assists, which represent the pass which leads to a pass. I have only chosen to exclude secondary assists, in equal parts because there are relatively few of them; they require the shot to go in, which defeats the purpose of tracking potential assists to begin with; and, ironically, the hockey analytics world has moved away from using secondary assists as a measure of player skill, as they appear to be much more random than repeatable.

Traditional usage rate can be split into "scoring" and "turnover" components. This gives us the three ways a player can "use" a scoring chance. In turn we can more directly compare scoring and playmaking to define player roles. The three usages then sum to "Total Usage" as a measure of overall offensive responsibility:

Average Usage Rates by Position
2019-20 NBA - positions via Cleaning the Glass

Position	Scoring	Playmaking	Turnovers	Total
Point	19.4	15.8	3.4	38.5
Combo	18.2	11.7	2.7	32.6
Wing	16.8	6.7	2.0	25.5
Forward	16.6	6.8	2.0	25.4
Big	16.0	5.5	2.3	23.8
LEAGUE AVG	17.0	8.1	2.4	27.5

Each usage rate can be read as the number of "attempts" per 100 chances[21] in each bucket.

Calling attention to a couple of things:

- Playmaking usage is just under half of scoring usage on average, which seems about right. Assists are awarded on around 58% of makes, while just over 50% of attempts occur where the shooter has had the ball less than two seconds and taken fewer than two dribbles.[22] Scoring chances which end in free throws are "assisted" far less frequently than shot attempts, pulling the overall ratio of playmaking attempts to scoring under 1:2.

---

21. *Chances*, not possessions.

22. The slight difference between those two figures represents both the minor discrepancy between assists as awarded by scorekeepers and those which would have been, according to strict application of the "under 2" method, as well as the degree to which potentially assisted shots go in at slightly higher rates than unassisted. The gap in *efficiency* between assisted and unassisted shots is much larger than the gap in accuracy, as assisted attempts are much more likely to be three-pointers, a topic discussed at much greater length in Chapter 8.

- The sharp-eyed observer will note that this scheme means offenses "use" more than 100 chances out of 100. This is intentional. Traditional accounting doesn't really allow for either the splitting of credit between passer and shooter or much credit at all to the passer in terms of offensive load. I would rather credit both and try to sort it out later than erase the involvement of passers on missed shots.

Further, the degree to which a team's total usage exceeds 100 tells us something about how cooperative their offensive play has been.[23]

This methodology also allows for resolution of some of the problems of TOV%. Passers now can lower their turnover rate relative to offensive role by both shooting *and* creating shots for teammates.

Whereas the old method was:

TOV% = Turnovers / (Turnovers + FGA + .44*FTA)

it can now be measured as:

True Turnover Rate = Turnovers / (Turnovers + FGA + .44*FTA + Potential Assists)

So instead of the issue where skillful playmaking merely avoided increasing a player's TOV%, each potential assist instead reduces their ratio of turnovers relative to offensive involvement. I think this more accurately reflects a ballhandler's ability to avoid miscues.

To illustrate the improvement, recall that point guards tend to have the highest TOV% in the league. In 2019–20, the league-average turnover percentage was around 12.4%. Among point guards it was 14.6%. As they have the ball much more than other players, we would expect them to have a higher volume of turnovers.

---

23. All else being equal, more cooperative play is better than more individual play. Across the tracking data era, potentially assisted shots have been more efficient than self-created shots by around 10 points of eFG%. Of course, many top offenses have had relatively low playmaking rates because of the dominance of superstar scorers.

To put it another way, point guards are selected largely for their ability to protect and distribute the ball. Since they have the highest turnover percentages, either coaches are systematically picking the wrong ballhandler or, much more likely, the metric sucks for its intended purpose.

We're more concerned with how well the player helps the *team* avoid turnovers. According to "True Turnover Rate" point guards had miscues on around 8.6% of chances used, on par with every other positional group, aside from big men. This probably still underrates the ball security of point guards, but at least better reflects their effectiveness running an offense.

So with this new information in hand, how might the comparison between Lin and Nash have looked under these metrics?

Linsanity and Nashty Redux
Estimated via Basketball-Reference.com

Player Run	Scoring	Playmaking	Turnovers	Total	True TO%
Linsanity	25.1	21.8	6.3	53.2	11.8%
Nash MVPs	17.4	27.5	4.2	49.1	8.6%

Nash was a far more effective playmaker and took care of the ball much better, turning the ball over at basically average rates. Lin was the more dynamic scorer while also doing plenty of playmaking, but he turned the ball over a ton. Among NBA point guards in 2019–20, the highest true turnover percentages were Trae Young's (10.0%) and Ben Simmons' (10.4%); given that during his run Lin substantially outpaced those rates, turnovers were in fact a bit of a problem, even accounting for his absurd production.

Chapter 4

Goodhart's Law:
On Playing the Drill

"When a measure becomes a target, it ceases to be a good measure."
—Anthropologist Marilyn Strathern

I n 2016–17, Russell Westbrook averaged 31.7 points, 10.7 rebounds, and 10.4 assists per game for the Oklahoma City Thunder. It was the first time a player had averaged a triple-double over a full season since Oscar Robertson in 1961–62 for the Cincinnati Royals.[1] Westbrook cruised to his first MVP award on the strength of this legendary feat, garnering 69 out of a possible 101 first-place votes.

Despite this landslide, there was grumbling in the more data-driven corners of the NBA world that though he had a fine season, he had only been the second-, perhaps even third-best player over that '16–17 season.[2]

---

1. A decade later, the Royals became the Kansas City–Omaha Kings, before leaving Omaha and then finally the Midwest altogether for Sacramento, where at some point in the late aughts they became the KANGZ of today, proprietors of the longest playoff drought in the NBA at 14 seasons and counting, having gone through 10 coaches, four general managers, and one video of the team's primary owner demanding the selection of "STAUSKAS" in the 2014 draft.

2. James Harden finished second with 22 first-place votes, while Kawhi Leonard was third with nine first-place votes.

For example, Kawhi Leonard finished ahead of Westbrook in two leading player value metrics,[3] while James Harden outpaced him in one of three and was well within the margin of error in a second.[4]

MVP Metrics Comparison
2016-17

Player	RAPM	EPM	PIPM
Russell Westbrook	+1.5/100	+6.7/100	+4.5/100
James Harden	+1.7/100	+6.5/100	+1.7/100
Kawhi Leonard	+2.5/100	+6.9/100	+3.2/100

"But he averaged a triple-double!"[5] was the retort. Which, while true, sort of missed the point.[6]

Though Westbrook's totals were gaudy, they only told part of the story. By all accounts an incredibly driven player, Westbrook openly chased the

---

3. "Single-number" metrics will be discussed at length in Chapter 6.

4. In the ever-changing landscape of player metrics, neither "Estimated Plus/Minus" (EPM) nor "Player Impact Plus/Minus" (PIPM) had been invented by that season, but each is representative of a particular style of metric. Of the three, PIPM places by far the most weight on box score statistics. It is thus not surprising that PIPM rated Westbrook more highly than other metrics, given the whole triple-double thing.

5. It is not without irony that the MVP debate from that season neatly mirrored one which occurred five years previously in baseball, when Miguel Cabrera of the Detroit Tigers won the award despite Mike Trout having a significantly superior season on almost every holistic measure of player contribution. But Cabrera won the Triple Crown, leading the league in batting average, home runs, and runs batted in, the first time that feat had been accomplished since 1967. It is perhaps a sign of progress that the gap shrunk to only five years despite baseball's nearly 20-year head start on the NBA in kicking off its own statistical revolution.

6. To be scrupulously fair, a number of voters were convinced of Westbrook's case not merely by his gaudy per game numbers, but also by his clutch performance. Defining "clutch" as any time a game had a scoring margin of five or less with under five minutes remaining in the fourth quarter or overtime, Westbrook led the league in clutch scoring while his Thunder won almost five games more than would be expected from their overall play, largely on the basis of strong play in late/close situations. However, even that rubric tilts toward other candidates. Westbrook finished eighth in "Clutch Win Probability Added"—a metric combining accuracy and game leverage of clutch shooting calculated by Inpredictable.com, a website we will meet again in Chapter 5—with Leonard finishing fourth in the same metric, while Westbrook's third-place finish in overall "kitchen sink" win probability added saw him trail Harden in first.

achievement of a seasonal triple-double. To the extent that pursuit was his focus, Westbrook's season demonstrated the economic maxim known as Goodhart's Law. Or, in more familiar sporting terms, he was playing the drill.

If "basketball ability" is the degree to which a player positively affects his team's chances of winning, directly measuring that ability is quite difficult. The mere existence of this book is pretty strong evidence for that proposition. If it were easy, all these fancy stats would be so boring and unnecessary.

Without that direct measurement, we instead search for indicators of this latent characteristic within each player. In other words, we use stats.

However, "good stats" are not a player performing well. Rather, they are a frequent *byproduct* of playing well. Not that thing itself, but an indicator that thing—good play—is present. What happens if a player ceases to focus on the goal of helping his team win, and instead just goes after stats? The numbers become unreliable as indicators of good play. Goodhart's Law in action.

Essentially, it is an argument about causality.

There have been studies over the years purporting to measure teamwork and its effects on winning. A common observation has been that the best teams tend to engage in a lot of encouraging "tank-filling"[7] behaviors on the floor. They high-five a lot. Naturally,[8] some coaches saw these studies and thought to themselves, "By golly, if high-fives are the key to victory, we are going to be the high-fivingest goddamn team of all time."

Of course, once the players knew that high-fives were being tracked and treated as a measure of their performance, guess what happened? "High-five rates" exploded. Whether or not high-fives were deserved, they were given. And the relationship between high-fives and high performance was sundered.

But back to Russell Westbrook and Goodhart.

---

7. As opposed to tank-draining. Experts suggest that to maintain a healthy relationship, the ratio of positive tank-fillers to negative drainers needs to be 5-to-1 or greater.

8. And by naturally, I mean apocryphally, though there are the occasional preseason stories about how some college or pro program has rededicated itself to teamwork and culture and are very intently tracking high-fives for the coming season.

To better explain, it is useful to discuss statistical accumulation in the NBA. In Chapter 2, we saw how stats attempt to turn action on the court into digestible chunks, our vocabulary for discussing the game, while in Chapter 3 we covered the difference between team and individual stats, and how there is a difference between a player "producing" in a way which adds to the team's total output vs. merely hoarding the statistical credit for the team's achievement without doing much to advance it further.

"Replacement level" is a somewhat nebulous but necessary concept for viewing basketball through a statistical lens. Essentially, the idea is that if a player was taken off the team, their contributions would not be completely zeroed out. Whoever appeared in place of the vanished player would certainly produce *something*.

In 1992–93, the last season before his first retirement, Michael Jordan played 3,067 minutes for the Chicago Bulls. This represented 15.5% of the 19,830 total minutes available, and 77.3% of the maximum any one player could accumulate.[9] In 1993–94, as Jordan was toiling for the minor league baseball Birmingham Barons, Chicago players totaled 19,780 minutes. The following season, with Jordan returning for the final few weeks of the season, they were back up to 19,830 minutes. In the 1.8 seasons without Jordan, the Bulls were not forced to play 80% of their minutes with four players. Pete Myers was announced as a starter, and along with other players he filled the 2-guard slot, albeit far less capably than MJ.

And it wasn't just the minutes. The shots Jordan took? Myers took some of them; others were lost to the Bulls' slower pace of play, two fewer overtime periods, and the decline in extra chances Chicago generated. The Bulls went from league leaders in offensive rebound percentage and turnover rate in 1992–93 to 11th and 16th, respectively, in '93–94. But even that bit of evaporation off the top still left over 1,000 field goal attempts to be distributed to other members of the team.

---

9. Chicago players totaled 19,830 minutes played, representing 3,966 minutes of game action. In an 82-game season, a team will play 3,936 minutes, plus five minutes for every overtime period in which they participate.

There is a similar story with respect to points, rebounds, assists, steals, and blocks. The Bulls were worse, as one might expect, what with the GOAT[10] suddenly departing the roster at the height of his powers. But they weren't Michael Jordan–amount worse. The next-best guy Chicago could find was also really good at basketball. Which in a roundabout way returns us to replacement level. Myers wasn't a great NBA player, but he was *an NBA player.*[11] You put him on the floor and he will do some things.

Even the worst NBA teams imaginable are filled with players elite enough at basketball for whom that is true. These players are why the team starts with the 80 points and so on we discussed as a sort of door prize just for being around at tipoff. The baseline then for a player's contribution is not zero, but rather the level of performance indicated by those bare minimum achievements.

In many ways, a team's style of play serves as a method through which these door prizes are distributed. The bulk of the rebounds are going to be grabbed by the guys playing close to the basket. The lead ballhandler is going to rack up assists, and of course shots turn into points at varying exchange rates. A primary offensive option getting all the best candies from the statistical gift bag is why it is such a highly coveted role to begin with.

Most times, individual statistical accumulation and additional value to the team go hand in hand. Before it became A Thing in its own right, the triple-double was a useful concept, illustrating the contributions of players who were bringing their team that value in multiple areas.

The triple-double brand was popularized in the 1980s as a way of illustrating Magic Johnson's superb play for the Showtime Lakers. Prior to Johnson, there had been a number of guards who combined big-time scoring with

---

10. At least to that point in time. The Jordan vs. LeBron debate is one of those unresolvable arguments in which the position one takes says more about the factors one deems important rather than the relative greatness of either player.

11. There are two ways to interpret the phrase "an NBA player." The first is literal—he appeared in an NBA game and is therefore an NBA player definitionally. However, it is also sometimes used to indicate that a player is good enough to be on the floor in an NBA game and not be a total liability. Sometimes through exigencies of injuries, development of young players, or poor talent identification, teams trot guys out who aren't really competitive at this level of play. While as amorphous as is the concept of "replacement level," I find this a useful construct in terms of looking at teams.

a hefty dose of assists,[12] but not since Robertson[13] had there been a player with the on-ball mastery to score and dish while also possessing the size, strength, and willingness to be a big-time rebounder at the same time.

In Johnson's case, those rebounds frequently started the fast breaks which populate his highlight reel of no-look passes and acrobatic scoop layups still shown to this day. With that backdrop, it's no wonder that "triple-double" became synonymous with "all-around awesome."

It's worth zooming in on the trends which led to Johnson's dominance, as the shifting league landscape is an important factor in why Westbrook's triple-doubles should be discounted a little.

Taking a 10,000-foot view of NBA reveals a long-sweeping arc in which the competitive returns to size have slowly but continuously given way to an ever-improving level of skill in the game; shooting, passing, ballhandling, and so on. In this narrative, the entrance of Johnson and Larry Bird into the league—inextricably linked as they are going back to their college rivalry which culminated in "The Game of the Century" between Johnson's Michigan State and Bird's Indiana State—represents an inflection point.

Prior to that, the game's biggest stars, those recognized as its best players, had nearly always been the behemoth centers. George Mikan. Russell and Wilt. Kareem. Bill Walton. Interior players had dominated the game to such a degree that from the introduction of the MVP award for the 1955–56 season until 1982–83,[14] 22 of the 28 awards went to centers, with another three going to power forwards. Only Bob Cousy, Robertson, and Julius Erving won the award playing on the perimeter.

From Bird's first MVP in 1983–84 through 2019–20, only three times have centers[15] taken home the prize. Karl Malone also won two as a more or less "traditional" power forward. Even the winners who would morph into

---

12. Nate "Tiny" Archibald was the last player to lead the league in both scoring and assists, in 1972–73.

13. Robertson himself led the league in scoring and assists in 1967–68.

14. The season before the first of Bird's three consecutive MVP awards.

15. One win apiece for Hakeem Olajuwon, David Robinson, and Shaquille O'Neal, though O'Neal's dominance from the late 1990s through the mid-aughts could easily have brought a few more.

5s as they aged and the league downsized[16] were much more comfortable operating away from the hoop, employing the same range of passing, shooting, and ballhandling skills as their smaller competitors. Those perimeter skills are the defining characteristics of 2020–21 MVP Nikola Jokić's game.

I'm not a historian, so to make sure the above checked out, I asked someone who is. Curtis Harris is the proprietor of the @ProHoopsHistory Twitter account. He describes the broad strokes of the league's transformation as follows:

> The Age of the Big Man (c. 1945 to 1980) was itself a distinct era. When Mikan began playing it was assumed men his size (6'10") were TOO tall to be of any practical use on the basketball court. Most centers topped out at 6'5" or 6'6". So even though he wasn't the fastest guy around, he was far more mobile than previous men of his size, hence why he trounced the league and sent everyone looking for other athletic behemoths.
>
> The Magic and Bird entry into the league serves as good a point as any to mark the decline (but not end) of the Big Man. Kareem and Moses Malone still dominated the early 1980s. But once Bird gets his first MVP in 1984 things turn against the Big Man, at least in terms of awards. Curiously, though, DEFENSIVE awards have gone the opposite way. Perimeter players used to split Defensive Player of the Year with the bigs in the 1980s, but it's been an almost exclusively Big Man award for the last 25 years.

The implication is that the height of basketball skill was no longer considered to be, well, height. Rather, the ability for one player to do *everything* was what teams wanted. Stuffing the entire stat sheet became the thing. The ability to grab a defensive rebound, dribble the length of the floor oneself, and either finish at the rim or find a teammate for a dunk of their own, or, in more recent years, to knock down a transition three—*these* were the superstars that every team came to covet.

---

16. Tim Duncan (twice), Kevin Garnett, and Dirk Nowitzki.

If nothing else, accumulating at least 10 points, 10 rebounds, and 10 assists in a single game,[17] i.e. the triple-double, provided a very useful shorthand for this all-court mastery. Messing around and getting a triple-double was in fact a good day, or at least a good game. So much so that players became very aware of the plaudits attached to a triple-double, leading to some very obvious stat-chasing, whether in the form of rebound-stealing or patently obvious assist-hunting from players just a tally or two short toward the end of a no-longer-particularly-in-doubt contest.[18]

Perhaps the apotheosis, or really nadir, of the triple-double chase occurred in 2003. In the closing seconds of a blowout win over Utah, the Cavaliers' Ricky Davis was one rebound short. Davis intentionally missed a layup in order to grab the miss and secure his 10th rebound. Which is all well and good, except his intentionally missed shot was *at the wrong basket* with no defense in sight. Needless to say, this did not count as a rebound and Davis was not credited with a triple-double that night.

While that incident was embarrassing, it also illustrated some of the silliness of an artificial milestone imposed by our inherent love of round numbers. Davis had what appears to be a fantastic outing that night, putting up 28 points, 12 assists, and nine rebounds in a game his team won by 27. I will admit to not having broken down the tape possession-by-possession of this one, but it would be pretty hard to have those numbers (on efficient shooting) in a game your team wins with a sizable margin and have had a *bad* game, regardless of how much one thinks stats can lie. But that one extra rebound would have somehow validated the performance over and above what little value that rebound would have provided.

---

17. Triple-doubles have occasionally been achieved with blocks or steals instead of one of the other categories. Since 1983–84, there have been 68 triple-doubles with at least 10 blocked shots (spread among 24 players) and eight (from seven different players) featuring at least 10 steals. There were 1,785 regular season triple-doubles recorded from 1983–84 through 2019–20 by 311 different players. Ricky Davis is not among that 311; more on him shortly.

18. Harris adds, "The NBA was also expanding its stat box starting in the mid-1970s, so quantifying triple-doubles in the 1980s can be seen as an outgrowth of that. For around 20 years after the league started tracking rebounds and minutes, the box score didn't change. Then in 1973–74 they started tracking steals and blocks. In 1977–78 turnovers were added. It appears there was a greater desire to quantify what was happening on the floor."

In fact, the "rebound" is one of the areas where allocative incentives are most at play.

There is measurable value for a team to grab the board and thus "get the stop." In Chapter 3, we looked at how the player ending up with the ball isn't really responsible for the entirety of the value brought to the team. Still, one player ends up with the stat. If the focus of everyone involved is purely on winning, the assignment of credit doesn't really matter.[19]

However, in a situation where a player or team is acting on, shall we say, other incentives, this no longer holds true. We must then turn a more skeptical eye to the stats accumulated. The incentives for a player to "stat-hunt" are obvious. Stats equal dollars, and while this is truer for some stats than for others,[20] getting big numbers is a great way to get bigger number$.

For a team, the rationale for nudging the distribution of stats in certain directions is more subtle and ranges from the largely benign and possibly even helpful to less salutary efforts at self-preservation. As an example of the former, perhaps a solicitous home scorekeeper can goose a player's totals in stats that come down to judgment calls, such as assists or blocked shots. More impressive marks might help a player's case when it comes to award and All-Star voting. Perhaps a player who receives such recognition is happier, a better locker room presence, more amenable to coaching, and above all else thinks kindly of the org so won't agitate for a trade.

Other motivations are less helpful, perhaps even damaging. Imagine an executive who is feeling a bit of pressure to keep their job. They need a particular draft pick or free agent signing to work out.

"Coach, can you help us out here?"

And suddenly the player in question has a "breakout season," which is actually just the normal level of performance leading to more impressive top line stats via the five extra minutes of playing time he's getting per game. Similarly, a rookie might be force fed minutes and touches to appear to be contributing at a higher level than they might otherwise be if playing time and touches were being awarded on a more meritocratic basis.

---

19. Though we still must be very careful in conflating the team value and the player value.
20. Yay Points!

Somewhere between those extremes is a situation where a team wishes to trade a player and seeks to "showcase" them by giving them a more expansive role to make him a more attractive target for acquisition by a rival. Anecdotally, this doesn't seem to work often. There are few secrets in the NBA, and if word gets out that a team is trying to move a player, and that player suddenly goes from 25 to 35 minutes per night, two and two get put together in 29 other front offices, and the stats discounted accordingly. Usually.

These are just some of the ways in which the assumption that statistics have been accumulated in the normal run of play by players and coaches attempting to win games above all else might not always be completely accurate.

Which brings us back to Westbrook. As part of his quest for triple-double seasonal averages, he worked overtime to ensure he gobbled the lion's share of "free" rebounds, those misses abandoned by the shooting team in favor of transition defense. Over his final three seasons in Oklahoma City, no player in the NBA totaled more uncontested defensive rebounds than Westbrook:

Defensive Rebounding 2016-17 to 2018-19
(via NBA.com)

Player	DRB	Contested	Uncontested	Cont. %
Russell Westbrook	2057	307	1744	14.9%
DeAndre Jordan	2335	647	1680	27.7%
Andre Drummond	2427	859	1548	35.4%
Giannis Antetokounmpo	1884	477	1392	25.3%
Karl-Anthony Towns	2176	786	1385	36.1%
Rudy Gobert	1881	559	1310	29.7%
LeBron James	1562	345	1215	22.1%
Anthony Davis	1854	671	1178	36.2%
Nikola Jokić	1744	597	1135	34.2%
Hassan Whiteside	1799	664	1129	36.9%
James Harden	1364	251	1104	18.4%

For sake of context, around 25% of defensive rebounds were "contested" leaguewide over this time frame.

Now since Russ was snagging all of the freebies, there were fewer to go around to his teammates. One of the chief victims from the standpoint of statistical accumulation was Steven Adams. Despite being one of the more physically imposing players in the league, Adams averaged just under 4.8 DRB/36 minutes, a hair above league average and sandwiching himself between Kelly Oubre (4.7 DRB/36) and Chris Paul (4.9 DRB/36). Not great for a center. But Adams had to "earn" an unusually high proportion of those rebounds.

The chart below compares DRB/36 to the proportion of those rebounds which were contested for players who totaled at least 1,500 minutes in those three seasons:

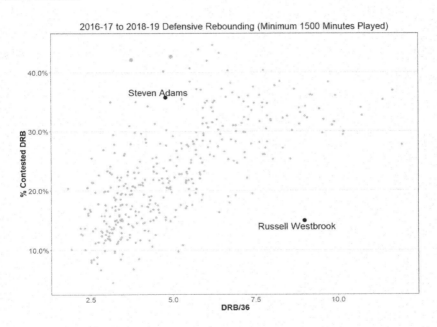

Adams didn't grab many defensive rebounds, but few players had to work harder for those they did snag, while Westbrook grabbed a ton, but didn't have to fight for many of them.

This is not a critique of Westbrook per se. This accumulation of rebounds didn't *hurt* the Thunder; they still ended up with these rebounds. Further, defensive rebounds from point guards tend to lead to more fast break opportunities than do those secured by other players. The offense does move more quickly if you can "grab and go" rather than needing to first complete an outlet pass. Westbrook's thirst for rebounds is a big part of why his teams play in transition far more often with him on the court than off.

But from the standpoint of rebounding and rebounding only, Adams may have been more valuable to the Thunder. According to Defensive Rebounding RAPM[21] for those three seasons, Westbrook's impact on Oklahoma City's defensive rebounding was essentially neutral. That is, once we account for the other nine players on the floor, Westbrook didn't really move the needle either way in helping OKC rebound a larger share of opponent misses. Meanwhile, Adams scored in the top 10% of all players on this metric. Much like the indications that Brook Lopez would be useful to our defensive rebounding when we considered signing him in Milwaukee, the Thunder were not just better but a *much* better defensive rebounding team with Adams on the floor, while Westbrook barely moved the needle.

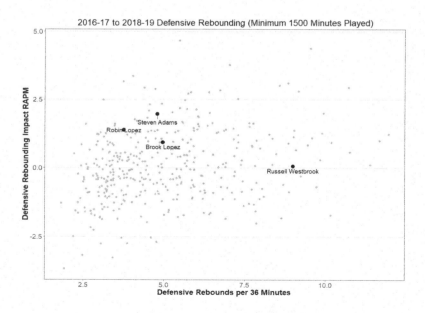

21. Much more on RAPM and other metrics based on regression models in Chapter 6.

Westbrook's rebounding contained a lot of empty calories, while Adams was eating his spinach to make the Thunder strong.

But the best players do everything. And especially after Kevin Durant departed for Golden State, Westbrook wanted to be known as one of the best players. Thus, the rebounds, the triple-doubles, and poor Steven Adams doing the dirty work for little recognition.

Players responding rationally to incentives shouldn't be a surprise, nor will they always be especially subtle in those responses. Toward the end of 2016–17, as Westbrook was chasing triple-double history, Maurice Harkless of the Portland Trail Blazers had his own individual goals in mind. Harkless, a sub-30% three-point shooter[22] through his first four seasons, had a clause in his contract which earned him a $500,000 bonus if he ended the season shooting above 35% on threes.

Heading into the homestretch of the season, Harkless was *just* short of that mark. Entering Portland's 77th game of the season, his season average was 34.6%. That night, he turned into a veritable flame-thrower from the outside, knocking in 3-of-5 and raising his season average to 35.2%.

What happened next shouldn't be a surprise to anyone with a passing familiarity with economics, or really human behavior in general. In Portland's next game, Harkless missed his first three-pointer, dropping his seasonal average to 35.1%—really 35.05%, but we go to one decimal for most things in the NBA. He had used up his cushion.

For the rest of the season, he simply stopped shooting.

In fact, he removed the temptation to even attempt a shot. One can go back and watch all of Harkless' touches over his last three contests that season (he sat out Portland's 81st game), and there is nary a "record scratch"—one of those jarring moments in a game where the ball swings around the horn to an open shooter who catches the ball in perfect rhythm and…doesn't shoot. Harkless avoided so obvious a non-attempt by sticking inside the arc as much as possible; you can't shoot a three if you're never standing in three-point territory.

---

22. Just barely: 29.978587% on 467 career attempts.

Over Portland's first 77 games, Harkless averaged around 3.5 catches in the corners[23] per 100 possessions. Over his last four games, he only caught the ball in the corners once. Total, 0.4 corner catches/100. Rather than put himself in a position where he might have to obviously turn down an open look to make sure he secured the bag, Harkless safely hung out along the baselines instead.

Was he hurting the team with this change? Perhaps. In those last four games, Portland averaged 108.1 points/100 possessions with Harkless on the floor compared to 113.0/100 over the rest of the season. It's a small enough sample that it doesn't really prove anything, but it's not hard to argue Harkless had goals other than the team's success in mind.

There was no real harm done in any event. The Blazers had already secured their playoff berth and Harkless' teammates and coaching staff were fully supportive of him getting paid a little extra. Who among us wouldn't take a 5% annual salary bump for doing less for one specific week of work?

This isn't to cast shade on Harkless, or to suggest there was anything unique about what went down. Rather this was a recent and highly visible public example of a player maximizing toward a different goal than purely team victory. If teams didn't want players to chase bonuses, they shouldn't put bonuses in contracts to be chased.

Returning again to Goodhart's Law, Harkless' bonus was ostensibly an award for providing a shooting threat to help the Blazers spread the floor for Damian Lillard and company. By targeting the measure, Harkless acted precisely opposite the intent of the bonus. Record-scratching "anti-shooters"—those who do not even attempt open threes—are less effective

---

23. Players for whom the three-pointer is the bleeding edge of their range, such as Harkless, find a high proportion of their three-point attempts in the corners where the shot is slightly closer to the basket. Through the end of 2016–17, 52.5% of Harkless' career three-point attempts had come from the corners, one of the highest proportions in the league.

floor spacers than all but the lowest accuracy players.[24] At least for the final few games of the season, an anti-shooter is what Harkless became.

Westbrook and Harkless are simply two examples, one big and one little, of how changed goals can affect the way statistical production should be interpreted.

As a postscript, the novelty factor of hitting arbitrary benchmarks does wear off. Nobody remembers the second four-minute miler, and Westbrook went on to average triple-doubles each of the next two seasons and then did so again in 2020–21[25] while not receiving a single first-place MVP vote in any of those seasons.

---

24. The easiest recent example of this is Westbrook's longtime OKC teammate, Andre Roberson. Roberson has never been a great shooter. But more pertinently, he is one of the more *reluctant* shooters in recent memory, to the point where teams simply stopped guarding him to provide extra help on Westbrook and Kevin Durant. Correctly so, given Roberson's low volume of attempts. His average of 3.1 3FGA per 100 possessions in his three seasons alongside Russ and KD were among the lowest for any off-ball perimeter player in the league over that period. I have posited that a non-shooter in the corner was more damaging to an offense than a *bad* shooter. I have dubbed this the "Roberson Corollary." My theory is that Roberson could make literally every corner three he attempts and the defense would still be better off by having the extra defender in Durant's lap rather than pretending to guard Roberson on the 96.9 other possessions. Of course, if Roberson really did make every shot, he'd shoot more, so it is an inherently absurd illustration. But the point remains that from a floor spacing standpoint, willingness can be as important as accuracy.

25. In the process breaking the all-time record for triple-doubles by a single player, finishing the season with 184, passing Robertson's mark of 181 in the closing days of the 2020–21 season.

Chapter 5

But Who's Counting?

"On two occasions I have been asked [by members of Parliament], 'Pray, Mr. Babbage, if you put into the machine wrong figures, will the right answers come out?' I am not able rightly to apprehend the kind of confusion of ideas that could provoke such a question."

—Mathematician and inventor Charles Babbage

The numbers are not the game.

As with any set of recorded statistics, what shows up in the box score is an abstraction, a simplified representation. They provide a conversational shorthand so that we don't have to use the kind of exhaustive description which led off Chapter 2 to make the subject of discussion clear. We understand that the neatly recorded columns summarizing events aren't the whole truth.

But what if they aren't "true" at all?

The game's basic stats are very much products of the understanding of basketball at the time they were first codified. At that point, there were also technological limits on the gathering, transmission, and storage of information. But, as the apocryphal Einstein maxim states, not everything that counts can be counted and not everything that can be counted counts.

Moreover, just because things have been counted, collated, and cataloged does not prove the counting to be accurate.

Recording statistical observations of complex phenomena can be fraught with confounding variables, squishy definitions, and extraneous information which is attention-grabbing but ultimately extraneous information immaterial to the purpose for which the data is being collected. Imagine trying to quantify every important aspect of human social interaction, such as office dynamics or the dating scene at a local hotspot. The difficulties of producing a useful dataset from such complex environments should be obvious.

Cognitive psychologist Robin Hogarth has described learning as occurring in one of two types of environments: kind and wicked. A "kind" environment is one with well-defined rules, constrained actions and answers, and ready, accurate feedback from decisions and experiments. A "wicked" environment is much the opposite. Decisions are open-ended; rules are ambiguous; feedback is either rare, untrustworthy, or both. Obviously, these descriptions represent archetypes, with most real world situations having aspects of each.

Office politicking or the singles scene at a bar perfectly embody a "wicked" environment for statistical tracking. Meanwhile, in a "kinder" statistical environment, the definitions of items being recorded are concrete enough to allow for application of easy heuristics and perhaps even automation. Determinations of what is and is not important have already been made for the collector. Situations follow consistent and readily observable patterns, reducing ambiguity. Sports are far down toward the "kind" end of the range.

The rules are well established. The statistical record, whether via box score, play-by-play logs, or even player tracking, is meant to be a repository of the history of the game. With that, a certain degree of internal consistency is required. A defensive rebound grabbed by Bill Russell in 1965 should be roughly the same thing as one awarded to Rudy Gobert in 2021.[1]

---

1. The *value* of the event might have changed substantially based on game context, but the fact that each represents recovery of the ball following a missed shot by an opponent is crucial for analysis or comparison to have any validity whatsoever.

This need for consistency has led to a robust set of parameters which serve to define how each stat is recorded.

These rules are both formal and informal. The NBA Statisticians' Manual provides criteria for the award of each box score stat. On top of that guidance, decades of application have further codified a sort of "common law" understanding of what each of these things are. Players, coaches, fans, and scorekeepers have had thousands of reps recognizing these events. With definitions broadly known and well understood, feedback and correction of mistakes is no big deal. It's about as good an environment for collecting consistent data as one could hope for.

That said, the historical depth and apparent consistency of sports data does not conclusively demonstrate that the data is right. There are many nooks and crannies in the NBA statistical world where little inconsistencies and inaccuracies can jump from the shadows to bite the unsuspecting on the ankles.

Shot Flavor

One of my go-to examples of this is the "shot type" information found in the NBA play-by-play feed. Since play-by-play was introduced, qualitative descriptions of many events have been attached. For example, rather than listing shots as simple makes and misses, there are almost always distances and quite frequently some detail about the shot included.

Rather than

Harden 3FGM

the play-by-play might read

Harden 26' 3PT Step-Back Jump Shot

At first glance, this appears to be a treasure trove of information, with the promise of being able to collate a player's accuracy on very deep three-point attempts[2] or on step-backs. Did Tim Duncan really shoot an otherworldly percentage on bank shots? Is Kyrie Irving "automatic" on floaters? What about the "Dirk-step" one-legged fadeaway?

The data as collected will "answer" those questions. Unfortunately, those answers will be meaningless insofar as they are meant to accurately summarize events. It isn't that these descriptions are *wrong*. If one watched clips of every Harden three-pointer which was labelled "step-back" the majority will be recognizable as step-back jumpers. However, if one watched *all* of Harden's three-point attempts rather than just the subset labeled "step-back," there would be plenty of jumpers that were at least arguably step-backs but were not recorded as such.

Worse, those step-backs which were missed by the play-by-play feed, recorded as simply "3PT Jump Shot," aren't a random sample. Made shots are more likely to have had the "shot flavor" added in.

Jump Shot Efficiency
via 2019-20 NBA Play-by-Play

Shot Description	FGM	FGA	FG%
3PT Jump Shot	21270	60065	35.4%
3PT Pull-up Jump Shot	3351	9296	36.0%
3PT Step-Back Jump Shot	1916	5008	38.3%
3PT Running Jump Shot	622	1565	39.7%
3PT Running Pull-up Jump Shot	448	1132	39.6%
3PT Fadeaway Jumper	64	221	29.0%
3PT Jump Bank Shot	96	188	51.1%
3PT Turnaround Jump Shot	21	92	22.8%
3PT Floating Jump Shot	5	24	20.8%
3PT Step-Back Bank Jump Shot	14	22	63.6%
3PT Driving Floating Jump Shot	1	17	5.9%
3PT Turnaround Fadeaway Shot	0	12	0%
3PT Turnaround Fadeaway	4	4	100%
3PT Driving Floating Bank Jump Shot	1	3	33.3%
3PT Turnaround Fadeaway Bank Jump Shot	3	3	100%

---

2. There is no "official" designation for what constitutes a "very deep" attempt, sometimes referred to as "four-point range." I have found that 28 feet is a reasonable cut off point, though of course players like Damian Lillard, Stephen Curry, and in a pickup setting my former colleague and the Bucks' Senior Director of Scouting Matt Bollero routinely pull up from 32 feet and beyond.

Were the data presented in the previous table to be taken at face value, the *worst* thing a player could do is take a boring old catch-and-shoot three. Put some sauce on it instead and watch the efficiency rocket upward!

What's actually happening here is that these details, these little bits of commentary, are more frequently added to makes than misses. This discrepancy has gotten better through the years but is still present across the full range of shooting situations, from pull-up bank shots to post-ups and even to layups and dunks. Running, floating, driving, or finger-rolling is always "better" than simply laying the ball in, at least if play-by-play descriptions are to be treated as gospel truth.

This effect is especially prevalent when a player has a signature shot or move. A scorekeeper is likely primed to notice these specialties, such as Harden's step-back or Damian Lillard's deep three-point pull-ups.

This situation developed for understandable reasons. The goal of including shot description data in the play-by-play was not analysis.[3] Rather the intent is and was to provide some color and feel of the game to people "watching" via one of the various "game-time" dashboards and apps which sprung up as the Internet developed.

If the purpose is to emphasize highlights, bricks off the glass[4] might not be worth describing as any different from any other miss. But the "bank is open" chuck that misses just badly enough to kiss off the glass and go in? Make a note of that so fans of the opposing team can scream "Bullshit!" at their phone screens while they continuously refresh.

Additionally, the scorekeeper simply has more time to enter the fun stuff on a made shot than after a miss. When the ball goes through the net, there is a break in the action—a short break, but still a pause to catch one's breath before the ball is inbounded and play continues. On a miss, not only does the shot need to be recorded, but also a rebound, perhaps with an ensuing tip-in attempt or rapidly developing fast break the other way.

The descriptor is nice, but the only truly vital things to capture are the shooter, whether it was a three-point attempt or not, the approximate location of the shot, the approximate timing of the attempt, and of course the

---

3. The shot type data is not, to my knowledge, considered "official" in any way.
4. "Thumpers" in the parlance of longtime Bucks broadcaster Jim Paschke.

result. Only those aspects are part of the "official" statistical record. From an analysis perspective, we're often better off leaving the rest alone.

Mike Beuoy, proprietor of the sports analytics website Inpredictable, points to a similar issue from the NFL, where studies[5] have shown how recording bias in down-and-distance data has clouded analysis of fourth-down conversion rates. Though both might be recorded as "4th & 1" in the NFL's play-by-play data, there is a significant difference between "4th & an inch" and "4th & 1.99 yards" in terms of conversion rates. Teams understand this, so choose to go on fourth down more frequently in "4th & a short 1" than "4th & almost 2."

As Beuoy says, "That skews your 'success rate,' and maybe makes you a bit too confident in terms of conversion. One way you can address that is to look at third-down situations where teams always obviously go for it on third down. If you have good working domain knowledge, you know that a 3rd & 1 situation is going to be very similar to a 4th & 1 situation. That's one way to insulate yourself against bad or skewed data; knowing how to approach a problem in different ways and from different data streams."

If inconsistent data can lead down analytical dead ends, perhaps even leading to counterproductive strategic suggestions, what happens if the data is altogether wrong?

The Analyst's Armageddon

Let me tell you a story of how it can all fall apart. To be clear, this is entirely my subjective experience. For reasons which should be understandable shortly, nobody directly involved has been much interested in speaking on the record about these events.

Prior to the 2017–18 season, the NBA implemented a new courtside statistical entry system. The league was changing primary data providers and decided to update the courtside tech at the same time. The old system had the all the normal issues which arise from using an aged process, with various patches and little fixes. It was time.

---

5. Such as those conducted and publicized by that league's head of analytics, Mike Lopez.

The new system streamlined many of the processes to allow for quicker transmission from courtside entry to the feeds and APIs which power game-time apps.[6]

Sadly, some of the features that slowed the old system down mattered. For example, a player couldn't be awarded a stat if the system didn't know they were in the game when the play occurred. There is enough going on during an NBA game that a scorekeeper occasionally missing or mis-entering a substitution is something that is going to occur, though hopefully only rarely. The old system would catch that error by informing the operator that a player more than likely did not just throw that alley-oop from the bench, so maybe go back and make sure you didn't omit something?

Similarly, there were error-checking routines which prevented the entry of events in impossible sequence. For example, if the home team made a shot with 6:25 left in the first quarter, there is no sequence of events which allows for the next recorded event to be another shot attempt from the home team with 5:40 left in that quarter. *Something* had to have happened in the interim given the constraints of the 24-second shot clock and the fact that possessions alternate between teams. The old system would have required the operator to address the "So, what happened in that 45 seconds that you aren't telling me?" question.

With these guardrails removed or altered as part of the streamlining of the new system, all hell broke loose.[7]

Information on a single possession not being recorded may seem minor, but several complex systems are built on top of the play-by-play feed. Certain aspects of the data critical to those systems needs to be 100% accurate. And

---

6. Which have only become more important to how many consume the game following the invention and widespread adoption of smartphones.

7. Actually, minor amounts of hell experienced mostly by a few people in very specific roles broke loose. Being one of those people at the time, it sure seemed like all of the hell in the moment.

it was reasonable to expect that level of accuracy, considering it had been demonstrably reliable for many years.[8]

As an example of the things that build off and assume the accuracy of the play-by-play, the NBA collates a range of situational stats. These include fast break points, points off of turnovers, and second-chance points. The stats are tracked by looking at the immediately preceding play-by-play event to a score. Points in transition aren't credited because a scorekeeper decided "That was a fast break." Rather, a scoring event occurred less than eight seconds[9] after the ball changed possession between teams without an intervening stoppage such as a timeout, foul, or ball tipped out of bounds.

Obviously, a befouled play-by-play renders those stats inaccurate or at least unreliable. Far more pertinent to the modern analyst is the degree to which the use of tracking data requires clean play-by-play.

Eight seasons in, tracking data is so ingrained that how the sausage is made can be forgotten. But it's important to understand what is going on underneath the hood. The actual data is simply the output of multiple[10] cameras recording the positions of all 10 players and the ball (approximate to within a foot or so) and doing so 25 times per second. In raw form, this information is essentially useless. Each tracking "frame" is simply a list of player IDs and coordinates. Even stringing several frames together is just moving those dots around.

The real insight comes from analysis of patterns within the movement of those dots. The service provided by a company like Second Spectrum isn't just the collection of the raw location data. As important is the creation

8. There were a few situations the prior system did not handle well. The most common was in the proper ordering of events when the offensive team recorded multiple rebounds and subsequent putback attempts in quick succession. These near simultaneous events sometimes found their way into the play-by-play record out of order. This was annoying, but ultimately a straightforward fix when parsing events from the play-by-play logs. There were other similar situations, none of which were likely to recur more than a few times each season. My recollection may be fuzzy, but I think the oddest discrepancy I found was an instance where a player was awarded two free throws, took the first attempt, and was ejected from the game before the second attempt. The system did not have an event code for that happening.

9. Or Less—hence Mike D'Antoni's design of the mid-aughts Phoenix offense and the wonderful Jack McCallum book of the same name which chronicled a season for the Steve Nash–led Suns.

10. Initially four when Stats INC. ran the SportVU system in NBA arenas, six since Second Spectrum took over the collection process prior to the 2017–18 season.

of algorithms and heuristics to pull out what Maheswaran, the Second Spectrum CEO, calls "basketball words in the data."

One of the main reasons spatio-temporal data—AKA "tracking"—has been so successful in sports while similar technologies have at times faltered[11] in more open-ended environments is that the computer processing that data doesn't need to teach itself the rules. There are important contextual clues within play-by-play which steer processing algorithms in the right direction to successfully turn the dots into basketball data.

Once the machine understands the rules and some basic vocabulary is taught, the raw data turns into recognizable events. A particular sequence and pattern of movements by multiple players can be identified as a "pick-and-roll." Not just the fact that a pick-and-roll occurred but also more specific elements such as the identities of the four players involved (two on O, two on D), the location of the screen, how each defender attempted to guard the situation, and so on.

Of course, the most important things recorded was the end result of the play. Did the offense score? And if so, was it directly from the pick-and-roll action or later in the possession?

But before the machine can learn to diagnose the pick-and-roll, it needs to know some things.

Each player in each frame is recorded as a set of X/Y coordinates[12] located (approximately) at the center of the player's mass. The dot doesn't have arms or limbs. It doesn't have a face, or eyes, so the computer doesn't know which direction a player is facing[13] or even where they are looking. Most importantly, dots don't have hands.

As the saying goes, the hand is part of the ball. If the dots have no hands, no dot "has" the ball. And here's where a jacked-up play-by-play file creates a problem. The algorithm defining the events from a tracking sequence doesn't need to identify which team has the ball. Because we *know* who has the ball from other sources, i.e. play-by-play.

---

11. I was told all cars would be self-driving by now.

12. With a vertical "z" coordinate also included for the ball.

13. This is frequently derivable from patterns of movement, but this derivation isn't as precise as direct measurement, and that lack of precision negatively impacts the ability to analyze a lot of the things for which facing would be very useful, especially on the defensive side of the ball.

If the Bulls are playing Charlotte, and Zach LaVine hits a three-pointer with 6:25 remaining in the first quarter, if nothing else has been recorded in the play-by-play, we know Charlotte has possession at 6:15.

With this knowledge, the system can look at a pattern of four players on the floor and say, "Charlotte is running a pick-and-roll. Terry Rozier is pretty close to the ball, so he's handling. P.J. Washington is close by, so he's screening for Rozier. Coby White is going 'over' the screen and Thad Young is 'up to touch.'"

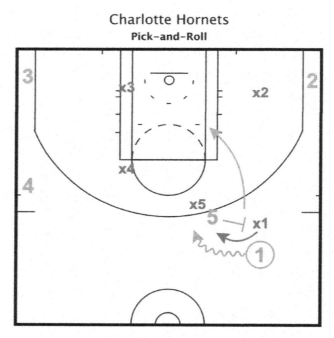

Charlotte Hornets
Pick–and–Roll

(Diagrams courtesy of Randy Sherman, Radius Athletics)

Now, at various points in this theoretical action, the ball might be just as close to White as to Rozier. Especially when we combine normal measurement error[14] with the dots representing center mass rather than arms or hands, there might be a few frames here and there where White appears to

---

14. The frame-by-frame "jitter" in the tracking data is typically several inches in one direction or another.

be *closer* to the ball than Rozier. But, since we know Charlotte has possession, the system can infer Rozier is in possession rather than he and White stealing the ball back and forth from each other several times a second.

Imagine this same configuration of players except for some reason—such as befouled play-by-play—the system thinks Chicago has the ball. Considering all the action is taking place close to the basket Chicago is defending, dots are moving in patterns which make little sense and certainly don't fall into any order the computer has been trained to recognize.

Charlotte Hornets
Pick–and–Roll

(Diagrams courtesy of Randy Sherman, Radius Athletics)

This was the situation for the first few weeks of 2017–18.

It wasn't every game. But it happened often enough that entire quarters of tracking data were unusable, at least without substantial reprocessing. I can assure you that the average NBA analytics department—heck, the *exceptional* NBA analytics department—was not well equipped to do so on a moment's notice.

There were players shooting at the wrong basket or for the wrong team. Three-minute possessions. *Possessions with negative duration.* It was all happening. Of course, it wasn't *actually* happening, but in the world of our most important data source it appeared to be. When the foundation of the statistical house suddenly transforms from rebarred concrete to sand, weird things start to happen.

An underground economy emerged between those in analytics roles. A text might read, "Hey, it lost track at 8:37 of the second quarter in our game last night. Rest of the quarter is broken," as we notified each other as to what portions of which games to exclude from reports and analysis while the bigger problem was addressed. No data at all is better than knowingly wrong data. From the standpoint of credibility within the organization, having no data is bad, but data describing literally impossible events is far worse. Trust is built slowly but destroyed swiftly.

The situation was largely rectified after the first few weeks of the season. But in the interim it was not a lot of fun to have to say, "I'm sorry, but there is no report on last night's game because the system broke. It's not my fault! Really!"

In short, this sucked. A common obstacle to the acceptance of analytics is the argument that since we can't explain *everything* in precise statistical terms, we can't really explain *anything*. The cause is not helped when we really can't explain anything.

While this was an extreme and thankfully unique example, it serves to illustrate the degree to which the data used for analysis rests on assumptions of accuracy and consistency which don't always hold.

Recall the definition of transition play; a fast break occurs if a shot, shooting foul drawn, or turnover occurs within seven seconds of the team acquiring possession. Precise timing of the preceding change of possession would be nice, but that level of precision is not necessary as long as the measurement is roughly consistent.

As an indicator, transition scoring matters far more in relative than in absolute terms. Whether the Pelicans allowing 15.1 fast break points per 100 in 2019–20 was a good or bad sign for their transition defense depended entirely on whether the league average was closer to 10 or 20.

(In fact, the NBA averaged around 13.5 fast break points/100, placing New Orleans 25th in the league, suggesting it was an area needing improvement.)

Assuming the distributions of time taken in "fast" possessions is relatively similar across teams, it doesn't much matter if the cutoff is six seconds or eight seconds. The teams which are better or worse at getting out and running themselves or preventing opponents from doing likewise will still be recognizably good or bad.

If the timekeeping is consistent.

If.

One of Beuoy's first big basketball projects was creating an in-game win probability model for the Inpredictable site. This model accounts for score margin, time remaining, which team has possession, and how many timeouts remaining or fouls to give each team has left, and from that information estimates the chances of each team winning the game from that point. Much like the rise of fourth-down "kick it or go for it" analysis in football, this estimate provides incredibly useful information for analyzing and informing game strategy. At what point does it become wiser to pull the starters because the game is out of reach? When should a team start intentionally fouling?[15] When *must* a team attempting a late comeback go for three as opposed to the dreaded "quick two"?[16]

To build this model, Beuoy needed to understand NBA play-by-play at an atomic level. A few seconds here or there, the presence or absence of an extra timeout or foul to give, can produce big swings in a team's chances of mounting a comeback or holding a lead. Precision in these "game state" factors was vital to properly calibrate the model.

Beuoy's day job—he is an actuary focused on health care—gives him an intimate understanding of the pitfalls of faulty data, so he knew to be on the lookout for problems and inconsistencies. Exploring the data, he found that though some pieces of the earliest years of play-by-play were inconsistently

---

15. As with most sports where similar exercises have been undertaken, Beuoy's analysis suggests teams don't recognize hopeless situations early enough. A team trailing by 10 points with six minutes remaining will win about one in 20 times. Similarly, teams go to extreme "underdog" strategies like fouling and forcing up quick threes until well after they should.

16. We'll get back to my personal end of game pet peeve, the "quick two" in Chapter 10.

recorded,[17] the feed had what was needed: "The key data elements seemed to be working. The time and score were right. Times for possession [starts] seemed to work. I think it was probably worse for trying to do plus/minus analysis with substitution data. Since that wasn't really needed for the win probability model it didn't break much of what I was doing."

As he explored further, he made some interesting discoveries. For example, the "pace" statistic might not always capture the true speed at which a team plays. "Pace was already established as kind of an 'advanced metric.' But it was always box score based. So it was always the average of the pace a team played on offense vs. your opponent's offense," Beuoy said. In other words, it wasn't just how fast a team played, but how fast they allowed or forced the other team to play as well.

Early in the Steve Kerr era in Golden State, Beuoy experimented with separating pace into offensive and defensive components: "The one thing that jumped out to me when I started splitting that out—everybody kind of knew the Warriors played really fast. But once I split out offense and defense, what really jumped out was they played insanely fast on offense. But their defense was so good, that they had one of the slowest paces on defense, because teams had to fight more to get a shot."

In 2015–16, Golden State finished second in the NBA in the league's official pace stat, averaging 100.2 possessions per 48 minutes. However, when Beuoy measured offensive and defensive possession lengths separately, Golden State had the fastest offense in the NBA by almost a quarter second, a sizable margin when the difference between fastest and slowest is just over 2.5 seconds. On *defense*, the Warriors forced the seventh-longest possessions.

Intrigued by this finding, Beuoy continued to examine the timing and sequencing of events in the play-by-play feed for other insights. By accident he stumbled upon something: time moves slower in some arenas than in others.

---

17. Most notably shot location and distance information.

As Beuoy put it:

> I noticed that for whatever reason rebounds on average will take 1.5 seconds in Houston. In a couple of other arenas it's longer than that, two to three seconds. There's some weird effect there that in the grand scheme of things probably doesn't matter too much, though it did skew one analysis that I was working on.
>
> I was trying to correlate possession length following a defensive rebound to efficiency. At one point, I think, 'You've got the inside scoop on this.' In the play-by-play [that timing difference] made it seem like teams got a lot more efficient, the correlation between efficiency and possession length shifted really dramatically. But it was a mirage, because it wasn't really the play on the court. It was just the timing for when possessions began after defensive rebound was recorded differently.

Average Length of a Rebound by Home Team
2019-20 NBA Season

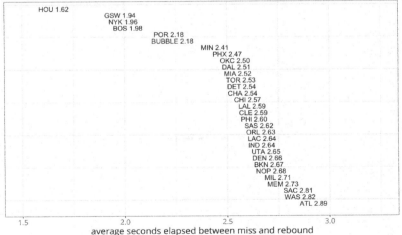

average seconds elapsed between miss and rebound

(Image courtesy of Mike Beuoy)

As a result of the quick trigger finger of the Toyota Center scorekeepers, the Rockets appeared to be much less willing to fast break at home than on the road. According to the calculations from Cleaning the Glass, Houston got out in transition on 22.4% of possessions at home, but 28.8% on the road. Considering the average team looked to fast break slightly more often (around 0.7 percentage points) at home, this would be quite the stylistic change. But the change didn't exist on the court, only in the data.[18]

There is a similar arena effect in PBP-based shot location data. Without access to tracking data, the precise coordinates of each shot is mostly a guess, though the general area of the court will be pretty accurate; in real time, it's far easier to note that a shot came from the left wing somewhere inside the arc than to narrow in on the exact square foot.[19] So rather than try to sort out exact locations, shot zones serve as a useful proxy for shot quality. On average, accuracy is far higher on attempts from the restricted area than on those from the rest of the paint.

Shooting Percentage by Zone
2019-20 NBA Regular Season

Shot Zone	FG%
Restricted Area	63.5%
Midrange	40.5%
In the Paint (Non-RA)	39.9%
Corner 3	38.9%
Above the Break 3	35.1%
Backcourt	1.7%

18. A separate oddity Beuoy found was that the timing of rebounds relative to missed shots changed dramatically before the 2017–18 season, right when the league switched courtside input systems. This change created an apparent trend which made pace appear to be more highly correlated with efficiency than in previous seasons. Really, the trend was illusory. Possessions on *made* shots end on the make, but possessions on defensive rebounds end with that rebound. Thus the extension of time between missed shot and rebound artificially extended the length of possessions ending with rebounds, possessions which are quite obviously lower efficiency than those which end with made shots. Once again, the game didn't change, just the data.

19. Or square tenth of a foot; the 94'-by-50' court is turned into a 900-by-540 grid for purposes of location entry.

However, as this data is recorded in real time with only one look at the play, there are plenty of judgment calls, especially on drives, where the shooter is moving rapidly toward the hoop. Whether the shot was released from inside or outside the restricted area can be ambiguous.

In real world terms, this doesn't really matter. There is no imaginary vertical wall on the edge of the restricted area which boosts efficiency if a shooter breaks the plane. But for purposes of analysis of shot selection, it's the difference between over 60% and around 40% expected accuracy. Which can be a *big deal* when evaluating a team's offensive or defensive structure if enough "extra" shots are assigned to one area or the other.

So long as there is consistency in the recording, the ambiguities of the "in or out" decision will largely even out. But much like Beuoy's discovery of variable timing of a rebound, there are some persistent discrepancies between arenas in the recording of shot location.

By measuring the proportion of paint shots which were judged to have been inside the restricted area, then comparing that ratio between a team's home and road games, we can estimate the degree to which a given arena is more or less generous in making the determination.

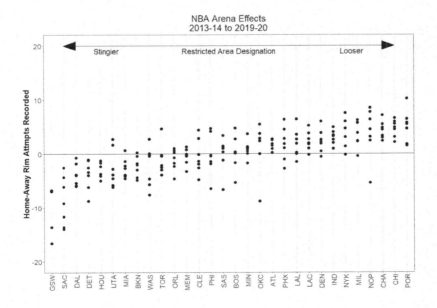

Each dot on the chart represents a single season; negative numbers mean a lower proportion of attempts were marked restricted area attempts in a team's home games than in road games, while positive numbers indicate the reverse.

The implication is that teams to the left have probably *appeared* to have slightly better defensive and slightly worse offensive shot profiles due to playing half their games in a "stingy" environment, while the opposite is true for the teams on the right. Again, this hardly matters for the play of the game, but for purposes of analysis can certainly shift the narrative interpretation behind a team's success or failure.

There need not be anything nefarious going on for this kind of effect to exist. They could result from different sightlines from different scorekeepers, or simply that scorekeeping crews are consistent in how they make these judgment calls year after year.

Basketball data is "clean" relative to that collected in most real world settings. But care must be taken to ensure the data accurately represents the events being recorded. As noted by Beuoy in a tweet revealing his rebounding timing findings, "The lesson here is to maintain a healthy skepticism of your data—it's not reality, but rather a human/machine's interpretation of reality. Having spent my career working with U.S. health data, that skepticism is *deeply* ingrained."

And yours should be too.

Chapter 6

Evidence of Things Not Seen: Impacts Behind the Box Score

"Occurrences in this domain are beyond the reach of exact prediction because of the variety of factors in operation, not because of any lack of order in nature."

—Albert Einstein

During the Miami Heat's run to the 2020 NBA Finals, coach Erik Spoelstra said of Jimmy Butler, "He's an anti-analytics guy because you can't put a number on how he impacts winning."

As interpreted by ABC's play-by-play man Mike Breen during a broadcast, Spoelstra was proclaiming Butler an "anti-analytic" player. This reading requires "analytics" to be synonymous with three-point shooting volume, which is certainly one common though faulty description. But using that definition and measured solely against a "layups and threes only" model of shot selection, Butler would appear to be a throwback.

Due to his propensity for shooting from the dreaded midrange areas,[1] Butler was last in eFG% among the thousand-point scorers in the truncated

---

1. Poorly. Butler hit less than 30% of his attempts outside of 16 feet on the season, whether they were three-pointers or long twos.

2019–20 season. Of those 65 players, only eight attempted fewer threes than Butler. Seven of those players were big men of some variety; the one perimeter player was the famously downrated-by-the-metrics-community DeMar DeRozan.[2]

From the standpoint of traditional statistics, Butler and DeRozan are quite comparable.

Jimmy Butler vs. DeMar DeRozan
Age 26-30 seasons

Player	G	MP	3PA	3P%	2PA	2P%	eFG%	FTA	FT%	ORB	DRB	TRB	AST	STL	BLK	TOV	PTS
Jimmy Butler	325	35.7	3.0	0.333	12.0	0.491	0.493	7.6	0.849	1.6	4.2	5.8	5.0	1.8	0.5	1.9	21.2
DeMar DeRozan	377	34.9	1.7	0.294	16.1	0.492	0.487	7.3	0.839	0.8	4.2	5.0	5.0	1.1	0.3	2.4	23.4

The per game averages of each player from the 2015–16 through 2019–20[3] seasons are very similar indeed. Both players were slightly less efficient than average from the field. Against a baseline rating of 100, Butler's eFG+[4] was 95, while DeRozan's was 94 for this period. Factoring in their foul-drawing craft and/or grift, their scoring is slightly more efficient than average; Butler's TS+ of 104 gives him the edge over the 101 for DeRozan. Both players contribute decently well on the boards and are much better playmakers and passers than their reputations—especially DeRozan's—would suggest. Overall, their basic statistical profiles are much more "pretty good" than "game-changingly great."

---

2. Somewhat ironically, DeRozan had one of the best seasons of his career in 2020–21 during the writing of this book. Not coincidentally, DeRozan embraced a more "analytics-friendly" style himself, shooting more threes while also functioning as a playmaking smallball power forward with multiple shooters arrayed around him.

3. These were the age 26-30 seasons for both players, with "season age" calculated as of February 1 in a given season. Though the two are approximately the same age, they were the seventh through 11th seasons of DeRozan's career as compared to years five through nine for Butler; DeRozan played only one year at USC, while Butler spent four years in college split between Tyler Community College and Marquette.

4. A relatively new suite of stats added to Basketball-Reference.com during the 2019–20 season which scale a player's shooting splits to the league average that season to allow for more apples-to-apples comparisons in a changing league environment. I'm a big fan of this sort of normalization process, but sadly even the statistically inclined have become so used to calculated percentages that replacing eFG% and TS% with eFG+ and TS+ will be a steeply uphill endeavor if anyone bothers to try.

Yet Butler has long been beloved by the "metrics community" while DeRozan is something of a punchline. If the difference between them is all the little things that Butler does—his heart, grit, determination, the sheer Wants-It-More[5]—how can we be so sure Butler has been better? You simply can't use "the numbers" to measure[6] the value of those contributions.[7]

What if I told you that you could?

"'Regularized Adjusted Plus/Minus,' or RAPM (as well as APM,[8] its predecessor), is estimating a player's average impact on margin of victory by observing how the score of the game changes when the player is on the floor while also accounting for the strength of teammates, opposing players, and home court advantage," says Joe Sill,[9] the researcher who first introduced RAPM in a 2010 paper at the Sloan Sports Analytics Conference.

Don't let the nomenclature and computational complexity obscure what is a straightforward concept. To restate Sill's description, RAPM's approach is to measure, once we consider the circumstances in which the player appears, whether his team performs better or worse with him on the floor, and by how much? There are worse possible answers to "How can we tell how good a player is?"

---

5. "WIM" is one of those things that is surely important and equally as surely applied retroactively to turn differences in skill and distribution of variance into supposedly immutable character traits. Joel Embiid is somehow less of a winner because Kawhi Leonard's last-second rainbow kissed the rim four times before dropping at the buzzer in Game 7 of the 2019 Eastern Conference Semifinals. Leonard's Raptors of course went on to win the title, while the Sixers jettisoned Butler—or Butler jettisoned them, accounts differ—re-tooled around a mammoth Embiid–Al Horford–Ben Simmons frontline, and promptly got swept by Boston in the first round of 2020. Results over Process indeed.

6. It is somewhat unavoidable that a discussion centered around regression modeling will be a *little* dense, but bear with me.

7. I'm being slightly coy here. Defense is a big difference between the players as well, but I've got a whole chapter on that later. Not that Chapter 9 has any definitive answers on how to best value or evaluate defense.

8. Adjusted Plus/Minus, which I describe shortly.

9. Sill currently works in the front office of the Washington Wizards.

The Personal Ratings Pitfall

In Chapter 3, we spent some time exploring the differences between the meaning of team and individual stats even for the same "stat," such as a "rebound." We are now moving into an area where keeping this distinction clear is absolutely vital. Since we are explicitly defining player ability in terms of moving the scoreboard in favorable directions, it is tempting to… simply look at how the team has performed on offense and defense with the player on the floor, and voilà. The lure is especially strong when trying to measure defense, where we are desperate for useful guidance.

Unfortunately, this pulls us toward a common mental trap, which goes something like this:

1. We need a good measure of defense.
2. Individual defensive rating is a measure of defense.
3. Individual defensive rating is therefore a good measure of defense.

Too which I have one response:

DEFENSIVE RATING IS NOT AN INDIVIDUAL STAT.

Let me explain.

In 2019–20 Enes Kanter had a solid year for the Boston Celtics. In his 17 or so minutes per game, the Celtics scored 113.8 points per 100 possessions while allowing 103.9, meaning Boston outscored opponents by just under 10 points per 100 possessions. Meaning Kanter had a 113.8 ORTG, a 103.9 DRTG, and a +9.9 net rating for the Cs, right?

Wrong.

The difference might appear to be semantic, but "The team did X while Player Y was on the court" and "Player Y *had* a net rating of X" are substantially different. The former is clearly just describing what happened. The second is at least implying causation, that the Celtics won Kanter's minutes by nearly 10 points/100 *because* of Kanter.

I get why the term "rating" entered the popular lexicon. When Dean Oliver wrote *Basketball on Paper* in 2004, the concepts of "per possession" or "per minute" stats were new and foreign to the basketball world.[10] Describing things in terms of "points allowed/100" looked math-y and might have been a bit of a turnoff. So it was instead called "defensive rating" to help the medicine go down.

Today, per possession stats are the norm rather than the exception and we're *awash* in rating systems. That name, "rating," is an unhelpful anachronism, implying some sort of calculation or evaluation where none exists. It's just points allowed/100, an expression everybody would now take in stride.

All of which is the long way to say that *offensive and defensive ratings are not individual statistics.* As such, *Kanter* did not have a 103.9 DRTG. The *Celtics* had a 103.9 DRTG with Kanter on the floor.[11] But the "ratings" are established well enough as labels that we're stuck with them, and it becomes a matter of constant repetition of the mantra

DEFENSIVE RATING IS NOT AN INDIVIDUAL STAT[12]

until that too becomes broadly accepted knowledge.

---

10. Oliver was hardly the first to cite per possession efficiency. Luminaries such as North Carolina coach Dean Smith did so decades earlier, but that was more an exception than anything close to industry standard.

11. Kanter ranked 649th out of 780 players in Defensive Regularized Adjusted Plus/Minus (DRAPM) for the three seasons ending in 2019–20, estimating that he cost his teams 0.77 points/100 possessions on defense. Based on that record, it is probably wisest to assume the Celtics performed well on defense *in spite of* rather than because of Kanter.

12. Offensive Rating as well. A further issue which tends to cause confusion when discussing Offensive and Defensive Ratings as individual stats is that while Basketball-Reference.com lists Offensive and Defensive Ratings for each player, these are entirely different stats! Remember how I just said that ORTG and DRTG are purely descriptive and contain no information about whether the player in question was responsible for a team's strong or poor performance? Throw that out. These ratings, created by Oliver, are explicit attempts to estimate points produced or saved by a player's contributions. Oliver's "Ratings" aren't used much these days, in large part because of the cumbersome calculations involved. According to the B-Ref glossary, Offensive Rating, the simpler of the two, requires 19 steps to calculate. Largely developed in the 1990s, the intricate formulae are attempts to infer on-court data for individual players in a time before the introduction of play-by-play. Though they can be useful to examine pre-1996 seasons, the ready availability of play-by-play for 1996–97 and beyond makes the convoluted arithmetic of these "Ratings" unnecessary. But regardless of derivation, they are very different stats compared to the more prevalent "Points Scored/Allowed Per 100 Possessions with this player on the floor" versions.

Reducing Lineup Noise

To elucidate why individual plus/minus, and by extension individual on-court ratings, shouldn't bear a lot of analytical weight, I'll cede the floor to coaching legend Gregg Popovich:[13]

> I don't look at that [plus/minus]. I've never looked at it, just because you don't know who was in the game at certain times. You could have a weak lineup or somebody could have played badly, which helps somebody else get a "negative game." It's the last thing I look at, if I do.

Pop has a reputation for cantankerousness and likes to portray himself as an old-school skeptic of new developments such as analytics. But he's been an incredible coach who, even if he has taken a different path to get there, has often ended up in a lot of the same places strategically that a metrics-based approach would suggest over the years.

Just as appearing with weak lineups or players on a cold streak can drag a player's plus/minus down, being the fifth wheel on a great team will allow a player to be in the room where gaudy plus/minus totals happen without necessarily doing a lot to make it happen.

In 2019–20, Wesley Matthews Jr. finished sixth in the league in total plus/minus. The Milwaukee Bucks outscored opponents by 454 points with him on the floor over the 67 games in which Matthews appeared. How much of that margin should be attributed to Matthews' own play? The other four Bucks starters were pretty good too:

- Eric Bledsoe—eighth in total plus/minus. Named to Second Team All-Defense.
- Khris Middleton—third in total plus/minus. Appeared in his second All-Star Game en route to just missing a "50/40/90" season, shooting 49.7% from the floor overall, 41.5% on threes, and 91.5% from the line.

---

13. Quoting from an August 2019 USA Basketball presser.

- Brook Lopez—second in total plus/minus. Named to Second Team All-Defense and would have gotten my vote for Defensive Player of the Year if I had had one.
- Giannis Antetokounmpo—led the league in total plus/minus at +682, *176 points ahead of Lopez*. All-Star starter, NBA MVP, and Defensive Player of the Year.

Also worth noting: Matthews' primary backup, Donte DiVincenzo, finished ninth in total plus/minus.

Matthews filled a valuable role, certainly *participating* in Milwaukee's dominant regular season. But just how much did a guy finishing 182nd in usage rate out of 187 qualified players contribute to that dominance?

On the other end of the spectrum, Draymond Green of the Golden State Warriors finished 493rd out of 527 players in total plus/minus during the season. By contrast, prior to 2019–20, Green had appeared in five straight NBA Finals, winning three titles, and from 2014–15 to 2018–19, finished second, first, second, 30th, and 12th, respectively, in total plus/minus. While we had to wait until the belated start of the 2020-let's-just-call-it-2021 season to know for sure,[14] Green did not go from one of the best to one of the worst players in the league overnight. Kevin Durant leaving via free agency, Klay Thompson missing the entire season after tearing his ACL in the 2019 Finals, and Stephen Curry only appearing in five games had a lot more to do with that ugly plus/minus than did Green himself.

Perhaps more importantly, how much does this data tell us about whether Matthews outplayed Green? The example is extreme enough to allow us to say, "Not much." Even when making more apt comparisons, we should still slow down; plus/minus doesn't get us to the finish line.

Who you're playing with and against matters a lot. So, how can we account for the scoreboard impact of any one player[15] while also acknowledging

---

14. Despite his jump shot largely abandoning him, Green was a strongly positive player for the 2020–21 Warriors, with his passing, screening, and overall intelligence serving as very effective amplifiers for Stephen Curry's scoring genius.

15. A pretty good definition for "How well did this dude play?" The scoreboard is our North Star.

that all 10 matter? This is precisely the sort of query amenable to regression analysis.[16]

This regression takes the form of trying to predict the change in score margin over a stint of game action from the 10 players on the floor. In lay terms, you take plus/minus, and then you adjust for the other players on the court. Hence, Adjusted Plus/Minus models,[17] usually simply called APM. These models calculate estimates of player "values" so that the observed scoreboard differential between lineups is as close to the predicted result across the entire season's worth of play.

For various math-and-stat-y reasons, APM isn't good enough for real world decision-making. A single season's worth of data isn't enough game time to fully explore the impacts of 450 or more players in various combinations. It does okay in terms of sorting players who got a ton of PT into ranges of good, bad, and indifferent. Sadly, the range of uncertainty around each player's estimated value[18] is so large as to make any sort of ordered list extremely unreliable.

According to Sill, "the APM framework was very valuable" in formal statistical terms, but was prone to "overfitting" to the data on hand. The model could accurately describe the results of the randomness of a season already

16. For the non-statistically minded, according to Dictionary.com, regression analysis is "a procedure for determining a relationship between a dependent variable, as predicted success in college, and an independent variable, as a score on a scholastic aptitude test, for a given population. The relationship is expressed as an equation for a line…or curve…in which any coefficient…of the independent variable in the equation has been determined from a sample population."

17. The creation of APM is generally credited to longtime league analyst and former professor of economics Dan Rosenbaum, who has had stints in the front offices of the Pistons, Hawks, and Cavaliers, among others. Rosenbaum introduced the technique in a 2004 article still available on 82games.com. As there are very few completely novel discoveries, APM itself followed on the heels of other models arising from similar logic created by, among others, Wayne Winston and Jeff Sagarin.

18. For example, an APM model might estimate a player was worth +2.00 points/100 possessions, with a standard deviation of 1.5. Rather than the 2.00/100 being taken as a literal and precise value, it is merely the midpoint of a range of possible outcomes, which will fall between -1 and +5—two standard deviations—95% of the time. I'm almost embarrassed to put a discussion of confidence intervals in a footnote, as it is a massively important concept and represents one of the key barriers to accurate communication between analysts and decision-makers who are unfamiliar with probabilistic thinking. But it's a huge topic and I'm nobody's idea of a statistics professor, so a footnote is what we get.

played. Which didn't do that much to address the important questions. Such as, "Who is going to help us win most next year?"

In a Sloan Sports Conference[19] paper introducing RAPM, Sill elaborated:

> Overfitting occurs when a model fits the training data too precisely, i.e., in such a way that the fluky peculiarities and noise of the data are fit, so that the model's predictive performance on future data is degraded. As a simple example, imagine a situation where a rookie NBA player has a FG% of 67% over the first 5 games of the season. Suppose the task is to predict the player's FG% over the course of the remaining 77 games. It should be intuitively obvious that the estimate which best fits the available data, 67%, is unlikely to be the optimal prediction for the entire season. The naive use of such an estimate for the purposes of prediction would be an instance of overfitting. A smarter approach would be to combine the data from the 5 games with prior information about the typical distribution of FG% which NBA players achieve over the course of the season. While it is true that APM models are often estimated over an entire season of data (or even multiple seasons) it is nonetheless the case that standard linear regression is prone to overfitting, since the data is so noisy and since so many parameters (one for nearly every player in the league) need to be simultaneously estimated.

The inability to make good predictions for future results isn't, strictly speaking, fatal to a model's usefulness. Though in a sport like basketball where the good players and teams tend to stay good, this failure is a significant drawback.

To address this problem, Sill applied an additional technique, "regularization." This is the "R" in RAPM. "RAPM uses prior information (AKA regularization) about...the likely range of player ratings...and blends this

---

19. Sill, Joseph. "Improved NBA Adjusted +/- Using Regularization and Out-of-Sample Testing."

prior information with the data," Sill says. The practical effect of this "prior" is that lower-minute players tend to get pulled toward a baseline rating. We know[20] that a player who only played 50 minutes was probably not worth 30 points/100 possessions to his team, so the regularization penalty would pull that rating, quite strongly in the case of such a small minute sample, down toward zero.

An RAPM model produces estimates which remain extremely noisy over even a full season, though substantially less so than APM. Throwing additional seasons of data into it improves the model enough that it produces a decent approximation of player effectiveness.

Effectiveness.

Not skill, nor talent, nor ability. And certainly not their *ranking* among players. Instead, the value spit out by RAPM should be interpreted as, "In the role in which they were used, this player added or subtracted an estimated X points per 100 possessions." To the extent a player's role remains consistent, RAPM can predict the future, at least a little.

"Heat Culture"

While in the process of trying to quantify the supposedly unquantifiable, we also need to make clear there are things we are not measuring nor are we attempting to do so.

The value brought by Butler's teammate Udonis Haslem is one such thing. Haslem has not received consistent minutes in Miami's rotation since the 2014–15 season, playing 580 minutes *total* through the end of 2019–20. However, he is widely credited with being a pillar of the organization's ethic, which prizes competitiveness, conditioning, and togetherness. In the

---

20. This is an example of the "Bayesian" reasoning that is so important to the statistical analysis of sports. Named for 18th century statistician and minister Thomas Bayes, Bayesian reasoning recognizes that for many phenomena we study we are not starting from a blank slate. Rather, past observation and experience have allowed us to form a prior belief (often shortened to simply a "prior") against which our future observations push or pull. In this case, long observation has taught us that the guy signed to a 10-day contract probably isn't the best player in the league.

locker room, what Udonis says goes, in ways that a member of the coaching staff could never replicate.[21]

I have no reason to doubt this is true. From an outside perspective, the Heat certainly appear to be one of the more coherently aligned organizations in the NBA.[22] Their culture likely benefits them on the floor in myriad small ways. Miami has had the foresight to identify the potential in players like Duncan Robinson, and then maintain both the patience to let them develop and the structure to allow those prospects to see the path forward. In short, it provides players the motive and opportunity to buy in completely. Haslem is a big part of that. But none of this reflects his time on the floor. Perhaps he is due a percentage of the credit for Robinson's on-court production, however measured, but that credit is speculative and attenuated.

In terms of off-court influence, intangibles remain intangible.

More or Less Than the "Numbers"

Unlike Haslem's locker room presence, the Butler on-court "intangibles" become very tactile via tools like RAPM.[23] For the five seasons ending in 2019–20, RAPM rated Butler as the sixth-most-impactful player in the league per possession.

---

21. In my observation during my time with the Bucks, admonishments from other players, even deep bench or injured players, carried different and often greater weight than anything a coach might say. This was observable even if the coach in question was a recently retired player himself.

22. The Raptors and Thunder would be my other two votes for tops in those areas.

23. There is no "official" version of RAPM. Numerous small model-building decisions can have a significant impact on the results, but for the purpose of this text I'm using the version calculated by Ryan Davis and available on NBAShotCharts.com due to the easy accessibility of one-, three-, and five-year models going back over more than a decade of play. Five ThirtyEight's RAPTOR player value model also makes extensive use of this version of RAPM as a baseline. Ryan has also made his results extremely easy to export and search, for which the analytics community is very thankful.

Top 20 in 5-Year RAPM 2015-16 to 2019-20
Values Per 100 Possessions - via NBAShotCharts.com

Player	RAPM	Player	RAPM
Stephen Curry	7.82	Jrue Holiday	4.51
Chris Paul	6.91	Nikola Jokić	4.43
LeBron James	6.62	James Harden	4.43
Kawhi Leonard	5.55	Draymond Green	4.36
Kyle Lowry	5.26	Damian Lillard	4.17
Jimmy Butler	5.12	Kevin Durant	4.13
Rudy Gobert	4.88	Jayson Tatum	4.07
Paul George	4.76	Kemba Walker	3.91
Joel Embiid	4.73	Patrick Beverley	3.68
Giannis Anetetokounmpo	4.68	Paul Millsap	3.62

Butler achieved this despite playing on four different teams, a situation which would usually serve to suppress his value.[24] Over the course of his tenure with the Bulls, Wolves, Sixers, and Heat, Butler went from unquestioned alpha to drill sergeant to sidekick to leader among equals, excelling in each role in turn.

Butler's RAPM value should not be taken literally. It is neither definitive proof nor really even an argument that he was the sixth-best player in the NBA over that time. While he was selected to four All-Star teams and made Third Team All-NBA three times in that span, he was never really considered among the *very* top players in the game, a designation reserved for the likes of LeBron James, Kevin Durant, or Stephen Curry.

Even in a five-year sample, RAPM is too imprecise to overturn those judgments. While many RAPM-style metrics are expressed to the second decimal place (as is Butler's +5.12/100 rating), we shouldn't confuse multiple decimal places for precision in the measurement. That +5.12 is merely the center of a reasonably wide distribution of possible values for Butler.

---

24. Players who change teams tend to regress toward the mean. The more impactful they were in a previous role, the more likely it was that role was one well optimized for their skillset.

Restating it another way, RAPM estimates +5.12/100 to be the point where his "true impact" is equally likely to have been higher as it was lower. How sure can we be that Butler was more impactful over that sample than Rudy Gobert,[25] clocking in seventh at +4.88/100, or that he was less impactful than Kyle Lowry, fifth at +5.26? Not especially, in the 52-53% range on either end.

While this uncertainty is such that the order of RAPM values should not be interpreted as "rankings," the values can be taken as strong evidence that all three of Butler, Lowry, and Gobert were *extremely* effective players over the half-decade covered by this version of the model.

It is no accident that players like Butler and Lowry and Jrue Holiday[26] (11th at +4.51/100) are clustered near the top of the five-year RAPM list. All three are frequently recipients of "you can't measure it on the stat sheet" praise, and with good reason.

Between 2009–10 and 2016–17, *every* team featuring Lowry, Butler, or Holiday had a better Net Rating[27] with those players on the floor than off. Though they weren't always fortunate enough to be on teams good enough to outscore the opposition, even on those occasions when they were over-matched, their teams lost by less with these players on the floor. Only in the last few seasons has Lowry's on/off started to fall off as he enters his mid-30s. The Raptors were *slightly* better with him off the floor than on in 2017–18 and 2019–20.[28]

---

25. More about Gobert when we get to Chapter 9 on measuring defense.

26. In July 2021, Holiday and the Milwaukee Bucks defeated the Phoenix Suns in the NBA Finals. Holiday shot only 36.1% from the floor in the series, including 31.4% on threes. But Milwaukee outscored Phoenix by 37 points with Holiday on the floor over the six games of the series, the largest plus/minus for any player, and did so in large part because of the degree to which Holiday's other contributions more than made up for the poor shooting to move the scoreboard in the Bucks' favor. Which is exactly the kind of impact RAPM is designed to pick up on.

27. It may seem hypocritical to cite on/off rating having just bashed the use of Net Rating as an individual stat, but used judiciously, comparing a team's performance with a player on the floor to when they sit has some use to illustrate concepts like "they were better with him on the floor" in more concrete terms than an RAPM estimate.

28. Toronto's strength-in-numbers approach and the emergence of the positionally similar Fred VanVleet in recent seasons are just the sort of contextual factors which make using on/off ratings as proof of performance so dangerous without deeper analysis.

Conversely, DeRozan was 133rd on the five-year RAPM list, estimated to have contributed +1.08/100 over this time frame. Unlike Lowry, Butler, and Holiday, DeRozan's teams have performed better with him *off* the floor every season save for one. Considering this is over 12 seasons, two teams, and a number of different roles, the consistency is striking. In fact, given that track record, DeRozan showing up as a positive player at all according to RAPM is a mild surprise.

YAPMs[29]

The search for a single number to describe a player didn't stop with RAPM. The requirement of a full or even multi-season sample makes that metric a bit unwieldy. For the purposes of in-season and partial season analysis, there was a need for something more bite-sized. This need led to the development of several "statistical plus/minus" models, or SPMs.

There were all-in-one metrics before APM, of which John Hollinger's Player Efficiency Rating is perhaps the most widely recognized.[30] The benefit of these box score based models is that the stats are already counted, and what remains is to weight them. These metrics varied greatly in assigning those weights.

Hollinger extrapolated from league averages to create weights before scaling the results to a mean value of 15.0.[31] Others used complicated formulas or their own regression models.[32] But these weights were all largely

---

29. Description of the differences between the various flavors of plus/minus metrics requires some explication of the math behind each. I've tried to keep the following discussion as abstract as possible, but some complexity is inevitable.

30. The individual Offensive and Defensive Rating metrics developed by Dean Oliver and available on Basketball-Reference.com are another, more computationally involved example.

31. As newer metrics have been developed, PER has fallen into a degree of disrepute in the analytics community, though I think it retains some usefulness as a quick point of reference for a player's (primarily) offensive production. Looking at an individual player's season-on-season changes in PER can provide a useful snapshot of whether a player had an up or down year, has grown into or aged out of a starring role, has recovered from injury or is still compromised, and so on.

32. A common problem facing these models was mistaking the value of a team-level stat for the value credible to an individual.

educated guesses, what with the lack of a reference value against which to measure.

APM provided just such a point of reference. In fact, Dan Rosenbaum introduced an SPM model[33] alongside his first pass at APM itself:

> I was always pretty skeptical of how useful adjusted plus/minus was in and of itself. The bigger breakthrough in some respects was the idea, "We now have this kind of unbiased measure of player impact, but it's super noisy." Is there anything useful that we can do with it? My thought was we have all these other kinds of all-in-one metrics that just guess at what the value of these various statistics are in terms of player impact. We could use this unbiased measure of player impact [APM] to get better coefficients for all those metrics. And so that was obviously motivation for this statistical plus/minus.

In 2004, the ability to better weight box score stats was a huge step forward.

As the regression models improved, so did the SPMs. The more robust Box Plus/Minus (BPM)[34] derived the value of box score inputs from multi-year RAPM, with the greater precision of RAPM allowing for better weighting of those inputs. An alphabet soup of competing plus/minus metrics were created, inspiring Nylon Calculus contributor Hannes Becker to bemoan the frequent introductions of "yet another plus/minus model."

One strand of these new metrics did turn out to be particularly useful. This offshoot is probably best described as a hybrid of an SPM and RAPM

---

33. Named "Statistical Plus/Minus." Which is more confusing now that it was then, as the entire category of APM- and RAPM-derived box score metrics are also known as SPMs.

34. Created by Daniel Myers.

itself. ESPN's Real Plus/Minus (RPM) in its current iteration[35] uses SPM prior, which includes both box score and player tracking data, to form Bayesian prior against which the RAPM regression pushes the value.

Dizzyingly, the creation of these hybrid models led to the creation of more, likely better SPMs. For example, Player Impact Plus/Minus[36] uses a combination of box score and luck-adjusted on-off data to provide an RPM analog calculable on a game-by-game basis.

This cycle of improvement continues, whereby a more predictive regression model is used to form the basis for a more accurate SPM, which in turn can be used as a prior for the next regression model. "I was thinking that hopefully the best player impact metric is going to be some combination of those two," says Rosenbaum, which is exactly what has happened.

Explainability Follies

All of this statistical legerdemain is well and good, but when these metrics broadly and significantly prefer Butler to DeRozan—as they do—the (several) million dollar question remains. Just what is Butler *doing* on the floor to appear to be so much more impactful?

For as useful as RAPM models have proved to be, the methodology is a near total failure in one key aspect: explainability. There is no way to identify exactly what it is that Butler does that DeRozan doesn't and vice versa. We could watch film for days and days to pick up on possibilities, but there would be no real way of knowing if we had hit upon the secret or just a stylistic flourish with no real impact. As former Jazz analyst Taylor Snarr says, often "you don't know what you're measuring, exactly. Some of what is impacting the metric might be noise; some of it certainly is noise."

---

35. Earlier versions did not incorporate tracking data into the statistical prior. The changes were made in part to address RPM's apparent tendency to overvalue stat-collecting yet otherwise defensively mediocre big men due to the scarcity of good box score indicators for defensive ability. Unsurprisingly, the inclusion of an entirely new field of data substantially changed the model's output. The re-factored metric is both too new and complex enough for me to have decided how much I like it.

36. Created by Jacob Goldstein, now with the Wizards front office.

SPMs appear to offer a path to explainability, with values and weights assigned to various statistical accomplishments. Those weights should be interpreted with care. These stats are *indicators* of impact rather than direct measurements. As we saw in Chapter 3, a "defensive rebound" is the capstone of a series of actions culminating in a defender ending up with the ball after an opponent miss. The player grabbing the rebound is due the credit for only a portion of those actions leading to the rebound. Something similar is going on with the weights used by an SPM.

According to Rosenbaum these "are measuring a combination of the value of that [box score] statistic and whatever that statistic happens to be proxying for. It was funny, early on so many people seem to think that a bug. And I thought it was a feature. Because I want to know, what if this is telling me something about defense I want to know about."

As an example, writing on Five ThirtyEight in March 2014, Benjamin Morris examined the value of each box score stat. To do so he "created a regression using each player's box score stats (points, rebounds, assists, blocks, steals, and turnovers) to predict how much teams would suffer when someone couldn't play."[37]

By Morris' calculations, a steal was "worth" the same as 9.1 points. Taken literally, this is nonsensical. As the NBA is not Rock-and-Jock Basketball, there are no nine-pointers. At most, a "pick-six" type steal which leads to a breakaway "dunk" produces at most a little over three points (the 1.1 or so points the erstwhile offense could expect from the possession ended by the steal, and the two points from the dunk). Even that feels like cheating, because the dunk itself doesn't add two points. No matter how the defensive possession ended, the thief's team was going to get the next possession on which they could expect to score around 1.1 points.

But those results shouldn't be interpreted in such a head-on fashion. In a number of contexts, steals have been correlated with player ability, and not just defensive ability. One of the strongest statistical predictors of NBA success for college prospects is their steal rate. There are many theories as to why; Morris summarized what is my favorite among them:

---

37. Morris, Benjamin. "The Hidden Value of the NBA Steal." Retrieved from https:// fivethirtyeight.com/features/the-hidden-value-of-the-nba-steal/

"Maybe steals are just a product of, as pundits like to call it, high basketball IQ." This tracks. As Jake Loos, head of analytics for the Suns, says, "The highest IQ players typically will show up as the high APM players."

So, perhaps the combination of pattern recognition skills, quick reaction times, and physical ability to actually get to the ball fast enough which allow a player to come up with steals make the stat a strong proxy for general basketball goodness. But the steal as a stat is just an indicator, not the thing itself. As we saw in Chapter 4, confusing the two leads us to bad places, incentivizing stat-accumulative rather than scoreboard-effective play.

Even as these models become more sophisticated, telling us more and more about a player's impact on offense, defense, and everything in-between, they don't tell us how. Nor do they offer any clue to when a player might be "playing the drill" and chasing stats.

In fact, as models become more sophisticated and precisely tuned, the "black box effect" of not knowing what's going on underneath the hood grows more prevalent.

According to Snarr, "It is a tough balance, because I think that there is some benefit to try to be more precise. Finding stats and variables that could help you assign credit more accurately is the end goal. But I think that you should tread into those waters very carefully."

This difficulty in practical interpretation of the outputs was a major obstacle to the adoption of analytics prior to the introduction of tracking data. If even the best top-down models struggle to decipher *why*, the ratings produced might be interesting but are almost certainly not actionable.

So how can these models be of more use than point-scoring in the Twitter debate club?

Microskills

If these all-in-one models only measure contributions in a given role, how can they be used as the basis for trading for a player, knowing he will have a different role?[38]

"With an item like RAPM, it's great to use proxies such as number of possessions played and a sparse collection of matchups to infer how much a player contributes," says Justin Jacobs, a statistical researcher and former collegiate player who has worked and consulted for numerous NBA teams. "However, without measuring and incorporating the actual actions taken on a court, we will be unable to determine how much of that impact is truly due to each player."

These "individual actions," the very sort of "basketball words in the data" being unearthed by Second Spectrum, SIS, and others looking at more granular statistics and information, are the next frontier in on-court analysis of players.

Given the similarities between the statistical production of Butler and DeRozan, yet the sharp divergence in their apparent impact, *how* Butler does it matters a great deal. A big part of that "how" is on defense, where in many cases the black box output of a RAPM model is the best we're going to get. Though the two were rated essentially equally on offense, with Butler 22nd in ORAPM compared to 30th for DeRozan, on defense there is a chasm separating them, with Butler fifth and DeRozan 871st (of 942) in DRAPM.

---

38. Recent research suggests that a player changing teams is likely to experience a decline in their RAPM rating in the new environment. There are at least two competing but not mutually exclusive explanations. First, players who are playing a large enough role to have a RAPM rating in the first place are likely to have already been in an above-median-for-their-skillset role. Given the thin margins in talent between, for example, a low-end starter and someone close to being out of the league entirely, the former is probably living his best life, and a new address will more often than not be worse. The second rationale was suggested to me by Simon Strachan of the consulting group Gain Line Analytics, which has found that players in sports such as rugby union or Australian Rules Football tend to show measurable declines after changing teams due to the unfamiliarity of the new environment. The lack of familiarity requires more frequent engagement of Kahneman's "Type 2" thinking, required for solving new problems. This is both slower than the more automatic "Type 1" system *and* occupies so much of the brain's working memory so as to degrade fine motor skills. In other words, in the early days in a new context, the player will both be late and execute skills poorly more frequently.

We'll get to defense more directly in Chapter 9, but Butler's rank still doesn't tell us why he has been so impactful on that end of the floor. We can make some guesses via his statistical résumé. Butler loves a steal, with his 2.5 STL/100 possessions ranking 12th among all players who played at least 5,000 minutes in the 2015–16 to 2019–20 period. But he has a very modest wingspan, is not explosively quick, nor is he the sort of big man who impacts a game quite noisily with their interior play and rim protection.

Rather than being an "anti-analytics" player, Butler is an analytically fascinating one. Our best estimates suggest he is very good defensively and far more valuable on offense than his box score numbers would suggest. The subtleties of what he does and how he does it are the reason why the numbers and the practiced eye work best in tandem.

Chapter 7

Mind the Cap: Player Value and Roster Construction

"We must consult our means rather than our wishes."

—George Washington

The Golden State Warriors had just blown a 3–1 lead in the NBA Finals. As the Cleveland Cavaliers celebrated on the Oracle Arena floor and the rest of the basketball world marveled over The Block, The Shot, and The Stop,[1] Golden State's brain trust must have been pondering a seemingly unanswerable question.

How could they make a 73-win team better?

The system was set up to make such a thing impossible. Yet for an organization which prided itself on being "light years ahead"[2] of the competition, it was not advanced analytics or a breakthrough in coaching strategy which propelled them into the second phase of their dynasty. It was simple accounting.

---

1. Courtesy of the Cavs' Big Three of LeBron James, Kyrie Irving, and Kevin Love, respectively.

2. As stated by team owner Joe Lacob in an April 2016 profile in *The New York Times Magazine*.

The Cap

Perhaps there was a time in the NBA when there was enough slack in the system that all it took to build a winner was superior talent evaluation. When there was a quorum of teams that just didn't know what they were doing—or perhaps knew *exactly* what they were doing[3]—there were enough cluelessly constructed rosters filled with inferior talent that just picking the right players was sufficient, even if those players cost top salary dollar.

That is no longer the case, nor has it been for some time. Both the ruthlessness of competition and the talent-assembly skill utilized has increased rapidly over the past decade or two.[4] Perhaps it is the increase in computing power, putting the tools needed for sophisticated analysis on the desks of every executive. Maybe it was the rise of fantasy sports, which turned general managers into heroes almost as much as players and coaches, leading to sharper and more informed outside criticism. Or perhaps the influx of franchise owners with backgrounds in finance, buying their stakes from those whose fortunes had come from manufacturing or retail, brought with them a mindset focused on optimization and demanded the same of those running their teams.

Now that everyone seems to be playing the same game, the main reason teams now focus so much on efficiency is because they have to. The rules all but require it. By the rules, I'm of course referring to the salary cap. Every dollar a team spends on one player reduces what is available to spend on another.[5] Salary efficiency is not just advisable but necessary.

---

3. While well down the list of reasons why he was terrible for the league, it has certainly been alleged that Donald Sterling had calculated that he could make more money off of national TV deals and revenue sharing than he could by trying to have the Clippers field a competitive team.

4. Though the history of how and why that shift came to be is well outside the scope of this book.

5. Salary caps are often considered anti-labor, and the concept certainly has its roots in wage suppression. However, there are plenty of examples of ruinous competition between franchises damaging an entire league. Protecting teams from the siren song of spending themselves into oblivion while making the players revenue-sharing partners might well be better for players long term. The cap has risen by an average of 8% in inflation-adjusted dollars per year since its inception in 1984. Meaning there has been a more than 15-fold increase in total player compensation, which offers some support for the argument that the system has worked out well for players. Or maybe that's just what I tell myself to allow me to participate in an inequitable system. To quote Doc Holliday in *Tombstone*, "My hypocrisy only goes so far."

Under the NBA's collective bargaining agreement, the league's players are guaranteed 51% of Basketball Related Income—"BRI"[6] for short—in salary, limiting the amount each team can spend on players to a fairly narrow range. While this does not eliminate the edge held by financially muscular organizations, it does impose significant restrictions. The big-market teams can "buy" wins more readily than teams in less media-saturated areas,[7] but even the most profligate franchise must pay attention to what they're getting for their money.

While much of the criticism of the influence of "analytics" on basketball centers around the degree to which performance metrics serve to commodify players, this is by operation of the salary cap as much as it is "analytics" per se.[8] To put it another way, players are going to be judged, compensated, and traded based on production so long as the continued employment of coaches and executives is determined by on-court success. We might as well value that production accurately.

Much of the "business" that drives the NBA is utterly incomprehensible without referencing the salary cap. While cap strategy and analytics are different fields, the two disciplines frequently work in tandem. The desirability of acquiring a player is almost as much a function of their salary and contract status as it is their ability and on-court fit within a team.

---

6. Each season, the cap number is hammered into 30 stone tablets and delivered to each front office, as it is essentially the word of the BRI god as interpreted by the league office. BRI is derived via a series of arcane formulas and classifications determining which portions of the money generated around the league's activities counts as arising *from* the league's on-floor product. I won't pretend to know anything more than that about how BRI is calculated. From the perspective of a basketball operations department the only thing that matters are the seasonal revenue projections which tell teams both how much they have to spend and how much they *have* to spend; each team is subject to a salary floor requiring them to spend at least 90% of the designated cap number on players every season.

7. In many cases, the financial power of large-market teams is more useful in terms of *buying out of* mistakes, which in a way is operating with a higher salary cap than teams who can't.

8. While analytics does not precisely dictate this sort of commodification, it is hard to argue with the notion that an approach to team building centered on efficiency correlates with the sort of cutthroat mindset which would also turn to statistical analysis to squeeze every possible edge.

A Primer on Player Value and Cap Economics

The cap rules themselves are as complicated (and as riveting a read) as the U.S. Tax Code, but understanding a few concepts helps us decipher the NBA's transaction game.[9]

There are two ways to think about player salaries: in dollars and as a percentage of the cap. As NBA salary information is readily accessible, it's simpler to reference the dollar figure. But in a league where the cap rises over time at an uneven rate, the percentage of the cap represented by each salary is often more useful in evaluating players as "contractual assets."

In 2011, a roughly average league starter making $12 million would have been wildly overpaid, pulling in 21% of the cap. By 2018–19, the same dollar figure would be a decent value at only 12% of the cap, around three-fourths of the going rate for starters. Without knowing the cap percentage, it can be easy to be overwhelmed by the sheer magnitude of the dollar amounts, losing sight of the fact that while the denomination of the chips in play have gone up, the stacks have the same relative value.

In the 2020 off-season, several non-All-Stars signed deals for more than $20 million per season. Which sounds crazy, but is perfectly fine value for players in that "very good but not quite a star" tier. In 2010–11, Rashard Lewis was paid around $19.5 million in what was seen as a substantial overpay for a player in the "very good but not close to being a superstar" class. In 2020–21, this is simply market rate for players at a similar level to where Lewis was in 2010, such as Malcolm Brogdon, Zach LaVine, or Jerami Grant.

A second necessary component is to define how we value player production. This is a two-part process; first determining the number of wins each player is likely to produce[10] and then estimating the cost of acquiring each win.

---

9. If those details *are* your bag, the single best resource is Larry Coon's CBAFAQ.com. Larry is the Information Technology Director at UC Irvine, but his basketball claim to fame is as the foremost expert on the CBA and the salary cap in general. To the extent that when the league is confused about a particularly complicated cap issue, they call Larry to sort it out. One of my proudest moments in basketball was stumping him on a cap question at Summer League in 2015.

10. Even though reducing a player to a single production number removes nearly all context from how they got there, when it's time to talk dollars, you do have to come up with a number. Estimating player wins is the worst way to do so, except for every other method we might try.

There are several ways to go about this task. My preferred method is to determine the marginal points a player added or is projected to add, in the form of a plus/minus metric such as those discussed in the previous chapter. As an example, in 2018–19, Seth Curry's estimated RAPM[11] was +.99/100, which we'll round up to say he played at a "+1 level."

We can't simply assume one point for every 100 possessions Curry played. An "average" NBA player producing at a +0/100 rate is still really valuable. Only 248 of the 529 players who appeared in 2018–19 had a RAPM exceeding zero. Players 249 to 400 still brought far more to the table than the best G-Leaguer was likely to, so the baseline needs to be set somewhere below zero.

In working with RAPM I've found that using a baseline of -3/100 produces a distribution of wins which largely aligns with the league's NBA's actual salary structure. Against that standard, Curry added four "net points" per 100 possessions.

Using the following:

Net Points = Impact * Playing Time

this rate of production over the approximately 2,900 possessions Curry played for the Trail Blazers works out to 116 net points. Every 30-35 additional points of scoring margin over a season adds one win to a team's expected record.[12] For sake of simplicity, we'll use the midpoint of 32.5 points per win. Curry's 116 net points was thus equivalent of him adding just under 3.6 wins.

Valuing wins can be tricky, as not all wins are created equal. In an 82-game season, the first 20 wins are virtually free. Teams who finish with substantially fewer have either worked hard to do so or been especially

---

11. Using the nbashotcharts.com calculations.

12. This is determined by the Pythagorean Wins formula, which projects a team's "expected" record based on their season-long point differential. Copious research suggests that this reflection of average margin of victory is a better predictor of future performance than a team's actual win-loss record, which can be heavily influenced by a few bounces of the ball in close games. The precise change in point differential required for an increase of one "Pythag Win" depends on the team's pace of play and the overall league scoring environment.

unlucky. In other words, they're either tanking or have been whacked by the injury stick multiple times.

While not quite free, the wins needed to progress from 20 to around 45 wins aren't especially costly. It is the next 10-15, which take a team from a solid playoff squad to one with genuine championship aspirations, where things get sticky and upward progress tends to stall.[13]

Adding wins once a team gets to 60 isn't usually about money; the opportunities needed to improve a team at that level are less a question of cost—these options tend not to be available at any price—than the unusually fortuitous confluence of circumstance.

That's on the team level. When considering the acquisition of a player, it must be remembered that wins are not an additive commodity. In Chapter 3, we discussed the importance of viewing stats in *marginal* terms; how much value is this achievement adding that would not otherwise have been realized?

It is no different with wins. If the new guy is going to be productive, he needs playing time. That burn is going to have to come from someone else. The player shifted to the bench presumably brings some value, however minimal, in that he is an NBA player. That prior level of production must be considered when calculating what the newbie will add. This mechanism as much as money is why it's easier to add wins to a bad team. For a cellar dweller, it's not that hard to find someone who can use minutes better than those currently on the squad. As a team improves, the marginal bar rises.

There is an inflection point in a team's growth when they shift from *having* to fill 240 minutes per night to only having 240 minutes per night to give. It's possible to get up around 50 wins with a "no bad players ever" approach. Even lacking stars, getting nothing but solid, competent, *professional* minutes every night will win a lot of regular season games. Some of Brad Stevens' early Celtics teams fall into this category.

---

13. Fifty-five wins (or 55-win pace in a shortened season) is a solid rule of thumb to determine if a team is a genuine contender or not.

Such a team is generally getting the bug-to-windshield experience in a playoff setting.[14] A year or two of that is enough for most coaches or execs to decide "we gotta go get some players," but upgrading on "solid" is surprisingly hard. There are only 125 or 150 players in the league who produce at a level sufficient to do so.

You can drive yourself crazy trying to perfect a sliding win value scale, but it isn't necessary to do so. We want to be able to compare players across teams, and tracking to factor in the difference in win value between the Cavaliers and Nuggets doesn't help us much. So league average value for a win it is.

In recent years, team spending has averaged about two-thirds of the distance from the salary cap figure to the luxury tax line,[15] which in 2018–19 worked out to around $2.8 million/win. Since:

Production Value = Net Points * League Value Per Win

Curry's production of those 3.6 wins was worth around $10.4 million to Portland. Considering he was on a one-year, $2.8 million deal, this was excellent value for the Blazers. Fortunately for him, Curry was able to turn that success in only his second season as an NBA rotation player—at age 28—into a four-year, $32 million contract.

To determine which teams are getting dollar-efficient production, this exercise is repeated for every player on every roster. Unless they go massively over the cap and into the luxury tax, a contending team is going to have to beat the league average in dollars per win by a significant margin. A team spending up to the tax line at an average rate of return would win about 43 games.

---

14. See Chapter 11 for a discussion on why.

15. The luxury tax is an escalating surcharge—starting at $1.50 for every dollar of overage with the per dollar charge increasing every $5 million—imposed on teams by the league for exceeding an amount set at around 21.5% above the salary cap for a given season. The proceeds of this levy are then distributed to all the non-tax teams, which in turn can make the first dollar spent over the tax line *very* expensive. Teams operating in the tax also are subject to some additional limitations on the flexibility in executing trades and other transactions.

The Three-Legged Optimization Stool

Money is not the only constraint on roster building.

Even without a salary cap, there would be limits to the degree to which throwing money at the team-building problem would be effective. There are only five players allowed on the court. Each game is 48 minutes long. Though the number has increased over time, there are a maximum number of players on each roster. And, of course, there is only one ball.

If one wants to be technical and/or exceedingly nerdy about it, assembling a winning team is a complex optimization problem which might be stated as "How many points can a team score and prevent given the constraints of available dollars, roster spots, and minutes?" It's a three-legged problem, with the most successful teams the ones who best balance their use of money, minutes, and roster spots.

We've covered per possession or per minute ability of players extensively in earlier chapters, and just got through discussing dollar efficiency. The final leg of the stool is efficient use of roster spots.

Many players can be *extremely* efficient under perfect circumstances. Matt Bonner was a gangly stretch 5 who, while playing for San Antonio, was in the top 50 single-year RAPM each season from 2009–10 to 2011–12, culminating with the fourth-highest rating (!) in 2011–12.[16]

Over those three seasons, "The Red Rocket" started a total of 11 games and played about 20 minutes per night. Since Gregg Popovich knows what he is doing, Bonner's limited playing time wasn't an oversight. He didn't play more because he was extremely effective in certain matchups, and largely useless in others.

If a player can only perform well in ideal conditions, there is a ceiling on their total contributions. With a limit of roster spots, a team cannot simply employ an endless platoon of specialists who can be subbed in continuously as dictated by matchups. The ability to produce in a variety of roles and situations is extremely useful, and though coming up with a metric

---

16. As mentioned earlier in this chapter, I don't recommend leaning too heavily on single-year RAPM as more than a directional indicator. But the arrow is only pointing one way in this example.

for versatility would be a chore, we don't need one, as minutes played is a decent enough measure of the variety in a player's game, at least relative to his teammates.

Maximizing one leg often comes at the cost of the others. An elite specialist might provide great value in terms of both money and minutes, but that spot on the roster would still be occupied by a low-minute, situational player. Meanwhile a productive starter who isn't quite a star will do well maximizing the roster spot, but will probably be expensive relative to their production[17] and middling in terms of minute efficiency.

NBA Roster Optimization
2017-18 to 2019-20 seasons

Player Salary Level	Player-Seasons	$Mil/Win	MP/Win	Wins/Spot
Max	119	3.68	273	7.48
>MLE	259	4.56	478	3.36
>MIN & <MLE	264	2.98	628	2.06
League Min.	354	1.45	778	0.83
Rookie Scale	433	1.45	623	1.90
League Average	1429	3.10	500	2.40

The challenge faced by teams is thus not simply "sign the best players." Every player represents a tradeoff. Is it worth the substantial salary premium to swap out a four-win player making $10 million per year for a player who will produce six wins in similar minutes but makes $20 million? Is it better to add an elite wing defender whose lack of shooting makes him a specialist, or an average but versatile player who can credibly but unspectacularly perform multiple roles? It depends on the team.

---

17. To estimate production, I've used a slightly modified version of "Player Impact Plus/Minus" while including only players who appeared in games in a given season in the analysis. PIPM was developed by Jacob Goldstein, now an analyst for the Washington Wizards, and is a useful companion to RAPM-style metrics with its better ability to assess low-minute players.

But there is one class of players where there are no tradeoffs. The answer is always "Yes, him!" when offered. These are the true superstars of the game. The problem is, there ain't many of them.

Maximum Scarcity

From 2017–18 to 2019–20, there were around 40 maximum salaries on NBA rosters in each season.[18] With how universally desirable players at that level are to teams, there aren't enough to go around. It's not possible to simply "make more."

Artificially inflating the number of "max players" by intentionally paying a non-star star money—because you need stars!—is a felony Goodhart's Law violation. The "not quite" class of players with salaries in the teens are already the least-dollar-efficient class of players in the league without goosing their salaries even more to add a "fake" max or two.[19]

Only emphasizing the scarcity is the existence of multiple levels of max contracts under the CBA:

- **"Rookie" max:** Players finishing their first contract will be eligible for a starting salary of no more than 25% of the salary cap in the first year of the new deal. There are some exceptions by which players who perform at an exceptionally high level in terms of All-NBA selections can earn up to 30% on their second deal under the so-called Derrick Rose Rule.
- **30% max:** A player with at least seven years of service is eligible to receive up to 30% of the cap, the so-called veteran max. A small subset of players are eligible for what is known as the "Designated

---

18. This is pretty close to the "right number," as between 40 and 50 players provide "max" production in a given season. Of course, not everyone getting max money is giving max production, and not everyone giving max production is getting max money.

19. If one was looking at dollar efficiency in a vacuum, it would be easy to conclude that these "not quite" stars are bad investments. However, though they tend to be more expensive in dollars per win, no other non-max performers produce more per minute or per roster spot. Elect to sign 85% of the player for 60% of the cost a few too many times and a team winds up with 85% of the wins and 0% chance at the title.

Veteran Player Extension," by which a player with under 10 years of service can receive the "supermax," but that is a rare situation indeed.

- **"Supermax":** Players with at least 10 years of experience are eligible for starting salaries of 35% of the salary cap on new contracts.

In the present cap environment,[20] this created a range of around $11 million between the smallest and largest "max" deals available. To be worth the supermax, a player has to "produce" around 3.5 more wins than he would to be worth the rookie max. This is an enormous gap in value produced; fewer than 25% of the players who see the floor in a given season produce 3.5 wins or more.

Just as there are three levels of max contract, there are three levels of max players. Between three and seven players per season are worth 12 or more wins, true "supermax" level. Another 10 to 15 produce between 10 and 12 wins, worthy of the 30% "veteran max." And 20 to 25 produce eight or more wins, justifying the rookie max.

Not only do these top players bring highly concentrated regular season value, they also take on massive importance in the playoffs. In researching "Championship Value,"[21] I have found that only players who produce 4.5 wins or more do much to increase a team's odds of a title or deep playoff advancement. From this relatively high baseline, the additional playoff value increases more or more rapidly the higher up the ladder of stars you go.

For any given player, the sixth win is "worth" more than the fifth but less that the seventh in terms of playoff value. This illustrates why First Team All-NBA level superstars have become so vital; teams have sacrificed several consecutive seasons on the altar of searching for one.

---

20. Just over $109 million per team.

21. My research in this area has been based upon and building off of prior work by ESPN's Kevin Pelton. Pelton originally created his "Championships Added" metric as a tool to assist in a historical ranking project. In replicating and extending that research, I found that the approach worked well almost regardless of the "wins added" metric being used. Irrespective of the wins metrics of choice, the distribution of "Championship Value" tends to segment the league into tiers of players of similar size across metrics. Though individual players might be viewed higher or lower by a given metric, I have found that creating a pyramid consisting of these player tiers is an extremely helpful lens through which to view the league's players and to help determine the difference between an impact player and the perfectly decent players who are known in league parlance as "just a guy."

Though a supermax level player might be worth 40-50% more in the regular season than a rookie max player, he provides *as much as three times the value toward winning a championship.*[22]

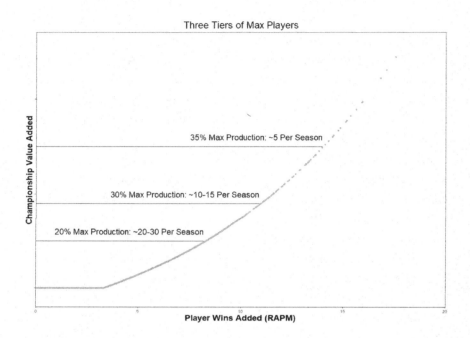

Three Tiers of Max Players

35% Max Production: ~5 Per Season

30% Max Production: ~10-15 Per Season

20% Max Production: ~20-30 Per Season

Championship Value Added

Player Wins Added (RAPM)

---

22. The "Championships Value Added" is illustrative of the importance of the elite of the elite to winning a title rather than as a literal, additive metric. Especially if the trend toward stars managing their minutes throughout the regular season continues or increases, strictly adhering to such a metric which rewards bulk accumulation can severely distort one's view of the landscape. For example, James Harden played 827 more regular season minutes than Kawhi Leonard in 2018–19, and did so in a system which maximized Harden's statistical accumulation. Interpreting this to mean Harden was massively more important to a championship team would have been silly to suggest in prospect and is quite obviously ridiculous in retrospect, after Leonard grabbed the title of "best player in the world" during that playoff run. Though LeBron James missing the postseason after eight consecutive Finals trips probably helped Leonard's perceived ascendance a touch.

The Bird Rights Trap

Teams navigating the intricacies of the cap make for great case studies on the law of unintended consequences. Provisions intended to increase flexibility and give previously capped out teams a little breathing room might present a quick fix, but that very flexibility allows deeper holes to be dug than had existed in the first place.

The use of "Bird Rights" are one such area of the cap. Let me first say that Bird Rights, or at least a similar mechanism, are all but essential to the operation of a league. A salary regime which didn't just encourage but *required* stars to leave top teams would not be good for the league as a whole. Avoiding that situation is worth a little bit of pain. Bird Rights have accomplished the main goal of letting teams keep their stars as long as both parties are amenable. However, the side effects have often trapped teams in cycles of "pretty good" while removing much likelihood of "great."

In the negotiations which led to the creation of the salary cap, one of the main concerns was that a team might find itself in a position where it could literally not afford to keep a superstar. This was especially worrisome for the best teams. Both from a competitive and business standpoint, it seemed shortsighted to impose such punitive rules on super teams.

The Boston Celtics of the 1980s were one such team. This squad featured the famed Big Three frontcourt of Larry Bird, Robert Parish, and Kevin McHale alongside an excellent backcourt of Dennis Johnson and Danny Ainge. Thanks to one of the sharper front offices in the league, the Celtics always managed to surround those starters with excellent role players, whether Tiny Archibald toward the end of his career, 1981 Finals

MVP Cedric Maxwell, 1986 NBA Sixth Man of the Year Bill Walton, or lesser but still productive players up and down the roster.[23]

As the salary cap discussions began to take shape in the early '80s, the Celtics' ability to keep Bird—both that specific situation and what it represented as an archetype likely to recur—came to a head. What would befall both the Celtics and the league were Bird forced to choose between getting paid commensurate with his contributions and staying with this iconic team?

Prior to the imposition of a salary cap, similar issues had played out. But those instances were more about skinflint ownership than an enforced ruleset. With the imminent likelihood of teams being bound to some sort of spending limits, the situation had to be formally addressed.

Enter the Bird Rights rule.

Under the premise that teams should be able to retain their own longtime stars without much regard to the salary cap, long-serving players would now be re-signable to any otherwise legal contract regardless of a team's salary cap situation. While the triggers which grant a team "Bird Rights" have changed over time,[24] it became a vital mechanism for long-term team construction, though not quite every player signed via Bird Rights is a Larry Bird.

As a result, nearly every team operates over the salary cap, often significantly so. Teams have taken advantage of the flexibility enabled by Bird

---

23. Including one of the great, lost to memory shooting seasons of all time from Kevin Gamble in 1990–91. Players like Gamble simply don't exist anymore, as he was a small forward who didn't shoot threes, get to the basket much, or do much else but score. But in that one season, boy, did he score efficiently, shooting 59.2% on two pointers, the second-highest mark for any perimeter player who averaged fewer than five free-throw attempts per 100 possessions, a qualifier attempting to account for players who rarely got to the basket in the time before universal play-by-play logs or shot charting. Chris Mullin, one of the purest shooters of all time, managed to hit 60.2% of his twos for Golden State in 1996–97. Basically, Gamble spent a whole season doing nothing but spotting up at 18 feet but still managed to score 15.6 per game on nearly 60% from the floor. As a golfer might say, that'll play.

24. Currently, a team is nearly always allowed to re-sign a pending free agent just completing his contract with the team. A player finishing a one-year contract which was also his first season with a team is due the confusingly named "non-Bird Rights," allowing a team to spend up to 120% of his previous salary. A player completing a two-year contract or with two consecutive years with a team generates "Early Bird Rights," allowing for the larger of 175% of his previous salary or 105% of the league average salary. "Full Bird Rights" allow a team to sign a player to any otherwise legal contract attached either at the end of a contract of three or more years, or three or more years of consecutive service with the team. There will not be a test later.

Rights to flex themselves into contractual straightjackets. In these circumstances, teams can either spend over the cap to retain their Bird Righted player or lose him, and, remaining over the cap, have little or no avenue from which to procure a replacement.

The implication of this "keep him or else" bind has been termed "The Bird Rights Trap" by former Grizzlies VP of Basketball Operations John Hollinger. Because of the inability to replace the player, this artificial scarcity creates a game of contractual chicken between player and team during which the team frequently blinks first, which in turn evaporates the team's options for future flexibility.

This creates a compounding effect over time. Because these contracts tend to be three or four years long, going over the cap to re-sign a star[25] in Year 1 likely puts a team over the cap in Year 2. In Year 2, another key piece is up for a new deal; the options are again to pay whatever is necessary to keep him or lose him for nothing with no way to replace him. Rinse and repeat, and it's not hard to see how teams get locked into rosters that top out at "pretty good every year, but not really a championship contender" level.

That isn't a *bad* spot to be, far better than the true mediocrity treadmill of teams finishing at the bottom of their conference standings year after year. That zone in the middle is sporting purgatory, never really a playoff threat but also never bad enough to increase its chances of getting a tentpole star in the draft. Being in the mix to advance in the playoffs and maybe make a Conference Finals or two if the matchups break right is more satisfying. But it still leaves the nose pressed against the glass just outside the high-roller suite of true title-chasers.

Even looking retrospectively, it might be hard to question any one move at the time. Faced with the choice of keeping "our guy" or taking a step back, it is almost always defensible. From the standpoint of continued employment for top decisions makers,[26] doing so is borderline required.

---

25. Or "He's a pretty good role player and we'd like to have him around because the fans like him." It happens not infrequently.

26. Getting worse to get better later has proven to be a tough sell to ownership, even if the logic is explained and agreed to beforehand.

The Cap Spike

Earlier, I claimed that teams with more than 60 wins generally have trouble adding more wins. Anyone with even passing familiarity with recent NBA history was likely wondering if I had just forgotten about Kevin Durant going to the Warriors.

I did not forget.

That situation is the rule proving exception, demonstrating how many things had to come together for a team which won 73 games the previous year to get unquestionably better. How was a team that was already a juggernaut able to make that kind of splash with a minimum of salary-clearing gymnastics? The entire system is set up to prevent such a competitive imbalance from arising.

Earlier, I said it would require a fortuitous confluence of circumstances. And so it was to be.

For starters, the Warriors had already been the beneficiaries of landing a player who literally changed the way basketball is played in Stephen Curry.

It's easy to say that now through the lens of perfect hindsight, because as a prospect, there were concerns about Curry's size, defense, and ability to stand up to the physicality of the NBA. Moreover, the sort of off-the-dribble, long-range shooting which made him such a great watch and tough cover in college had no real precedent in the NBA. In 2008–09, only 2.5%[27] of made shots were unassisted three-pointers; in 2019–20, that number had climbed to 6.0%.

Those questions and perceived need to adjust his playing style had him squarely in the second tier of 2009 draft prospects. Even looking back, it's hard to say the Clippers made the wrong choice selecting Blake Griffin first overall. James Harden went third to Oklahoma City. The other four players drafted ahead of Curry…yeah.[28]

---

27. About 1-in-40 when the average team accounted for 37.1 makes per game.

28. To be fair, Tyreke Evans and Ricky Rubio have had solid NBA careers, and I will stand on the table and shout that had he not torn his ACL as a rookie, Rubio would have become an All-Star. Not Stephen Curry, but not a drastic oversight. But, shit happens. Rubio did blow his knee out, and now he's here in this footnote alongside Evans and the true busts drafted before Curry in that lottery, Hasheem Thabeet and Jonny Flynn.

No other way about it, the Warriors hit the jackpot with Curry dropping in their laps with the seventh pick. The good fortune didn't stop there, as Curry's second contract was about to become one of the best values in the league. In his third year Curry appeared in only 26 games. The series of ankle injuries which had dogged him to that point required season-ending surgery.

Those rickety ankles made him something of a risk heading into his second contract. When Curry and the Warriors hammered out a four-year, $44 million extension, it was seen as something of a gamble, as hard as that is to believe in retrospect.

Even those most enamored with Curry's production and potential had concerns. ESPN's Kevin Pelton wrote:

> Going strictly by the numbers, no extension was a bigger bargain than the one signed by Stephen Curry. Over the last three seasons, he ranks slightly ahead of [rookie classmate James] Harden in terms of WARP, pegging him as a max-type player. Yet this contract is still fraught with risk because of Curry's chronic ankle injuries. After surgeries each of the last two summers, he still rolled his ankle in a preseason game without any apparent contact.

We know how the story ends. Curry's ankle problems never recurred in any serious way; he missed no more than four games in any of the next five seasons.

As important as that bit of accidental bargain-hunting was for Golden State, it was the explosion in league TV revenues which really did the trick. The flood of new money—remember, the players get 51%—wasn't unexpected; the extension to the media rights deal was signed on the eve of the 2014–15 season, but the new money wouldn't kick in until the 2016 off-season. After negotiations between the league and Players Association didn't produce an agreement to "smooth" the infusion of cash into the system, it all happened at once.

Prior to the 2016 off-season, the largest season-on-season increase in the cap had been $7 million, in 2001. The cap for 2016–17 was *more* *than $24 million larger* than it had been for the 2015–16 season, a 34.5% increase.

The effects of this sudden jump were profound. There was an entire class of free agents in the summer of 2016[29] who signed stupefyingly large contracts merely by being up for a new deal at the exact right moment. Even teams that had been Bird Rights Trapped under the pre-spike cap had millions and millions to play with.

With so much more money available—and as importantly so many more teams bidding—the value-to-production economics of the league were completely upended. Recall that the most dollar-efficient players are those on max deals, league minimum contracts, or still under the rookie scale. The "middle-class premium" received by players signing deals above the minimum but below the max is in the range of 30% to 35%. In the summer of '16, that premium was between 60% and 70%.

The spike could not have been timed more perfectly for the Warriors. Already a regular season wins record-breaking terror, their trio of All-Stars were suddenly being paid drastically under-market rates.

Entering the final year of that supposedly risky extension, Curry had just been awarded a second consecutive MVP while taking up around 17% of the cap—or around two-thirds of the 25% top players tend to make on their second contracts. That percentage declined to a borderline comical 12.9% of the cap once the spike kicked in.[30]

Draymond Green was a similar story for Golden State. An absolute steal of a draft pick[31] in 2012, Green signed a hefty five-year, $82 million contract after the Warriors' first championship in 2015. The first year of that

---

29. These deals, of which many were almost instantly underwater in terms of the ratio of production-to-cost, were dubbed the "Sour '16s" by Nate Duncan and Danny Leroux of the popular and cap-focused *Dunc'd On* podcast. Both Nate and Danny were extremely helpful in walking me through some of the cap machinations described in this chapter.

30. Players making around this proportion of the cap in 2020–21 include Tony Snell, Dillon Brooks, and Patty Mills.

31. Green is on the very short list of best players to come out of the second round of the post-2000 era, alongside Nikola Jokić and Marc Gasol. Perhaps not coincidentally, all are legendarily "high feel" players who overcame supposed athletic limitations to become All-NBA-level performers.

deal paid him just over 20% of the salary cap. By the summer of 2017, he was only receiving 17.4% of the cap.

If anything, that decline undersells the relative bargain the Warriors were getting. While the system is built with some degree of inflation in mind, the salaries of players who re-sign increase at a faster rate than the salary cap. Between 2004 and 2016, the cap rose by an average of around 4.1% per year. A player signing with a new team could get 4.5% annual raises, while a player re-signing[32] could see raises up to 7.5%.[33] So Green should have been getting more expensive relative to the cap, but his salary actually declined significantly in those terms.

Likewise with Klay Thompson, who signed an extension which kicked in for the 2015–16 season at $15.5 million, just over 22% of the cap. Heading into 2016–17, his $16.6 million salary was only 17.6% of the cap.

Instead of their three established All-Stars taking up three-quarters or more of the salary cap, they were due just under 48% of the cap, which left plenty of room to clear enough space for a fourth star to come on a max contract.

It just so happened that the highest-profile star to be out of contract that summer was Kevin Durant. Disgruntled after another disappointing loss in the playoffs (the Thunder coughed up their own 3–1 lead against the Warriors in the Western Conference Finals), Durant decided to sign on. And a 73-win team added one of the top five players in the game, just for good measure.

The Warriors' good fortune aside, the salary cap is the biggest obstacle to the rich getting richer. Though we've spent the majority of our time talking about one set of numbers—the analytics—which identify the players and skills that are desirable, it is that other set of numbers generated from the salary cap which limits what is possible. In the age of NBA optimization, building a title team without acing the tests presented by both simply can't be done.

---

32. Via most available mechanisms. Certain circumstances limit re-signed players to the lower raise amount.

33. In the current CBA, these percentages have been bumped up to 5% and 8%.

Chapter 8

The Midrange Theory

"And the Lord spake, saying, 'First shalt thou take out the Holy Pin. Then shalt thou count to three, no more, no less. Three shall be the number thou shalt count, and the number of the counting s hall be three. For shalt thou not count, neither count thou two, excepting that thou then proceed to three. Five is right out. Once the number three, being the third number, be reached, then lobbest thou thy Holy Hand Grenade of Antioch towards thy foe, who, being naughty in My sight, shall snuff it.'"

—Cleric, **Monty Python and the Holy Grail**

Three is greater than two. Thus explains the shift in how basketball— starting at the NBA level and trickling down—has been played over the last 20 years. Shortest. Chapter. Ever.

Of course, it is nowhere near that simple.

Perhaps no aspect of the analytics-era NBA has been as controversial yet simultaneously misunderstood as the explosive growth in three-point shots. The long-range revolution didn't just happen; several threads woven through the last two decades of NBA history came together to result in a tectonic realignment of offensive basketball principles.

The revolution started with a simple question: just what *is* a "good" shot?

The answer to that question sets the groundwork for the entire game, as shot selection represents the primary strategic battle between offense and defense. The purpose of offensive systems and defensive schemes has always been to allow your team to take good shots while preventing the opponent doing likewise. As Dean Oliver wrote in *Basketball on Paper*, "There is really nothing else in the game."

On a game-to-game level, shot-making and top-end talent might outstrip tactics, but over the long haul better shots mean better results. As strange as it may seem now, assessing shot quality empirically was nearly impossible for most of the history of basketball. There was intuition grounded in experience and logic that shorter shots were better, but there was no way to prove it. It was only in the last quarter century that the tools and technology became available to do so.

Court Geography

It was a stroke of luck for basketball as a spectator sport that the three-point line was invented prior to the ability to track and record shot locations. The game could have easily become borderline unwatchable with the order reversed.

Once that location data became available, the conventional wisdom that shorter shots were better was proven correct, at least partially. The most accurate shots are and have always been right around the rim. The surprise is the rate at which this accuracy declines as one moves farther away from the hoop. Or rather, the rate at which it *doesn't*.

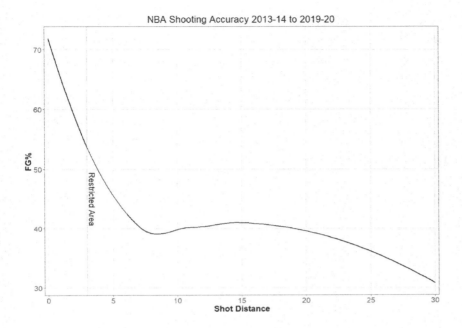

In a dataset spanning over 20 years, shooting accuracy holds more or less even on shots from about five feet out to around 24 feet. In other words, in a world where all shots are with two points, there are essentially two shot zones: the rim, and everywhere else.

With this information in hand, defensive priorities should be pretty obvious. The only reasonable strategy is to protect the paint at all costs. Similarly, on offense, getting shots at the rim becomes imperative. Well-designed games or sports allow for multiple plausible avenues that give reasonable chances of success. This is not that.

The dominance of the paint-at-all-costs strategy would lead to a mosh pit under the rim which would likely be ugly as hell if it was even recognizably basketball. But more problematically for the game as a spectator experience is that it would be *boring*. Soccer has a wonderful term for the tactic of flooding the goal area with defenders: parking the bus,[1] though with only five players on the floor and a much smaller area to cover, a bus might prove superfluous; a large Volkswagen would suffice. And nobody is paying to see a car parking.

Thankfully, shot location wasn't universally tracked until well after the three-pointer was introduced. Adding that extra point changed the geography, as the area of "high value" scoring zones increased substantially. Defining the offense's operating portion of the frontcourt as anything within 27 feet of the hoop, adding the area beyond the arc takes the high-value share from 2% to around 22% of that usable area.

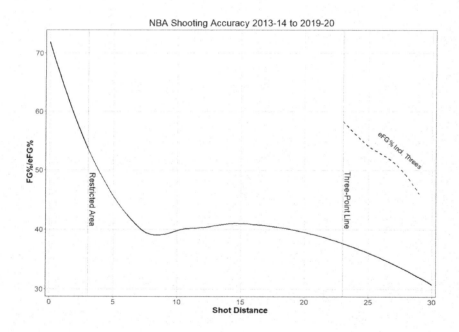

1. The intermittently successful and eternally quotable José Mourinho, who has managed several top European clubs, is credited with popularizing the phrase. During his first season coaching Chelsea of the English Premier League, he was asked about the opponent's tactics after a particular dour and defensive performance. He responded, "As we say in Portugal, they brought the bus and they left the bus in front of the goal."

Not only do these danger zones take up more area, the 1,000 square feet which make up the midrange between the basket and the arc could not be ignored either. Though defenses might be willing to concede shots from this Half-Donut of Doom, offensive players don't just occupy this zone but rather *travel through it*. Better to stop a driver at the free-throw line than to meet him at the rim where the defense risks fouls, offensive rebounds, and, most worryingly, getting posterized.

However, to force the defense to defend the whole floor, offenses had to start using the area beyond the arc. By which I mean, they had to be willing to shoot the three and continue to do so until the defense came out to stop them. While in retrospect offense developing in that direction was obvious and inevitable, it took some time.

Development of Modern NBA Shot Selection

With the exception of a three-year blip from 1994–95 to 1996–97 when the NBA experimented with a shorter three-point line,[2] the league was slow to adopt the three as an offensive staple. In 1979–80, the first season with the arc in place, the league took 2.7 3FGA/100 possessions. By 2011–12 this had risen to 20.0 3FGA/100.

The 17.3 3FGA/100 increase sounds like a lot, but spread over 32 seasons, the increase is somewhat glacial. Beginning in 2012–13, the increase in three-point-attempt rates accelerated rapidly. By 2019–20, the league averaged 33.8 3FGA/100. The last eight seasons have seen average annual increases around three times as large as the increases over the first 32 years of the three-point era.

---

2. The closer line was set at 22 feet all the way around the arc, as opposed to the former and current distance of 23 feet 9 inches across the top of the floor, tapering down to 22 feet in the corners.

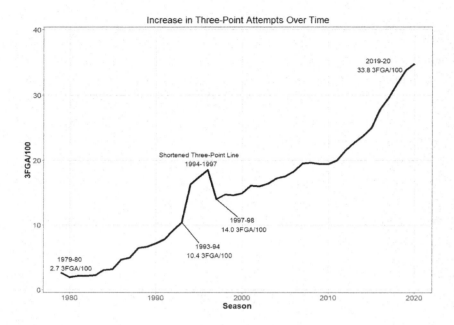

These are the facts, and they are undisputed.[3]

But what are we to make of these developments? The easy narrative is that the NBA had become soft; there were too many jump shooters settling for threes rather than working the ball inside to the post or operating from the midrange areas.

I have a different theory.

Let me walk you through it, step-by-step.

It's true that an increasing share of attempts are coming via the three, rising from 15.7% of all shots in 1997–98—the first year back to the modern "long" line—to 38.2% in 2019–20. Since we're talking about the share of shot attempts, attempts in another area or areas must have declined as a proportion of shots by similar amounts. The shifting of shots from other spots to three-point range does not mean the NBA has become a jump shooting league. At least it hasn't become *more* of one than it already was.

---

3. Ross, Smilin' Jack. *A Few Good Men.*

If teams and players were now abandoning attacking the rim to simply jack up treys instead, there might be something to the charge, but that's not what has happened.

In that 1997–98 season[4] when the arc moved back to the current 23'9" distance, almost precisely one-third, 33.3%, of all shot attempts came from within the restricted area. By 2019–20 this share of close-in shots—the dunks and layups and tip-ins lost to the gaping maw of the three-point revolution—had plummeted all the way to…32.3%. Over that time frame, shots from the rest of the painted area[5] actually *increased* slightly, from 14.1% of attempts to 16.2%. In other words, the proportion of attempts in the paint has been roughly level across this 24-season span.

What *has* disappeared are long midrange attempts, two-pointers from outside of the lane. Long twos made up 36.9% of attempts in 1997–98, but only 13.4% by 2019–20. Rather than sacrificing dunks and layups to facilitate threes, a good chunk of the jumpers the league was already taking have simply become jump shots from a little farther out.

4. The NBA has only tracked shot location data since 1996–97. However, the first season was the last season of the shortened three-point line, and the consistency of that location data isn't quite as reliable as we might like.

5. Copyright Hubie Brown.

Shot Distribution by Zone

(via NBA.com)

Season	Rim	Non-RA Paint	Midrange	3FGA	All Jumpers
1997-98	33.3%	14.1%	36.9%	15.7%	52.6%
1998-99	31.0%	15.2%	37.1%	16.7%	53.8%
1999-00	30.0%	15.2%	38.2%	16.5%	54.8%
2000-01	29.4%	15.7%	38.0%	16.9%	54.8%
2001-02	30.2%	14.6%	37.2%	18.0%	55.2%
2002-03	30.2%	14.8%	37.0%	18.0%	55.0%
2003-04	31.3%	14.4%	35.7%	18.5%	54.2%
2004-05	32.0%	13.1%	35.5%	19.4%	54.9%
2005-06	32.5%	12.9%	34.5%	20.1%	54.6%
2006-07	33.0%	12.9%	33.1%	21.1%	54.2%
2007-08	32.1%	13.0%	33.0%	22.0%	55.0%
2008-09	32.8%	12.8%	32.2%	22.2%	54.4%
2009-10	33.3%	13.2%	31.5%	22.0%	53.5%
2010-11	31.6%	15.3%	31.1%	22.0%	53.1%
2011-12	32.4%	14.9%	30.3%	22.4%	52.7%
2012-13	32.9%	14.6%	28.4%	24.2%	52.6%
2013-14	32.4%	15.0%	26.9%	25.8%	52.6%
2014-15	32.2%	14.9%	26.2%	26.7%	52.9%
2015-16	32.5%	14.6%	24.6%	28.3%	52.9%
2016-17	32.1%	14.2%	22.2%	31.4%	53.6%
2017-18	31.7%	15.7%	19.1%	33.5%	52.6%
2018-19	33.1%	16.0%	15.2%	35.7%	50.9%
2019-20	32.2%	16.2%	13.4%	38.2%	51.6%

The critique used to attempt to dismiss "jump shooting teams" of the modern era, such as those of the Warriors dynasty, is nonsensical. The league has *always* shot a ton of jumpers. In 1997–98, 52.6% of NBA shot attempts were either two-pointers outside of the paint or threes. In

2019–20, 51.6% of shots were from these areas. Getting into the paint against an NBA-level defender is hard and 24 seconds is not a lot of time in which to do so.

Even if we count jump shots a little differently, considering only shots from 15 feet or more as "jumpers," the rate of such attempts has been steady since the 2004–05 season, inching up only slightly in the last season or two, to 45.9% of shots from 43.0%.[6]

So the league isn't taking more jumpers. Rather, what *has* happened is the league's offensive approach has changed substantially in terms of where those jumpers come from. Though the math of 3>2 probably meant the shift was coming sooner rather than later, a role-bending cohort of young stars and two sets of rule changes lit the fuse for the three-point explosion.

The Vanished Goliaths

The kind of shots which started disappearing in 1997–98 were in-betweeners. Not long jumpers, not layups, these were attempts outside the paint but shorter than 16 feet. These came in many varieties, from floaters and teardrops to pull-ups and runners. But there is one particular type which made up the bulk of the reduction: post-ups.

According to data from Synergy Sports,[7] back-to-the-basket play is a far less prevalent scoring tactic now than it was then. In the 2004–05 season, 16.1% of offensive plays in the half court were designated as post-ups by Synergy's play loggers.[8] By 2019–20, that number had declined to 6.5%.[9]

---

6. The 2004 off-season is important in this story, so we'll return there in a bit.

7. Synergy has tagged and tracked "play type" data for longer than any other company around.

8. In the Synergy dataset, "use" of a play—not a possession, this data is at the chance level—includes situations where a player posts up and either takes a shot, turns the ball over, or draws a foul for which free throws are awarded, meaning either shooting fouls or fouls on the floor with the defense in the penalty.

9. This likely understates both the initial popularity of the post-up and the degree of the decline in its use. Synergy only tracks play-*ending* actions; situations where a team "plays out of the post"—entering the ball to a player dangerous enough on the block to perhaps draw a double team—but the offense finishes some other way, such as a kick out to a shooter for a "Spot Up" or "Off Screen" attempt, are not included in the tally.

Percentage of Half Court Chances by Play Type

Season	Isolation	P&R Ballhandler	P&R Roll Man	Post-Up	Hand Off	Spot Up	Off Screen	Cut
2004-05	18.1%	13.1%	4.8%	16.1%	1.9%	29.0%	7.1%	9.9%
2005-06	18.7%	14.3%	5.1%	16.6%	2.1%	27.1%	7.0%	9.0%
2006-07	17.7%	14.7%	5.0%	15.2%	2.4%	28.6%	6.1%	10.3%
2007-08	14.6%	14.8%	5.9%	14.0%	2.9%	31.5%	6.3%	9.9%
2008-09	16.4%	14.5%	5.5%	12.8%	3.2%	31.6%	5.7%	10.3%
2009-10	16.8%	15.3%	6.4%	14.4%	3.2%	27.4%	6.1%	10.3%
2010-11	16.1%	15.9%	6.9%	13.5%	3.4%	26.8%	6.9%	10.7%
2011-12	14.2%	16.4%	7.8%	13.8%	3.0%	26.6%	7.0%	11.3%
2012-13	13.1%	17.5%	8.7%	12.7%	3.5%	26.6%	6.7%	11.3%
2013-14	11.1%	20.2%	9.1%	13.0%	4.2%	25.1%	6.9%	10.4%
2014-15	10.4%	20.6%	9.2%	11.5%	5.1%	25.9%	6.9%	10.3%
2015-16	9.6%	22.1%	9.3%	10.1%	5.6%	25.7%	7.3%	10.3%
2016-17	9.9%	23.0%	9.0%	9.0%	5.7%	26.2%	7.4%	9.8%
2017-18	9.5%	22.8%	8.9%	8.5%	6.6%	26.8%	7.4%	9.7%
2018-19	9.2%	23.7%	8.3%	8.3%	7.1%	27.1%	6.8%	9.6%
2019-20	8.7%	25.2%	8.3%	6.5%	7.0%	28.6%	6.5%	9.2%

This shift away from running offense through the post had multiple causes.

Starting with Kevin Garnett[10] the league saw an influx of players with center size but skills which were, if not guard-like, at least perimeter oriented. Though these players were adept in performing "big man" defensive responsibilities, specifically rim protection and rebounding, they preferred to and could face the basket effectively on offense. Instead of operating from the low block, these players played from the elbows and out far more frequently than the behemoths who came before.

The effectiveness of this archetype—Garnett was joined shortly by others like Dirk Nowitzki (drafted in 1998) and Lamar Odom (class of 1999)—saw teams begin to prioritize shooting, playmaking, and mobility from players occupying roles which had operated under the assumption that bigger is always better to that point.

---

10. Drafted straight out of high school in 1995.

As the perimeter skills of big men grew, the relative importance of back-to-the-basket post moves declined. Even dominant scorers like Amar'e Stoudemire, drafted in 2002, were more often finishers playing out of pick-and-rolls than they were stationary offensive hubs, planted on the block.

While this position-flexible evolution got rolling, a series of rule changes drastically altered offensive and defensive strategies. The first set of revisions made post-up play more difficult, while later revisions served to increase the value of perimeter creation to the relative detriment of the post.

In 2001, the NBA completely overhauled the rules banning zone defense. Prior to this change, players had to be either directly guarding a specific opponent or actively double teaming the ball. The first violation of this "illegal defense" rule in a game resulted in a warning; subsequent infractions meant technical fouls.

With this rule in force, creating space for post-ups was comically easy: simply station a couple players above the arc on the opposite side of the court.[11] That's it. Defenders were *required* to guard them, regardless of the shooting threat those "spacers" posed. Dikembe Mutombo was required to be guarded just as much as was Ray Allen.

This greatly benefited low-post scorers. First, they had plenty of space in which to catch the ball. Further, double-teaming defenders couldn't come until the player in the post had the ball, or at the earliest until the pass was in the air to them. The second defender had to wait to commit,[12] making reading the double relatively simple. Traditional centers were seldom noted for their passing skills, but the obviousness of help approaching made kickout passes to shooters or cutters easy enough for all but the most limited.

The liberalization of zone defense rules prior to the 2001–02 season changed all that. Gone was the complicated trigonometry of court zones and maximum guarding distances. Instead, there was one major rule:

---

11. This offensive style was so gimmicky that there was a rarely called illegal *offense* rule in place disallowing sets with more than two players above the break on the opposite side of the floor.

12. A subtle bit of gamesmanship under this system would be passers trying to "draw" illegal defense calls by pump faking the entry pass. Bite this fake too hard, and it was a violation. Which leads me to say, what a dumb rule! Why punish players for being alert and reactive to threats on the floor?

defensive three seconds. A defender could spend no more than 2.9 seconds inside the key unless they were actively guarding an offensive player.[13] Beyond that, anything goes.

As with any major rules change, the full implications took a few years to shake out. Among the most important were:

- Non-shooters were now worthless as floor spacers. Sure, a player with shooting range measured in inches rather than feet could still stand at the top of the key. But the defense was no longer under any obligation to guard them. Teams quickly ceased doing so.

- Without the requirement of closely attending to a specific matchup, players all over the floor could "shrink" off their assignment, putting bodies or at least arms in passing lanes. Post entry passes became more difficult. The increased traffic often forced passes into the post to be thrown wider and more toward the sidelines, pulling the offensive player well off the block. A catch at 13 feet was always known to be worse than receiving the ball at eight feet with one foot already in the lane. But because of now-available shot location data, just how much of a detriment resulted from the increased distance became clear. The gap between an eight-footer and a 13-footer is substantial; that extra five feet of ground to cover frequently meant the difference between a great shot and a mediocre one.

- Help defenders no longer had to choose between hard double teams and staying attached to their own matchup. Instead, they could "dig down," congesting the space around a post player as they received the ball or started their move, but were not required to fully commit to the ballhandler to do so. Defenders could "stunt and recover," faking a double team without ever fully rotating off of their assignment. Players in the post no longer had easy reads for passing out of double teams, and when they did decide to kick it back out, passing lanes were much more congested. This led to an increase in turnovers;

---

13. The intricacies of modern NBA defense and exploiting the practice of "2.9ing" to maximum advantage is well beyond the scope of this book. Suffice it to say that many present-day schemes attempt to play to the outer edge of the defensive three-seconds rule to enable a team's top rim protector to patrol the paint as much as possible.

according to Synergy data around 11.5% of post-ups resulted in turnovers in 2004–05, compared to just over 14% in 2019–20.

The upshot: less space to operate, more difficulty receiving the ball, and far more complex decisions. Not a great recipe for post-up success, all because of the relaxed rules on defensive positioning.

Shortly thereafter, during the 2004 off-season, the league re-emphasized "freedom of movement" rules. The goal was to reduce contact on the perimeter to allow for more flow in offensive play. The success of this initiative in turn enhanced the value of smaller but more skilled perimeter players.

Previously, defenders could hand check even out on the perimeter, "guiding" offensive players around the court with a firm hand on the hip. Size and strength in the backcourt was a huge defensive advantage. Though these big wings were generally slower and less skilled than their smaller and more elusive counterparts, that guide hand negated edges in quickness to a large degree.

Ron Harper, an athletic scorer in his younger years, started as the titular point guard for five NBA champions between 1996 and 2001. He was not a major offensive contributor for any of those teams, but his backcourt partnerships, first with Michael Jordan and then Kobe Bryant, were prime examples of the defensive effectiveness of two big, physical guards.

The removal of perimeter hand checking didn't change the league's competitive "meta" overnight, though it is no accident that the comparatively slightly built Steve Nash was the league's MVP in each of the two seasons immediately following the change. Over time, teams realized that a new generation of quicker playmakers, unburdened from the previously allowed physicality, could get into the paint at will against slower defenders. A player of Harper's profile starting at the point on anything other than an emergency basis would be seen as shockingly old-fashioned only a few years after the change.

Players like T.J. Ford (drafted in 2003), Devin Harris (2004), and especially Chris Paul (a 2005 selection) might have been viewed as too small to be top-level offensive players in the previous era. But with the ruleset rebalanced in favor of their talents, these players helped usher in the new era of guard-dominant attacks.

Though the increased scrutiny on perimeter contact didn't directly impact low-post scoring, the desirability of playing "inside-out" through the post declined as a result anyway. Those smaller, highly skilled guards led offenses to employ more pick-and-rolls and fewer post-ups[14] for offensive initiation. Once the big guy isn't being used in the post, where on the court does he go?

Productive Standing

Two out of every three shots which were long twos in 2004–05 had been replaced by three-pointers by 2019–20. The midrangers that went away weren't selected at random. Rather it was almost exclusively *assisted* midrange attempts that had been subbed out.

---

14. The line between a "post-up" and an "isolation" can be murky, especially for players who like to face up out of midpost and elbow catches, as Carmelo Anthony and Blake Griffin often did in their primes.

% Assisted FGM By Zone
(data via NBA.com)

Season	ATB 3	Corner 3	Midrange	Non-RA Paint	Restricted Area
1997-98	81.8%	93.6%	66.8%	43.4%	55.9%
1998-99	82.1%	93.4%	65.7%	42.1%	55.8%
1999-00	80.9%	92.6%	63.5%	45.1%	53.7%
2000-01	81.8%	94.7%	64.2%	44.9%	55.5%
2001-02	82.3%	95.1%	63.6%	44.2%	54.4%
2002-03	81.5%	95.0%	63.0%	42.9%	54.6%
2003-04	81.6%	95.8%	64.1%	43.1%	55.0%
2004-05	81.0%	95.5%	61.4%	40.7%	52.9%
2005-06	80.4%	95.8%	59.4%	39.1%	50.7%
2006-07	82.3%	95.9%	58.0%	38.4%	53.0%
2007-08	82.6%	96.5%	56.6%	37.9%	53.4%
2008-09	81.2%	96.5%	53.8%	35.7%	51.6%
2009-10	80.3%	95.5%	53.7%	37.7%	52.1%
2010-11	81.4%	96.5%	56.9%	38.0%	52.8%
2011-12	79.5%	96.3%	55.7%	38.4%	53.4%
2012-13	79.1%	95.3%	56.6%	40.9%	54.1%
2013-14	79.0%	96.2%	53.9%	41.2%	53.8%
2014-15	80.1%	95.1%	54.4%	41.8%	53.7%
2015-16	79.5%	95.2%	51.4%	40.5%	53.9%
2016-17	79.4%	95.6%	46.8%	40.7%	53.4%
2017-18	79.1%	95.7%	46.5%	40.6%	54.1%
2018-19	78.2%	95.1%	46.3%	42.5%	55.5%
2019-20	75.7%	93.8%	43.7%	40.9%	54.0%

For the most part, assist rates within each shot zone didn't change much, nor did the league's overall assist percentage. The one exception was in the midrange, where the proportion of assisted makes plummeted from 66.8% in 1997–98 to 43.7% in 2019–20.

Assisted jumpers usually come directly off the catch. Tracking data from recent seasons has shown that catch-and-shoot jumpers are much more open than pull-ups on average. Being open enough to simply catch and shoot usually means something has gone right for the offense; perhaps a defender was unable to navigate a screen. Maybe he was pulled away from his matchup to help contain dribble penetration and was unable to recover quickly enough to prevent the shot. Or maybe someone simply got caught ball-watching and lost track of his assignment.[15]

These are possessions the offense has "won." It seems silly to limit the size of that win by shooting an 18-footer worth only two points when a player standing just a stride farther away from the hoop would get a full extra point on a make. Even if that 24-footer might be slightly less accurate than an 18-footer, the efficiency from choosing the longer shot is massive. An 18-foot jumper might go in around 45% of the time, or 0.9 points per attempt. By comparison, the league hits around 38%[16] of its open threes, or 1.14 points per attempt, a gain of nearly a quarter point in expectation.

To put that in context, the 2019–20 Bucks lead the league with an average of just over 1.10 points per shot. The Warriors finished 30th at just over 0.99. The gain realized from swapping out the long two for three is twice as large as the efficiency gap between the best and worst shooting teams. The math here is simply irrefutable and the league has—perhaps belatedly—recognized that it's more sensible for players to stand at 24 rather than 18 feet from the bucket when they aren't in the play. This change, and the altered shot profile which it necessitates, explains a sizable chunk of the ramp up in threes.

---

15. Among the many things which make today's version of the NBA more physically demanding than previous eras is the fact that players need to be "on" and engaged in the play for a far higher proportion of their time on defense as compared to the more stagnant post-and-iso game of the late '90s through mid-aughts.

16. One of the subtle things which made the 2020–21 season so difficult to analyze was that the league as a whole shot 39.5% on uncontested threes, the highest of the tracking data era by a wide margin. Whether or not that increased accuracy will become the new normal when fans return to arenas in full in 2021–22 remains to be seen, with the result having huge implications for defensive strategy going forward.

Alone in the Corners

Modern offensive philosophy seeks to force the defense to guard as large an area as possible. Spreading the court creates openings to attack the basket, cleans up passing lanes, and makes defenders cover more ground to help, recover, and rotate. This in turn leads to better shots, fewer turnovers, and ultimately higher efficiency. At least that's the theory, and with average offensive ratings exceeding 110 points/100 for the first time in the last few years, it's hard to argue.

Part of stretching the defense is filling the corners with shooters capable enough that the defense feels compelled to guard them. Think of these players as pegs keeping the canvas of the defensive tent stretched taut.

Corner threes are overwhelmingly of the open catch-and-shoot variety. According to tracking data, just under 90% of corner attempts come with the shooter having at least six feet of space from the closest defender.[17] Generating a high rate of corner looks is usually a sign that an offense is working well; for a player to be open in the corner, something has had to pull a defender away allowing the open shot off the catch. Likewise, conceding relatively few augurs well for a defense.

But there is a paradox at work here. The corners are strategically vital, and attempts from these areas are a useful indicator of offensive process. But the ability to shoot them isn't actually that big a determinant of a game's outcome.

As I mentioned earlier, off-ball players have found good spots to stand where they require defensive attention but are out of the way of the team's drink-stirrers. For relatively low-skill players, the corners are the best places to do so.

---

17. Analysis of tracking data suggests that six feet is just about right as far as setting the dividing line between categorizing a three as having been "contested" or not.

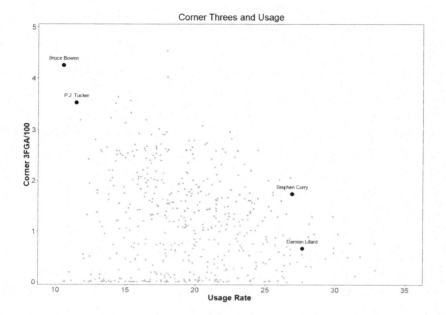

It's no accident that the most noted corner-three specialists—including perhaps the original "3&D" wing, Bruce Bowen—are the guys who did or do very little else offensively. On the other hand, the most dangerous long-range shooters simply don't end up in the corner that much. Among players with significant minutes since 2004, only two have averaged more than two corner 3FGA/100 while carrying a usage rate of 25% or higher, with both Paul George (2.01/100) and Michael Redd (2.05/100) barely clearing that threshold.

The same thing which makes the corners a great spot for a relatively unskilled player to stand make them a silly place to send stars. Those spots on the court are away from the main action, so why should the players a team *most wants in the action* spend much time there?

That said, even the highest volume corner-three shooters don't take *that* many. Only three times has a player made at least 100 corner threes in a single season, with P.J. Tucker's 109 in 2018–19 the all-time record. On the team level, the difference between mediocre and elite corner accuracy is about one point per game for the highest volume teams and much less for most. It's not nothing, but the relatively small impact illustrates that the corners are as much about spacing and presenting the defense with as many threats as possible as they are an offensive weapon unto themselves.

The Arrival of Stretch

The rule changes of 2001 and 2004 took the big man out of the post. Even as the offensive responsibilities of the center position changed and shrunk, the requirement of strong interior defense didn't. Rim protection remains vital, but the players who provide this presence had to find a way to not clog spacing when their team has the ball.

To some degree, this was accomplished by the switch from post-ups to pick-and-rolls. The "dive and dunk" role[18] allowed these players to continue to get all their shots from in close. But now, instead of *standing* near the basket to establish post position, they now *sprint into* the same space after setting ball screens. This more dynamic approach keeps space and driving lanes open, without these players needing the level of shooting skill to be effective spacers themselves.[19]

However, there were only so many with the requisite size, agility, and most importantly hand-eye coordination to go around. The ability to catch the ball in traffic while moving at NBA speeds, then maintaining the balance to be able to do something useful after the catch is rare. There have been many attempts to turn "bad hands" bigs into dive men. These efforts result in many more fumbled passes, charges, and ungainly travels than butterfly-like transformations of defensive plodders into offensive dynamos.

The realization dawned that instead of continuing to squish round pegs into square holes, why not take advantage of the increasing perimeter skills of taller players, especially shooting, and remove big men from the paint entirely? The pick-and-pop had long been a part of the league's offensive repertoire. Especially as he got older, Karl Malone started to space out for jumpers after screening for John Stockton with great frequency. But like most power forwards and centers, Malone was taking 18-footers, not threes,

---

18. Exemplified by players like Tyson Chandler, DeAndre Jordan, and, in more recent years, Clint Capela.

19. Remember, after the elimination of illegal defense, teams are free to completely ignore a non-shooter on the perimeter.

out of this screening action. In his 19-year career, the Mailman had 310 attempts beyond the arc, nearly a third of which came during the three seasons played with the shortened line.

Much like more productive standing was to be found at 24 feet, pick-and-pop bigs began to slide just beyond instead of just in front of the arc. The preparatory ball screen wasn't really necessary either. Removing the "pick" from "pick-and-pop," big men were used as pure spot-up spacers.

Under the old illegal defense regime, bigs had been stationed outside the arc. A few[20] even provided actual as opposed to rule-imposed spacing. Starting around 2012 or 2013, more and more centers started to get the green light to fire away.

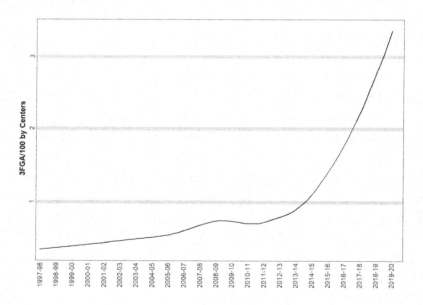

The result has been a sharp increase in the deployment and use of so-called stretch bigs. Offensively, these players operate much more like "3&D" wings such as Tucker and Bowen than centers from previous eras, while doing the same interior defensive work as the intimidators of old. For better or often worse.

---

20. Brad Lohaus, Matt Bullard, and Sam Perkins, to name three.

Teams today almost always play with four and quite often five legitimate spacers on the floor. According to NBA lineup data, the offensive player with the fourth-highest three-point attempts rate in 2019–20 takes them nearly as frequently (5.2 3FGA/100) as the *second*-highest propensity shooter in 2007–08 (5.8 3FGA/100). Meanwhile, the player with the *lowest* rate in a lineup takes over *10 times* as many threes (2.1 3FGA/100) as they did in 2007 (0.2 3FGA/100).

Earlier, I asked where the big guys had gone. More and more, they are out beyond the arc with the guards and wings.

The Map Is Not the Territory

Recent years have seen the "ideal shot chart" become almost a fetish object. Players are celebrated for their miniscule totals of midrange attempts. Which is all well and good. Most who end up with such a distribution are low-usage support players who make up for lack of star talent with a high degree of selectivity in their shot attempts. That doesn't mean merely efficient shot locations; as we've just discussed at some length, there is a lot more to a shot than a spot on a plot. While for a long time a display of shot locations enhanced understanding of how a team played, now that everyone understands where the most valuable shots exist, those charted locations might have begun to obscure as much about the play on the floor as they illuminate.

For most basketball fans, some variation of the pair of charts below is etched into their brains.

NBA Shot Distribution - 1997-98 **NBA Shot Distribution - 2019-20**

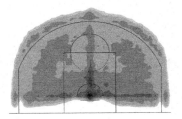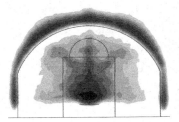

(Images courtesy of Owen Phillips)

Shot location is unquestionably important. In determining the quality of a given attempt, it might be the most important thing. But it is far from the *only* thing. As our tour through the recent history of NBA shot migration has illustrated, there is a lot more going on.

Hopefully, digging deeper into the league's changing shot profile has given a more complete understanding of the rate of threes attempted in today's game. The revolution sounds rather less dramatic once one recognizes that the main thing that has changed is that guys taking in-rhythm jumpers have simply taken one giant step back.

Which leads me to the final point to be made here: shot maps might have outlived their usefulness.

To reiterate a point, turning "basketball" into "basketball statistics" flattens the three-dimensional view from watching the game unfold into something that can be put on paper. Sadly, the moving pictures from the Harry Potter universe are not available to help preserve some of the more dynamic elements of the game as it moves from the court to the spreadsheet.

This flattening isn't inherently a bad thing. In fact, it's necessary, else we are required to recount proceedings in the painfully extended matter that led off Chapter 2. Many of the more important statistical tools used are chosen precisely for the ability to reduce dimensionality. What else is RAPM or the other models introduced in Chapter 6 other than a way to incorporate all the little things each player does in their time on the floor into one measure of performance?

But this can go too far.

As the game has become increasingly dynamic, the most prominent offensive strategies have changed considerably. In the pre-2001 world of illegal defense, a few players spaced to the opposite side of the floor while they watched a star player operate out of the post or in isolation. In today's game, offensive sets are a whirl of pick-and-rolls, dribble hand-offs, and misdirection actions that keep offensive players in near constant motion.

Of course, there are exceptions, such as the late-model James Harden–led Rockets. Those Houston teams were almost old-school in the way supporting players mostly stood and watched as Harden attempted to break the defense down by himself, much in the way Charles Barkley would as he tried to back his man down from 20 feet.

Those exceptions aside, modern offenses aren't static, and offensive plays are not just about where the shooter ended up. Perhaps equally or even more important as the shot itself is where the shooter came from and how the ball got there. None of which a shot chart can display.

Perhaps worse that stripping necessary context is abstracting so far or in such a way that the information presented is wrong. It's hard to compare the side-by-side shot maps and not conclude that the league has completely abandoned much of the court. Won't someone think of the widows and orphans in Midrangeville?

While there are fewer shots from those areas, that does not mean *no* shots. But what has happened is that a still sizable number of attempts has been spread over a much larger area. Much in the way a balloon starts to become translucent when stretched past a certain point despite containing the same amount of material as always, the midrange population has been rendered invisible by the space to which it is fit.

NBA Shot Zone Densities
(2014-15 to 2018-19)

Shot Zone	Locations	FGA	Density
Resticted Area	3729	340168	91.2
ATB 3 (< 28 feet)	22090	236157	10.7
Midrange	52278	225095	4.4
In the Paint (Non-RA)	19122	158929	8.3
Corner 3	5702	78748	13.8

Over the five seasons from 2014–15 through 2018–19, there were around 1.5 times as many shots attempted in the restricted area as from midrange. However, with the relative square footage of the two areas, that 1.5x ratio balloons to over 20 times the *density* of shots. Worse, there were more than 10 times as many shots taken from the midrange than from both corners put together. Yet the corners appear to be a hive of activity as tumbleweeds blow across the top of the key.

This conveys an almost wholly false narrative about the modern NBA. Because while attempts in the midrange have thinned out, those that remain are the most important shots in basketball.

Star Shots

One of the major critiques of the three-point era is that the game has lost the "art of the midrange." This charge gets the situation precisely backward.

While beauty is in the eye of the beholder, I don't think the painting envisioned by the Lost Arters is of a backup power forward spotting up at the top of the key for an in-rhythm 19-footer. They're thinking Chris Paul getting to his office on the right elbow and sticking a pull-up, Tony Parker's teasing teardrop which seemingly clears a defender's contest by millimeters, or Dirk Nowitzki bringing rain with a parabolic one-legged fadeaway. And I'm here to tell you these shots haven't gone anywhere.[21]

Not to put words in people's mouths or thoughts in their heads, but what we're really talking about here is bucket-getting. Star players breaking their man down and getting a tough two when their team needs a score. Among players with usage rates of 25% or higher, buckets are being gotten at or near all-time highs. In 1997–98, around 41% of these players' made shots were unassisted two-pointers. In 2019, nearly 49% were self-created twos.

Recall all that space offenses have worked so hard to create by having the "others" stand outside the arc and fill the corners, and by taking the big guys out of the post and having them either dive to the rim or space out themselves. This is what it has produced: providing superstars the room to operate and produce the new wave of masterpieces.

In addition, the modern masters have started using the whole frontcourt as their canvas. Stephen Curry and Damian Lillard, James Harden and Luka Dončić, have taken the art of getting buckets out beyond the arc.

---

21. Metaphorically, of course. While Parker and Nowitzki are retired, Mike Conley is still working his off-hand floater, while Nikola Jokić has turned the "Dirk-step" into his own "Sombor Shuffle," named for his Serbian hometown.

In 1997–98, unassisted threes were unheard of, accounting for only 2% of all made shots. This had tripled to 6% by 2019–20, with the increase concentrated in the highest-usage players.

For whatever else has happened in this era of basketball, preventing stars from "doing work" has not. In fact, these developments have crystalized just what it means to have star impact, at least offensively. I've repeatedly referenced how open threes usually require something good to have happened on a possession. The stars, the "drink-stirrers" as I like to call them, are the ones who make that happen.

They do this in a variety of ways. Some are so proficient at getting to the rim and finishing that it takes multiple players fully committing to the ball to stop them once they beat the initial defender. With a 4-on-3 situation on the rest of the court, someone is probably going to get open. Giannis Antetokounmpo and Zion Williamson represent this kind of battering ram. Others, like Curry and Lillard, are so dangerous off the dribble from beyond the arc that similar attention is required, but with more space to cover.

But the most common method by which stars break defenses down and give their less talented teammates opportunities is by turning what are otherwise bad shots into good ones. That is to say, they work the midrange. This operates in three ways.

First, a select few players are so skilled and athletic that almost any shot they take is a good one. Kevin Durant is a prime example, but there are other examples, such as Chris Paul and Kawhi Leonard. Defenses allow these guys to get into their bag at their own peril.

The second aspect is psychological. Even most star players aren't *quite* good enough to turn the midrange into an above-average shot. Nowitzki, without question one of the purist shooters of this or any other era, exceeded league average efficiency for all shots on his midrange attempts only three times in his career, and only in 2010–11 did he do so by a substantial margin, shooting 51.5% on twos outside of 10 feet against leaguewide 49.8% eFG%. But even getting close to average is enough to scare teams. Left open, Dirk would surely have punished teams.

The sight of even lesser shooters making a couple of pull-ups can be enough to draw just enough extra attention to create seams in a defense.

This help might be a mathematical mistake, but calling a star's bluff when they are essentially saying, "If you don't bring help, I'm going to beat you even from here" is a big ask.

The final prong is the shot clock. Twenty-four seconds is not that long, and even a "bad" shot is better than simply handing the ball to the ref when that time expires. Having a player who can bail out plays that don't find anything better late in the clock is a big deal. When certain classes of stars are referred to as "floor raisers," this is a big part of what that entails—taking a big chunk of the crappy possessions an undertalented team ends up with and turning them into non-terrible results.

So, while shots have moved out of the midrange, the midrange *game* is as alive and as absolutely necessary as it has ever been.

I can't convince you that you must *like* the modern style of offense. But I can hopefully help better explain it. All the ingenuity the modern basketball mind can bring to bear is aimed at creating the shots now known to be the best, and criticism. If this means a few more jump shots are taken from behind a line drawn on the floor, so be it.

One would never think to criticize a football team for choosing to go for touchdowns over field goals, nor should we do so in basketball. Perhaps if every team were doing the same things to create those good shots, the charge of stylistic boringness might stick. But this isn't so. Teams use the whole floor, and do so with more creativity and movement than ever before.

My midrange theory is this: with the extra bits cleared away, all that remains is the defense-shaking, shot-making artistry which caused us to fall in love with the game in the first place. The three-point revolution didn't kill the midrange game; it hardened and shaped it into a sparkling diamond.

Chapter 9

Chasing Ghosts: Evaluating Defense

"The most savage controversies are about matters as to which there is no good evidence either way."

—Philosopher Bertrand Russell

How do we count all the things that don't happen?

In March 2021, Philadelphia 76ers President of Basketball Operations Daryl Morey appeared on the *Rights to Ricky Sanchez* podcast, a popular Sixers-centric show.[1] Asked about the state of public metrics measuring individual defensive impact and how they compared to teams' proprietary models, Morey scoffed: "I would say public domain all-in-one defensive measures are all really bad. I think internally several teams have some pretty *okay* ones, not good."

It is with mild embarrassment that only now, just over eight chapters and tens of thousands of words into this text, our attention turns to the question

---

1. *RTRS* is generally credited with popularizing the "Trust the Process" mantra with respect to Sam Hinkie's strategy of extreme short-term tanking in the hope of acquiring one or more championship level superstars. Sports talk radio will be debating the merits of The Process up until the heat death of the universe.

of evaluating defense. This delay was not an oversight so much as a reflection on the state of knowledge regarding defense from a statistical standpoint. We simply know more, *much* more, about assessing offensive skills and production than we do for defense. There are some methods which are "pretty okay," in Morey's words, to measure defensive impact. But very few that describe the skills which create that impact, in large part because we tend to think about defense all wrong.

Eyes Off the Ball

Most stats involve action around the ball. Each tally represents an instance where a player has either shot, caught, or lost the rock. Focusing on the ball provides a decent first pass at a player's offensive role and value, but a similar approach tells us little about a player's defense.

For starters, the level of involvement is different. The best defenders guard the ball less frequently than the best offensive players make use of it.

I've already noted at several points that though baseball's own statistical revolution has been quite helpful to basketball analytics overall, it occasionally steers us in unhelpful directions. Defense is prime territory for that sort of misdirection, starting with the concept of usage.

For an offense in baseball, there is no such thing as usage. Rather, the batting order is set; when a player's turn to hit comes up, they step to the plate. In basketball, there are no turns. Stephen Curry could theoretically take every shot for the Warriors. Mike Trout will only ever account for one-ninth[2] of the Angels' plate appearances.

The ability of the offense to choose[3] who is "up" renders the concept of a "defensive go-to guy" an impossibility. Even if the offense did nothing but play one-on-one, there isn't a single defensive "stopper" who would be in the spotlight on both nights if his team played Curry and the Warriors one game but faced Joel Embiid and the 76ers the next.

Of course, NBA offenses are far too advanced to default to one-on-one isolations. Especially in the postseason, offensive philosophies aim

---

2. Or just over one-ninth, factoring in the batting order.
3. Or perhaps "strongly suggest," with the defense also having some input.

to attack the opposition's weakest defenders. Whether the tactics chosen force poor defenders into guarding top offensive players or require slower— either moving or thinking—defensive players to make tough decisions, bad defenders can be targeted while better defenders are avoided or minimized.

Looking at an average of usage rates of who each player has guarded[4] as a measure of defensive usage, the distribution of offensive usage is much broader than defensive usage. According to tracking data from recent seasons, the average defensive "matchup usage" was between 18% and 22% for 90% of players, while only one in four had offensive usage rates in a similarly narrow range, demonstrating that defense is almost inherently more collaborative than offense in today's NBA.

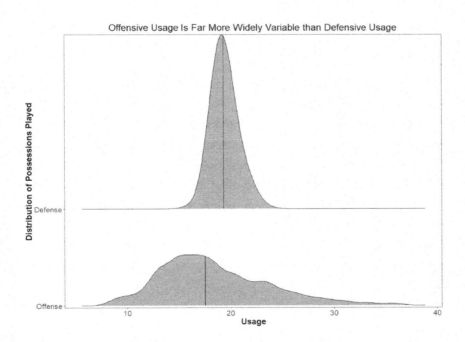

Offensive Usage Is Far More Widely Variable than Defensive Usage

---

4. This kind of data is a bit tricky to work with, as results can be sensitive to definitions used; who is guarding whom on a possession where the defense switches multiple on- and off-ball screens, for example?

Even examining defensive responsibilities within the framework of usage misses the point a little. On most offensive possessions, one or two players will be primarily responsible for the outcome. The other players on the floor matter, but the player with the ball is the most important. Which is of course *why* offenses give their best players the ball more often to begin with.

On most defensive possessions, all five defenders are at least moderately involved. Though some have come close,[5] no player in the league handles the ball for more than half of the time his team is on offense. The majority of a player's defensive contributions arise from off-ball play. This is the case even if they happen to be guarding the eventual shooter.

Recall the Duncan Robinson three which opened Chapter 2, where he shook free enough to catch the ball, set his feet, and launch a shot. Whether that shot had gone in or not, it was a bad outcome for the defense. But this failure had little to do with what any defender did *after* the catch. At that point, the die had largely been cast.

Success in this situation would be Robinson never getting open enough to catch and shoot in the first place. But how do we account for all the times an offensive player didn't get open? Balancing the good and the bad is always a challenge, especially when each defender has multiple responsibilities on every possession, which sometimes pull him in opposite directions.

Which gets us to the underlying question for defensive evaluation: who gets the credit or blame? As often as not, giving up an open three isn't primarily the "fault" of the player guarding the shooter. Something else happened in the possession to allow the player to get open, and we might have to rewind several seconds to pinpoint exactly where the breakdown happened.

---

5. According to tracking data, a few "heliocentric" stars like James Harden, Luka Dončić, and Trae Young have had the ball in their hands for upwards of 40% of the time their teams spend on offense with a given player on the floor, but these are outliers; most lead ballhandlers have the ball around 35% of offensive possession time.

Five Guarding Five

On that same *Ricky Sanchez* episode, Morey opined that the reason defense is hard to measure is because "it's so dependent on what the coach wants them to do." If we don't know what each defender was supposed to do, how can we determine fault of Robinson getting free?

A single defender being able to stop the ballhandler on his own is a wonderful result. However, coaches realized long ago that NBA-level playmakers are simply too good for that to be a realistic expectation on every possession. Breakdowns are going to happen, and each team teaches their own highly intricate dance of help, recovery, and rotation to mitigate those breakdowns. When Morey mentions "what the coach wants them to do" on defense, this is what he's talking about.

What limited existing defensive counting stats we do have are beholden to these schematic concerns. Perhaps the most notable example comes from the collegiate ranks. When interpreting the results of a draft model, analysts have learned to mentally downgrade perimeter players coming out of Syracuse as due to the Orange's unique style of zone defense; guards from that program rack up steals at higher rates in ways that are less reflective of player ability than the same accumulation would be for a man-to-man team.

These contextual effects are subtle at the NBA levels, as there isn't the same degree of stylistic divergence across the NBA as there is across NCAA play. But if one of the main uses of statistical analysis is to compare the performance of one player to that of another, the comparison should be if not apples-to-apples than at least apples-to-some-kind-of-fruit.

Creating the "defensive box score" is a frequent suggestion. The idea comes from the right place; defensive achievements are just as worth memorializing as those attained an offense. Perhaps if a "defensive triple-double" were possible,[6] we would notice and reward those contributions at least similarly to the way which offensive plaudits are distributed.

---

6. I suppose it's *technically* possible that a player could have 10 defensive rebounds, 10 steals, and 10 blocks in a game. Of the 24 times a player has recorded at least 10 steals in a game, the highest blocked shot total was five. I don't think we want the bar for defensive recognition set at "Holy shit, that's the greatest stat line of all time."

It just doesn't work, as defense messes with how we are used to tallying things. The defensive side of the ball is not merely the mirror image of the offensive. On top of the normal fuzziness of credit assignment,[7] add in higher degree of cooperation required on defense and the closest defender is even less to blame for the creation of an offensive stat than the offensive player was due the entire credit.

Back to our open shooter. Many times, his getting open is a product of design.

Not that teams are happy to concede open looks.[8] At least not anymore, with most current players representing at minimum a plausible threat from beyond the arc. Rather, the choreography of help and rotation which make up a defensive scheme gives each defender rules for when to leave their putative matchup to supply help elsewhere and when not to.

For the most part, teams do not *want* to be in help-and-recover situations. But NBA players are good, as are NBA coaches. Offensive sets are designed to put talented players in the right spots to force just the sort of multiple-players-to-the-ball-or-else near panic which is the frequent precursor to an open three. The breakdown which *caused* the open three is often much earlier in a possession than even the pass to the shooter.

Determining when and why a team's defensive "shell" got cracked is the sort of detailed inquiry which is not exactly amenable to a 10,000-foot, big-data solution. Rather, the best currently available tools tend to operate at a higher level of remove. The inferential effectiveness drawn from RAPM-style metrics[9] are useful in this regard.

Those metrics at least provide an estimate of which players' time on the floor most correlates with the opposition having a hard time scoring.

---

7. See Chapter 3.

8. Nor is there much evidence that better defensive teams achieve those results by "leaving the right guys open." This most persistent of myths is one of the first things brought to the table when an otherwise mediocre defensive team rides a run of poor opponent outside shooting to a string of good results. The tendency toward optimism then leads people who would be rightfully skeptical of such a claim with respect to a team they didn't follow or work for to argue that against all previous precedent the dice now have memory, and opponents hitting 31% from long range is the new normal. Regression to the mean is just the slap to the face needed to wake them from this trance-like cognitive slumber.

9. As described in Chapter 6.

Deciphering the how or why of that estimate is tricky, but at least we have *some* insight that a given player is doing something right. But all the normal caveats about small sample sizes and fit within a role or system attendant to top-down methods apply here. On top of which sits opponent shot-making variance, further confounding statistical analysis.

Control and Compensation

This inability to properly account for defense isn't new, nor are the effects of this evaluative difficulty. Any number of studies over the years have examined the degree to which offensive play is better compensated than defense.

The application of analytics and statistical rigor hasn't done much to change this fact, though it may have altered the contours. The "Yay Points!" volume scorer[10] who was seen as an unquestioned star is now treated with much more skepticism. However, this has merely led to a more efficient allocation of salary dollars in rewarding offensive impact rather than a shift of rewards from offense to defense.

It should be noted that the mere fact that offensive players are better compensated doesn't prove that scoring contributions are overvalued. At least on an individual level, offense appears to be more important.

Offense largely controls the style in which any game will be played. Looking at descriptors of style like pace or shot profiles, the consensus is the offense has about twice as much control as the defense at both the NBA and NCAA men's level. From a conceptual standpoint, it isn't much more complicated than the fact that the offense has the ball and thus gets to make the first choice about how a given play will unfold.

Part of the "offense chooses" aspect is the team with the ball decides where they want it to go on each play. Hence "go-to guys" and the wide dispersion of offensive usage noted earlier.

Offensive players also get paid because this proactivity makes offensive skill more versatile. A high-level offensive player is useful regardless of opponent. A wing scorer brings something to the table even if the opposition

---

10. "Volume scorer" is a nice way of saying "chucker" and has generally applied to those who rack up points, but need a bunch of shots to do so.

has Tony Allen, Marcus Smart, and Scottie Pippen rolled into one. A scorer simply occupying the attention of that elite defender is helpful in its own right.

By comparison, an elite post defender doesn't really offer much against teams which never play through the post, at least not with that particular skill. While having a great matchup for the handful of remaining post threats in the league has some value, it's easier to justify paying someone who can contribute across all 82.

Even if a player's offensive style becomes passé relative to the league metagame, they can still be effective. In fact, if they are good enough, having a countercyclical skillset might serve to enhance their value. To stick with the example of post players, Joel Embiid likely benefits from just this phenomenon. Conversely, a player's defensive skillset can very well become obsolete or at least less valuable as the league's offensive approach changes. When weighing whether to offer a player a long-term contract—the deals which typically carry the highest annual dollar figures as well—the chance of a guy suddenly becoming unplayable[11] represents another reason to pump the breaks on paying heavily for defense.

Finally, the very fact that offense is easier to measure makes it a surer bet. Signing an albatross contract via misjudgment of player ability is one of the better ways for a GM to become a former GM. Therefore, it shouldn't be a surprise that the big splash on offense is more popular than for a supposed defensive star who might turn out to be anything but.

Visible Efforting

I'm not here to bag on college basketball. The NCAA product is not my cup of tea, but I try not to judge. With one exception, which is when commentators or fans opine that the college game is better because the players "actually try on defense."

There are two things wrong with that statement. First, it's bullshit. Sure, you can find clip packages of James Harden checking out on a few defensive possessions, but that's an exception rather than the rule, even for supposedly

---

11. Roy Hibbert was great on *Parks and Recreation* though.

lazy defenders. Watch, really watch, defenders off the ball trying to navigate the myriad actions a modern NBA offense presents them with and then come back and tell me they aren't working hard.

NBA players are much better at working *smart* than are college kids. We all had more energy than sense at 18 or 20, so this shouldn't be a huge surprise.

Looking at tracking data, players in their first and second years in the NBA tend to do more "work" on defense than in later years of their careers. Perhaps not coincidentally, first- and second-year players also tend to be bad defenders.

Which leads us to the second and more insidious aspect of the "college guys actually play defense" trope. "Defense" and "effort" are not synonymous. Defensive execution takes recognition and reaction speed. It requires technique, understanding, and discipline. Sure, you have to play hard for those traits to matter, but undirected work is wasted work.

In fact, activity without direction might not be much of an improvement over lack of effort. A lazy defender can at least be counted on to be stationary in a certain spot. Their teammates know where they will be and can adjust accordingly. The rookie moving at maximum velocity in a different, seemingly random, direction on every play? That's harder to work with.

But the human eye is drawn to movement. The sprinting, gesticulating, floor-slapping live wire, the guy who "gets after it," sure looks like they are doing something. In short, they are visibly efforting. To overrate the efforter is to violate the famous John Wooden maxim to "never mistake activity for achievement."

Sometimes the visible efforters are elite defenders. Other times, not so much. In many cases, that efforting is only necessary because a defender lacks the early recognition and proper positioning which are the hallmarks of working smarter.[12]

Not only can efforting be an indication of poor defense, but it can be counterproductive in and of itself. A common drawback of the "physical pest" style of defender which is embodied by many efforters is that they give points away at the free-throw line.

For example, these players tend to commit more "bonus fouls," non-shooting fouls which still put an offensive player at the line for two.[13] Other than fouling a jump shooter,[14] there is perhaps no worse play a defender can make. Not only does giving away two free throws turn a chance with an expectation of somewhere between 0.9 and 1.0 points to one where the offense can expect 1.5 or 1.6,[15] it also depresses the value of the ensuing offensive possession. To simplify, it probably hurts the fouling team on the order of a full point.

Now, these things happen. NBA defense requires more than a little physical contact, and much of the contact is in the gray area where fouls might get called but often aren't. Still, some players are consistently handsier than others, and get whistled more frequently accordingly. Over the past decade or so, here are the top 20 biggest culprits:

---

12. As a thought experiment, imagine a defense being put into a rotation situation whereby a ballhandler penetrates and then kicks the ball out to the top of the key, after which the ball is swung to a shooter in the corner. We're more likely to notice the player desperately sprinting to the corner to try and contest the shot than we are the player who is already down and in his stance in the catch. The latter is substantially better, more effective defense, but without close attention would never even get noticed.

13. NBA teams are allowed four fouls per quarter before the "bonus" kicks in on the fifth team foul.

14. Which either turns the play into the best shot in basketball—a fouled three, worth around 2.3 points per attempt—or turns a defensive midrange attempt into the same two free throws as a foul in the penalty.

15. Based on league average FT%.

Bonus Fouls Commited Above Average

Min. 20,000 Possessions Played 2011-12 to 2019-20

Player	Bonus Fouls	Possessions	Extra Fouls/100
Mario Chalmers	106	22143	0.27
Corey Brewer	120	26592	0.24
Iman Shumpert	88	22784	0.18
Patrick Beverley	95	24966	0.17
Marcus Smart	85	24159	0.14
Avery Bradley	113	32484	0.14
Austin Rivers	95	27573	0.13
Devin Booker	80	24331	0.12
Alec Burks	70	21732	0.11
Chris Paul	126	39900	0.11
Kent Bazemore	77	24454	1.00
Isaiah Thomas	96	31340	0.10
Garrett Temple	71	23708	0.09
Vince Carter	75	25993	0.08
James Johnson	66	23061	0.08
Matt Barnes	64	22912	0.08
P.J. Tucker	113	3930	0.07
Devin Harris	59	21164	0.07
Kelly Olynyk	63	22053	0.07
Lance Stephenson	66	23467	0.07

The "extra fouls" column represents the rate at which each player has committed *more* bonus fouls than average accounting for playing time and the changing league environment.[16]

---

16. Interestingly, the rate of fouls committed in the bonus has declined over time even as possessions per quarter has increased. While this reflects something about the league's style of play leading to fewer fouls overall, it is still notable given that with the team foul count resetting at the end of each quarter, more possessions per quarter would lead to an increase in bonus fouls all else held constant. Fourth quarters and overtimes are not included in the analysis, as bonus fouls committed in the closing stages of a game are often either strategic—"take" fouls committed while trailing late in a close contest—or immaterial, as in the case of those committed in garbage time.

Occasionally these fouls are worth it, just the cost of a few extra gambles going for steals or trying to draw charges. Chris Paul has been caught with his hand in the cookie jar more than most, but is also one of the best thieves in the league. Annually among the leaders in steals for the bulk of his career, he also rates highly in RAPM models estimating his impact forcing turnovers of all stripes.

Paul aside, the list is full "visible efforters." Some appear to have made strong defensive impacts according to DRAPM and other metrics, but there are also a few who have "elite" defensive reps while impact metrics suggest they have merely been very good. These extra fouls could explain some of the discrepancy between reputation and impact; as each additional bonus foul costs around one point, the rate at which those fouls have been committed is a decent estimate of the degree to which fouling has been a drag on the player's defensive impact.

The same overexuberance which leads to these giveaways also can lead to fouling jump shooters. While data on the location of shooting fouls is imperfect, Avery Bradley and P.J. Tucker are both in the top 10 most frequent foulers on jumpers—midrange and from three—over recent seasons. But we notice the fouls from contested shots and struggle to count all the fouls that *didn't* happen on more skillful and under-control challenges.

The Myth of Three-Point Percentage Defense

Even previously hardest-learned lessons on proper evaluation of basketball statistics fail us on the defensive end of the floor. For example, we know that to value a player's box score contribution, the marginal contribution to the team's totals is more important than mere accumulation. To differentiate between fattening up on the "we put five guys on the court for 48 minutes" stats and bringing additional substance, we have to consider the efficiency with which the player used all the minutes, shots, and touches it took to achieve those numbers.

In a similar vein, why can't we just compare the difference between opponents' normal shot efficiency to the percentage recorded against each defender, and use that difference to measure defense?

As elegant and straightforward as this sounds, we might as well fit a model to atmospheric noise. While there are certain situations—rim protection foremost among them—where this approach can provide insight, those are the exceptions. For the most part, percentage allowed is not a useful measure of individual defensive ability.

Let's be clear what I'm not saying first, as the fine distinctions matter here. There are quite clearly better and worse ways to contest a jumper. A clean block on the release is a perfect contest. On the other hand, either a complete non-effort or worse yet *fouling* is a total fail.

More than that, things like "getting closer to a shooter" predictably suppress shooting percentages. Publicly available data only allows for this to be viewed by bands of distance between shooter and defender. Since tracking data estimates player positioning by "center mass," these distances are chest-to-chest rather than how far the contesting hand is from the jumper at the point of release. A defender with NBA wingspan is arm's length from a shooter at right about four feet of separation.

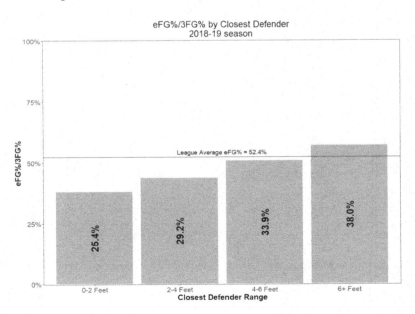

This chart illustrates the degree to which defensive proximity affects results, at least on aggregate.[17] Accuracy gradually increases with the distance of the closest defender until the shooter has about 10 feet of room. After which point, they're all basically warmup jumpers, which the league as a whole makes around 41% of the time during game action. But if defensive distance is the biggest determinant of jump shooting accuracy, we still need to ask, how much of being closer, on average, to opposing shooters is an individual skill, and how much results from defensive schemes, matchups, and the general breaks of the game?

Moreover, while getting closer to shooters will help induce more misses, it will also cause potential shooters to do something else with the ball. The framework of comparing makes and misses as a mode of evaluation fails to account for a second, and perhaps more sustainably positive defensive outcome: covering the player well enough that there is no shot to begin with.

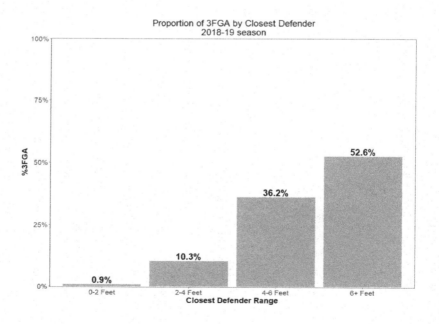

---

17. Looking at defensive pressure as a continuous rather than binned variable traces a similar path, just without the sharp artificial jumps between 5.9 and 6.1 feet of space on the shot.

This illuminates the problem with statistical measurement of individual defense well. While on the offensive side of the ball, the combination of player decision-making and ability to execute on those decisions can be rolled together in the evaluation, this isn't really true on the defensive end. Trying to replicate this on defense leads to not a measure of defensive ability, but of who the defender guarded and a whole lot of variance.

Rim Protection

In his *Ricky Sanchez* interview, Morey opined, "Bigs are a little bit easier to view defensively than non-bigs. Because bigs drive a lot of defensive value and their ability to both make paint shots harder and discourage paint shots, and then finish it off with the defensive rebound. That turns out to be the most measurable part of defense."

Whereas jump shot and especially three-point *percentage* defense is not really a thing on the individual level, the opposite is true for shots at the rim. Though we can prove this statistically, it is worth explaining conceptually as well. We just talked about how defensive action and attention which might suppress jump shot accuracy also tends to make the player decide to do something other than take a jumper, this dissuasion effect is not as prevalent nearer to the rim.

Unlike on threes, where close defensive attention suppresses shooting percentage to the point where the shot shouldn't be taken in the first place, even heavily contested shots at the rim are at least *decent* looks. Especially factoring in the increased likelihood of shooting fouls or offensive rebounds from close-in attempts, it is rarely much of a mistake for an offensive player to at least try to score at the rim. Thus, a greater proportion of scoring chances end up as one of the "true outcomes"—makes or misses—with far fewer instances of a would-be shooter doing something else than is seen on prospective three-pointers.

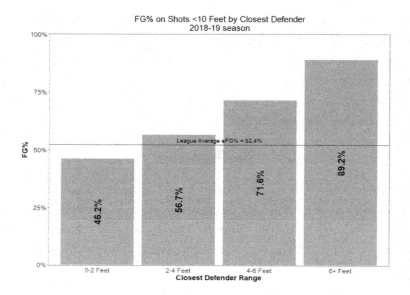

In part because of the resulting cleaner sample, FG% allowed against contests at the rim is somewhat consistent by defender, especially so for power forwards and centers. Offensive players usually struggle to finish against Rudy Gobert or Brook Lopez while they tend to have far more success against Enes Kanter and Kevin Love.

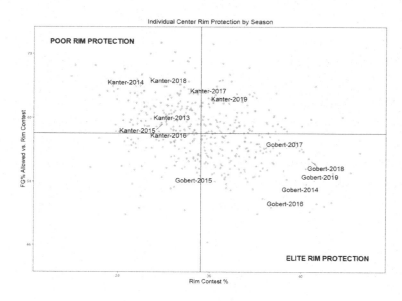

Seeing the Whole Board

There is still an element of scheme and context involved in rim protection. How often each player is in position to defend shots at the rim is partially a function of defensive tactics; the aggressiveness with which a big man chases out to the perimeter usually means less frequent contests. This relationship is one of the selling points of the "drop coverage" fad of the last few years, whereby less mobile but very tall and sturdy bigs sag back when defending pick-and-rolls to almost invite smaller guards toward them for challenged layups and floaters.

This leads to a few different problems. The first is nothing new: untangling player contribution and ability from team context. The bigger issue is that defense must be viewed holistically. Care must be taken when examining defense in microscopic detail, as zooming in too far can blind us to the tradeoffs being made.

Keeping with the rim protection example, while the effectiveness of a given player's contests at the rim is relatively easy to interpret—lower is always better—other aspects are less straightforward. The proportion of opponent rim attempts a player contests is generally a positive indicator as well, but there is a balance to strike.

In the previous chapter, we discussed how in today's game, a defense is forced to worry about two widely separated areas of the court: the basket area and the three-point arc. Focusing overly on one can leave the other open. An interior defender who is overly intent on defending the paint could be doing so at the expense of helping his teammates protect the arc.

This is perhaps better illustrated with reference to a related concept, rim deterrence. While the defense has *far* more control over opponent accuracy on rim attempts than on shots from farther out on the floor, it is still better to limit opponent attempts at the rim to begin with.

Having a big that can patrol the paint well enough to dissuade those attempts and force them farther out on the floor is great…all else being equal. That deterrence can come at the price of not providing enough support to the three-point arc.

"Rim Adjusted Deterrence" is an RAPM-style estimate of an individual's impact on the proportion of opponent shots which are taken in the restricted area. Some of the "top" centers in RAD (Lopez, Nikola Vučević, Nikola Jokić) are frequently used in drop coverage, to the point their teams struggle to defend the arc. Focusing solely on rim deterrence obscures whether that deterrence is helping the overall defense. Perhaps the player effectively walling off the paint allows his teammates to apply more pressure on the perimeter—á la Gobert—or maybe they're simply hiding near the basket and conceding too much on the perimeter.

Until we get to the point where we can actually see players affecting and influencing offensive choices, we'll likely be left with a combination of blunt measures, careful observation, and guesswork. It's unsatisfying, but "I don't know" is usually a better answer than the false projection of confidence, and when it comes to defense, there's much more that we don't know than that which we do.

Chapter 10

Two for One and Other Trivialities: The Little Things

"The inches we need
are everywhere around us!"

—Tony D'Amato, *Any Given Sunday*

I n 2018–19, the average NBA score was 117–105. That average margin obscures how many close games are played in an NBA season.

Of the 1,230 contests, 634 were decided by nine points—three possessions—or less. There were 400 two-possession finishes and 192 where the final margin was within a single possession. The NBA.com default definition of a "clutch" situation is any possession where the score was within five during the final five minutes of the fourth quarter or later. There were 620 games that had at least one play which met those criteria in 2018–19.

Moreover, these games were expected to be close. The closing betting line[1] was 10 or more for only 18.3% of games. According to

---

1. As reasonable an approximation as any for how closely matched any two teams were perceived to be. Thanks to Matt Moore of The Action Network for the historical spread information.

Basketball-Reference.com's Simple Rating System,[2] only seven of 435 possible matchups were a mismatch of larger than 15 points/100 and only 59 where the better team had an edge of at least 10 points/100. In short, the NBA is extremely competitive on a nightly basis.

Individually, any one innovation, adjustment, or maximization might not mean much. But in a one-possession game, the losing team performing just 2% better or the winning team 2% worse would flip the outcome. The league pays just over $3 million in salary for a win, while the value of an extra victory in a seven-game series is worth almost incalculably[3] more; grabbing an extra game here or there is huge.

While noisy "this changes everything" discoveries get the headlines, chipping away at these small margins are where an analyst can make subtle but significant differences. Listing every possible angle would be impossible, but here are just a few examples of the little things that can add up to become big impacts.

Splitting the Pair

Most of the time when a timeout is called during a stoppage for a shooting foul, the TO is administered prior to the first free throw. Automatic "media timeouts" work this way, and for the most part, coaches who choose to use timeouts at this point in the action usually call them either before the first or after the last shot. Occasionally the coach "defending" the free throws will instead call the TO between the first and second attempt of a two-shot foul. This is a tactic that should probably be employed more often.

Between 2014–15 and 2018–19 there were around 117,000 two-shot fouls during regular season play. The league collectively shot 73.7% of the first attempt but made 78.2% on the second.

---

2. Essentially Net Rating adjusted for strength of schedule. Even over a full season, the imbalance created by conference and to an extent division-heavy schedules mean that the team with the easiest schedule will play opponents who are around 1.5 points/100 worse than the team with the hardest schedule, equivalent to the difference between playing a 38- to 39-win opponent compared to the difficulty of going up against a 43- to 44-win squad. These comparisons assume the game is played on a neutral court.

3. We could totally calculate it. I'm just not going to right now.

On this evidence, shooters *seem* to get more comfortable at the line after the first attempt.[4] It appears this increase in accuracy is more about "range-finding" with consecutive shots from exactly the same spot than it is shooters catching their breath. "First-of-two" attempts directly following timeouts, allowing even more time for rest than between free throws, were made...73.7% of the time, the same as without a timeout.

The possible impact of using a timeout to split the pair is somewhat speculative, as teams have employed the tactic timeout around 100 times per season in recent years. But on that limited sample, the league has made only 72.9% of second free throws immediately after a timeout, suggesting around one extra miss for every 20 times a shooter is "iced" in this way. It may not be much, but a free nickel—the difference is almost literally 5 cents on the points-dollar—is a free nickel.

The Offensive Rebounding Equation

The NBA has been trending away from offensive rebounding for some time. To some degree this is a byproduct of other rule changes or unrelated strategic choices. The increase in three-point shooting along with the simultaneous decline in post play puts fewer offensive players in rebounding position to begin with on most possessions. However, it is also a strategic choice; the tradeoff between pursuing offensive rebounds and transition defense is intuitive. For years, coaches have preferred the "transition defense" side of the ledger over gambling for extra possessions.

I *think* the league has gotten too conservative with this "get back at all costs" mindset, even if just a touch. The tough part is figuring out just where the opportunities for chasing additional offensive rebounding arise.

Studying new or unusual strategies presents a unique challenge.

I was once asked to project how a lineup of five centers would look compared to a lineup of five point guards. Frankly, I was at a loss for how to proceed past making an educated guess. Aside from the occasional snippet of garbage time, these tactics haven't really been tried, especially

---

4. The effect does not compound with each additional shot. The third of three attempts saw similar accuracy to second attempts.

not at the same time. We can speculate where the advantages would lie, but in the absence of any real world evidence, how confident should we be in the opinion that the interior defense and rebounding prowess of the Five Center Death Punch would overcome the lack of shooting and lateral quickness? Would the Monstars even be able to get the ball over half court consistently? Such an outlandish scenario is more an exercise in curiosity than a useful research question. But similar problems of extrapolating from limited samples often arise when considering a novel strategy.

For as many rebounding chances as there are within a game, fewer of them illuminate the question of when to crash than one might think.

NBA players are NBA players because they are the elite of the elite at making good decisions on the floor. They identify situations where they have little chance of getting an offensive rebound well and know to get back on defense. This is only emphasized by coaching reinforcement; give up an extra run-out dunk or two off of a reckless attempt at a rebound, and there is at least an ass-chewing but more likely a benching in store.

Even with detailed tracking data, there just aren't many instances of players crashing the glass in poor spots, and without routine line-stepping, it can be hard to discern exactly where the line may be. This makes the analysis of risks and reward more theoretical than empirical.

However, the theory is straightforward, so we don't need a precise solution to come up with a good general rule. An attempt to crash the glass is worth it when

%Chance Additional Offensive Rebound * Points Per ORB

is greater than

%Chance Additional Opponent Transition * (Transition Pts / Chance—Half Court Pts / Chance)

To restate, it's only a good idea when you can expect to gain more points than you give up.

By way of illustration, let's hang some numbers on that theoretical skeleton. In 2018–19, an offensive rebound added a scoring chance worth around 1.06 points.[5] On the other side of the ledger, a fast break after a defensive rebound produced a little over 1.17 points. Since the average half court play garnered just under 0.95 points, giving up that fast break "cost" the defense about 0.23 points. As 1.06/0.23 = 4.6, each additional offensive rebound was worth giving up 4.6 additional transition chances.

Now, there are good reasons to suspect this is overly optimistic in the pro crash direction. There is a lot not being factored in: the downstream effects of giving up more transition plays; the likely increase in efficiency of those transition plays;[6] committing more loose ball fouls—especially detrimental if they lead to "bonus" free throws—and so on. A safer estimate is probably closer to needing an extra rebound for every 3 or 3.5 additional transition chances allowed.

Determining which spots clear that bar might be more educated guess-work than empirical proof, but just knowing what "good enough" means will help make those choices.

Hidden in Plain Sight

Good players who don't put up big numbers in any one area are often complimented as having "a good floor game." This somewhat malleable description usually means they do stuff like deflect passes, take charges, and come up with loose balls frequently. They help you win the possession game. And perhaps the most important aspect of winning the possession battle is avoiding turnovers.

As we discussed in Chapter 3, turnovers tend to come with the territory of doing useful things on offense. The best players usually have high turnover totals. It is difficult to notice players who are better than others at avoiding turnovers. Much as in evaluating defense, counting all the bad things a player prevented from happening is quite the challenge.

---

5. Using data from the excellent Cleaning the Glass website. According to CTG data, "putback" chances were worth just under 1.1 points per chance as compared to just under 0.95 per regular half court chance, and just under 75% of offensive rebounds led to "putback" chances as opposed to resets into normal half court chances.

6. The additional offensive rebounders committed likely mean more frequent 3-on-1 transition situations, resembling fast breaks after steals which currently produce 0.2 more points per chance.

It is not enough for a player to simply commit a low number of turnovers. Low-usage specialists often have miniscule turnover rates. This doesn't reflect elite ball security so much as it does coaches sending poor ballhandlers to stand in the corner, take catch-and-shoot threes, and try not to mess anything else up.

Though they will have far more turnovers than those specialists, the most effective ballhandlers and playmakers tend to be those who help the *team* reduce turnovers even if they are credited with committing a considerable number themselves. Though we can't see turnovers not happening, we can assess the ability to prevent them, to a degree.

Recall the Regularized Adjusted Plus/Minus (RAPM) techniques discussed in Chapter 6. Though more commonly used to estimate overall impact on score differential,[7] RAPM-style methodology can also help identify players adept at reducing their squad's miscues.

According to "Turnover RAPM" for the 2015–16 through 2019–20 seasons, the most ball-secure players include some of the more effective backup point guards in Monté Morris (13th of 942 players appearing in those seasons), Tyus Jones (fourth), and Ish Smith (third). The league's top point guards are represented as well: Kyrie Irving ranked 20th. Damian Lillard was ninth, Mike Conley eighth, and Kemba Walker second. High-volume isolation scorers often grade out well on this metric, illustrating why good-but-not-great iso scorers can be effective floor raisers[8] and are somewhat more valuable than suggested by their individual scoring efficiency numbers. To that point, LaMarcus Aldridge was 16th and DeMar DeRozan fifth. Kawhi Leonard's ability to get where he wants to go at the speed of his choosing puts him 10th, while even in the twilight of his career, Dirk Nowitzki provided elite scoring punch in part because offenses built around him rarely turned the ball over, as evidenced by him placing 12th.

But a special place should be reserved for Chris Paul, the unquestioned master of the possession game. Nowhere is Paul's genius-level feel better

---

7. Hence "plus/minus."

8. "Floor raisers" have the skill profile to help a bad team become competent and a competent team good, but unlike "ceiling raisers" struggle to help a good team become great.

demonstrated. Not only did Paul lead the league over this time frame,[9] but he was also amongst the players whose floor time lined up with opponents turning the ball over more.[10] Rather than try and describe it, I'll let a picture tell the story:

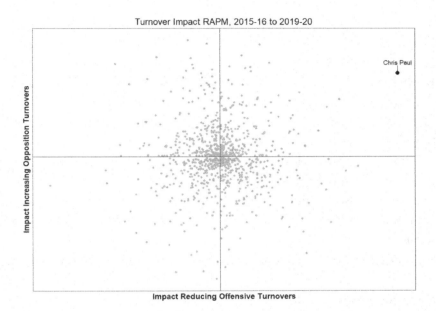

If there is a better illustration of being an all-time great floor general than the above, I have a hard time imagining what it could be.

One-Point Five, Not Two

Visualize a scenario with me. The Portland Trail Blazers inbound the ball with 38 seconds left in the second quarter. Damian Lillard catches the inbounds pass and speed dribbles upcourt. Just past half court, he hits his defender with an in-and-out fake crossover before side-stepping to his right and launching a leaning 27-footer with 31 seconds remaining.

---

9. And by a wide margin: the estimated gap between Paul and Walker in second is larger than that between Walker and Leonard in 10th.

10. Among the reasons you live with his propensity to commit an extra "bonus" foul here or there.

I might be wrong, but in your head you just shouted, "Two for one!"

For all the attention given to maximizing points per possession, the object of the game is to outscore the opponent, not "out per possession" them. Gaming the timing at the ends of quarters is one of the few ways to grab an extra possession in a game that might just come down to that one extra chance. The league has certainly caught on. Looking just at the first three quarters of games[11] in 2004–05, the average contest saw 1.8 shots attempted with between 29 and 37 seconds remaining on the game clock.[12] By 2019–20, this had risen to nearly 2.5 attempts. Considering there are only three quarters to work with, that's a massive increase.

Failing to properly execute a two-for-one is giving away free points, right? Not so fast.

The situation is a little messier than simply taking a shot in the right time frame to ensure getting the ball back one more time. Offensive rebounds, fouls, turnovers, and other events can change the situation. Even analyzing just shot attempts for sake of simplicity, we've been talking about it all wrong.

If all possessions or shot attempts were created equal, getting that one extra look is a clear win. However, we know this isn't the case. A fast break possession following a steal at the top of the floor is worth far more than walking the ball up dejectedly after being on the receiving end of a thunderous dunk.

Much as the event prior impacts the next play, so too does the time an offense has to operate.

This is true throughout the game, not just ends of quarters. The earlier in the shot clock a team can *start* their offense, the better the outcome, even if the play goes deep into the shot clock, proving the coaching aphorism "make them guard for the whole shot clock" correct.

---

11. The time and score imperatives of fourth quarters or overtime are often different than earlier in the game because being ahead by one is just as good as a five-point lead at the end of the fourth quarter, but the larger lead is much better at the start of it.

12. This is the approximate range where following the first shot attempt there is just enough time remaining so that the opponent will be forced to end their ensuing possession with a few ticks on the clock, while also not being enough time for them to flip the script and execute their own two-for-one.

I've analyzed this a number of different ways and have consistently found that each second earlier a team initiates its offense increases efficiency by right around one point per 100 possessions. The possible edge to be gained from this insight isn't huge; the range of "average initiation times" between teams isn't that wide, with the difference between the quickest and slowest being around 1.5 seconds.

Even though that might not sound like much, this is exactly the kind of small edge which, if pushed repeatedly, can add up quickly. The efficiency gain from that 1.5-second gap is worth around four wins over an 82-game schedule, all else equal.

Having time to work with matters, which brings us back to the two-for-one.

The end-of-quarter possession is shorter than 24 seconds and in some cases much shorter, as one of the goals of these "last shots" is to end the possession with so little time remaining in the quarter that the opponent has no opportunity to take a *last* last shot. The ball has to be in the air with under four seconds or so remaining on the game clock. With such narrow time constraints, it stands to reason that shots taken within that window are going to produce lower than average efficiency.

And they do! In 2018–19, shots taken with under two seconds on the clock in the first three quarters of games had an average eFG% of 30.6%.

It's probably a little more complicated than saying the "squib" possession at the end of a quarter is worth 0.6 points on average. Free throws, turnovers, and not getting a shot off in time all impact the efficiency, but 0.6 is a decent estimate.

While not to the same extent, the front end of the two-for-one features its own limited window in which to shoot. While leaguewide eFG% has been in the 52-53% range in recent seasons, 1.05 or 1.06 points per shot, shots taken within that 37-29 on the clock time frame are only around 50% eFG%.[13]

---

13. Interestingly, eFG% on shots in this window has been remarkably steady over the last 15 years, at almost precisely 50%, while overall league eFG% has risen from 48.2% in 2004–05 to 52.9% in 2019–20, suggesting the two-for-one might have become less valuable even as it has become more prevalent.

Let's say a normal possession late in a quarter is worth one point, roughly league average in the half court. The choice facing the team with the two-for-one is this: either they play it straight, and can expect to "win" the remainder of the quarter by four-tenths of a point—1.0 for compared to 0.6 against—or they can attempt to gain a bigger edge by shooting quickly. The first shot needs to be worth over 0.8 points—40% eFG%—to break even.

That's not a huge lift. But you also can't just come down and chuck up any old bullshit. Other things can go wrong playing quickly as well. The ballhandler could rush into an offensive foul, get the timing wrong, and allow the opponent to hold for the last shot. They could barf up such a poor shot attempt that they give up an easy fast break. Any of those eventualities is a disaster, relative to the situation.

So when coaches are less gung-ho about the quick attempt, it's not clear they are making a huge mistake.

Suppose the average team gets one reasonable opportunity at an extra two-for-one each game. With top-notch execution, perhaps they manage to get all the way to one point per chance on the first possession. Instead of the 0.4 point edge they could expect from playing it straight, they manage a net 0.6 gain on average. Over 82 games, this works out to an extra 16 or 17 points, or about one expected win every two seasons. Nothing to sneeze at, but the amount of "everything going right" needed to get to even that point does dampen the urgency.

But if it's there, it's worth trying. Players who are experts at executing in this situation—such as Lillard, who has led the league in two-for-one attempts *six times* while managing 51.2% eFG% on those shots—add just a little something extra for their teams by being able to do so.

Aside from giving us another avenue to appreciate Dame's greatness, there is some use in knowing that two-for-ones are nice but not vital. Practice time and mental energy for strategic thought are limited. Giving a coach peace of mind that this is something they *don't* need to think about frees up that space for other things with larger impacts.

The Quick Two and Other End-of-Game Nonsense

Speaking of other things, let's enter the tricky world of end-of-game scenarios.

There are endless permutations of the last few minutes of games. Time, score, timeouts remaining, and fouls to give. The free-throw and three-point-shooting ability of each team. The details can get complicated. However, unlike earlier in the game, where the impact of any one play on the game's result can be hard to discern, the effects late in the game are more easily quantifiable. Back in Chapter 5, we met Mike Beuoy and his website Inpredictable.com. Tools such as his win probability[14] model allow for end-of-game strategy to become something akin to baking, with precisely measured ingredients, times, and temperatures, whereas the strategic approach to most of the game is more "a pinch of this and a dash of that" cooking.

As an example of how such a model can help determine end-of-game strategy, I want to focus on a particular pet peeve of mine: the obsessions with the "quick two." While watching a game, whenever an announcer opines, "They don't need a three here," they almost certainly *do* need a three there, and have probably needed a three for a good while.

That the trailing team should seek to "extend the game" is a fallacy popular in many sports, of which basketball is not an exception. This line of thinking forgets that the goal is not to lose more slowly. Rather, as long-time NFL coach and commentator Herm Edwards once bellowed at a press conference, "You play to win the game!" While "We haven't lost, yet" might seem like progress, that progress is illusory.

Managing to force overtime isn't the same as winning. Indeed, during the compressed calendar of an NBA season, the additional wear and tear on top players is not ideal even if the team should prevail, let alone "extending the game" another five minutes and still losing.

---

14. There are other WP models including some proprietary to teams, but Beuoy's is probably the best known and most easily accessible of the public models. While every variety of WP model might view each situation slightly differently, these discrepancies are minor, and the analysis of most events will be similar.

With the proper goal in mind, Inpredictable's win probability model illustrates the degree to which "game extending" strategies are often a mistake.

Consider a team trying to decide how to proceed coming out of a timeout, with the ball but trailing by four with 20 seconds remaining in regulation. Using Beuoy's calculations, a team in this situation will win about 3.7% of the time. Assuming it will take them around five seconds to get a shot off, they will be down either one, two, or four points with 15 seconds remaining.

This is a frequent "don't need a three here" spot for broadcasters and some coaches. Their logic is that if the trailing team misses, the game is basically over. So take a two-pointer which will go in more often to keep the game alive. While based on a reasonable premise—win probability drops to 0.6% after a miss and defensive rebound—the logic doesn't hold.

In this spot, a team down two will win around 7.1% of the time. Reduce the deficit to a single point and their win probability jumps to 16.9%. Thus, the two-pointer needs to be around 2.4 times as accurate as the three to be the better option.

If even a poor attempt from three goes in 30% of the time, the "quick two" has to be converted nearly three-quarters of the time to represent an equally viable strategy. I ask you, if a coach has a play that reliably produces a 70% shot in their back pocket, why has that play been saved until after they've basically lost already? Of course, there is no "easy button" which spits out layups and teams can't count on a 70% shot in this spot.

This analysis holds true for a wide variety of late-game situations where a team faces a decision between going for two or three. Though the percentages might be slightly more or less favorable to the two depending on things like each team's shooting skill[15] or the number of timeouts each team has left, these small adjustments only matter if the underlying math is close.

A seemingly nightly scenario is questioning whether a team trailing by two with the ball and the shot clock off should go for the tie or take the three for the win. In general, playing for the win is the move. Let's consider

---

15. Beuoy's public mode is agnostic of these team-specific factors.

the best-case scenarios, where the trailing team makes the shot. What's the situation now?

After a made three, up one with 15 seconds remaining, win probability is 62.4%. After a made two, the game is tied, resulting in a win probability of 37.9%. Sometimes the breaks of the game dictate that a drive to the basket is the better option. A two-pointer needs to be made around 55% to produce similar win probability as a 30% three. Doable in the right circumstance, but the three is usually the best first choice.

So instead of getting cute and trying to play the game out longer, shoot the damn three already.

Chapter 11

The 82 and The 16: Playoff Game Theory

"My shit doesn't work in the playoffs."
—Former Oakland A's GM Billy Beane, *Moneyball*

A s a thought experiment, I often wonder how much different the NBA would look if games were played on a football (or even *fútbol*) schedule. With five or six days between games, what would change?

No back-to-backs. A set weekly schedule allowing for proper rest, recovery, and training focused on capacity building. The health impact and the disruption of traveling to road games would be minimized. Top players could play more. Minor ankle sprains or jammed fingers might actually have time to fully heal during the season, leading to fewer absences from the lineup due to flareups of nagging conditions.

As a result, depth would become less important, with fewer absences and tighter rotations. This in turn would raise the bar required to be a contributing player, heightening the overall level of ability on the floor at any given moment.

The competitiveness of each game played would also ratchet up. After all, dropping to one or two games per week would necessarily mean fewer games in a season.[1] Fewer games means more importance on each game, as an extra win or loss is far more likely to determine playoff seeding, home court advantage, and even admission to the postseason to begin with.

There would be multiple days to prepare and practice for each new opponent.

Shortened benches, extended minutes, more importance placed on any given game, and deeper, more opponent-specific game planning? Described that way, we already have some idea of what a "Sunday! Sunday! Sunday!" league would look like: the playoffs.

The analogy is imperfect. In the earlier rounds, there are more days between games in the postseason than the regular season. However, by the second round and especially the Conference Finals, the schedule moves back to every other day. That said, the reduced travel demands would still provide some respite.

Once we hit the postseason, the need to manage conditioning and health for a long season is gone. The season is almost over, one way or another! Certainly, more detailed preparation for a specific opponent—even if for up to seven games over two weeks rather than a single contest—is a major feature of the playoffs.

The game thus changes in subtle ways. Over time, player and team postseason performance diverges even amongst those with similar regular season profiles. Warriors star Draymond Green describes the difference as "82-game players vs. 16-game players." The implication is that for a team with championship aspirations, the focus should be on acquiring those 16-game players.

There is some appeal to this formulation. The same players and teams tend to advance deep into the postseason year after year. Between the 2011

---

1. Assuming the NBA returns to an 82-game schedule for the 2021–22 season and beyond, there is *a lot* of slack in the schedule in terms of games that could be removed before there is much competitive impact. For competitive purposes there isn't that much value gained from the last 15 or 20 games of the 82. Insofar as the purpose of the regular season is to allocate playoff berths and seedings, a shorter season would do just about as well. The overwhelming majority of playoff teams are in playoff position by 66 games into a regular season, and further supermajorities are within one seeding spot of where they end up in the final standings after the same number. Almost a fifth of the season simply doesn't matter, a fact teams have realized by adopting strategies to manage the season possibly at the expense of maximizing their chances of winning on any particular night.

and 2020 playoffs, LeBron James reached the NBA Finals a staggering nine times. The only comparable level of success for a star player in NBA history was Bill Russell during the Celtics dynasty of the late '50s and '60s. With all due respect to Russell, making the Finals is a tougher ask today.

However, James' omnipresence in the season-capping series says as much or more about the importance of having superstar talent[2] as it does about the 82-and-16 issue. Knowing the very best players are game-breakingly powerful in the postseason is an insight not especially valuable for building a playoff-ready roster; every team is always on the lookout for those superstars. The question is much more about how to find the playoff-viable talent to surround the superstar or superstar-adjacent meal ticket.

Running Out of Playoff Talent

Is there something that made Robert Horry a postseason force while an occasional All-Star such as Carlos Boozer seemed to disappear?

Horry wasn't a "better" player than Boozer. The latter made two All-Star teams, averaged over 20 points per game twice,[3] and had five seasons averaging a double-double, while the former never sniffed an All-Star spot, averaged double figures only three times in his career (the last in his fourth season), and came off the bench for more than half of his appearances.[4]

In the grand accounting of how the league viewed the two players, Boozer more than doubled Horry's career earnings, even adjusting for salary cap inflation. Scaling to 2019–20 dollars, Boozer made over $169 million, while Horry managed "only" a bit under $77.5 million, despite playing three more seasons. However, Horry has seven rings, while Boozer's teams never made the Finals and appeared only once each in the Western and Eastern Conference Finals during his time in Utah and Chicago, respectively.

Some of this is situational. Horry played alongside Hakeem Olajuwon, Clyde Drexler, Shaquille O'Neal, Kobe Bryant, Tim Duncan, and Manu Ginóbili on his title-winning teams. Other than being in Cleveland for

---

2. Discussed more fully in Chapter 7.

3. When averaging 20 meant a lot more than it does in today's era of juiced-up offenses.

4. Horry started 43.4% of the games in which he appeared, while Boozer started 90.0% of his games.

LeBron's rookie season and with the Lakers for Bryant's late-season return from an Achilles tendon tear in 2014–15, Boozer's best teammates were Deron Williams and Derrick Rose, the latter of whom blew out his knee at the end of the first game of the first round on what was probably the best team on which Boozer played.[5]

Still, Horry routinely elevated his game for the playoffs, while Boozer's shrunk.

Why is it that some players don't perform well in the postseason? In popular conception, the narrative is frequently that the moment becomes too big for some, drawing out a character flaw which prevented a player from being *truly* great. Horry's penchant (or good fortune, take your pick) to pop up in big moments earned him the sobriquet of "Big Shot Rob." This was chalked up to a winner's mentality, Horry possessing the fortitude that a player who saw his effectiveness decline sharply in the playoffs like Boozer lacked.

I've never bought that sort of character-based narrative. Nearly every player has had to climb an enormous mountain to reach the NBA in the first place. Perhaps there was a point at which the rewards of being in the NBA were not well understood, but that was generations ago. Even an NBA minimum contract can be more than 10 times larger than the most a player could make in the G-League.

These financial rewards lead to *incredibly* fierce levels of competition to move up the ladder, a vicious knockout tournament which can start before a player is even into their teens in the American system. The players who reach the NBA have won this tournament at every level. This has been by dint of their ability in part as well as the good fortune to have the requisite

---

5. That Bulls team as well as the 2013 Thunder who lost Russell Westbrook to his own knee injury in the second game of the first round are prime examples of the kind of bad luck that can derail a postseason. I've long thought that 2012–13 OKC team is one of the very best of this era to fail to reach the NBA Finals. Every year, there is debate about whether the title-winning team got lucky. Maybe an opposing star got injured, or a potentially tough matchup got bounced in an early round. Perhaps they advanced to the next round after a Game 7 in which the opposition missed 27 straight threes. But that seems unlikely. However, even if it is only the absence of bad luck of their own, *every* championship team got lucky in one way or another. The Warriors were blessed with not only amazing health for their top players during their run of three titles in four years from 2015 to 2018, but even before the playoffs started, the universe aligned to allow them to sign Kevin Durant, as detailed in Chapter 7. It is not an "either/or" with luck and skill, it's "yes/and."

mix of size, strength, and speed. But it required considerable determination and hard work along the way.[6]

I'm reminded of the story of Gus Caesar from Nick Hornby's wonderful *Fever Pitch*. Caesar was a *very* suspect defender for Hornby's beloved Arsenal Football Club in the late 1980s. Hornby ruminated at length as to what it meant to be mediocre at the First Division[7] level of competition:

> Did Gus commit himself to the life he had picked? You don't get anywhere near the first 11 of a major First Division football club without major commitment. Did he know he was good? Yes he did, and justifiably so. And think about it. At school he must have been much, much better than his peers, so he gets picked for the school team, and then some representative side,[8] South London Boys[9] or what have you; and he's still better than everyone else in the team, by miles, so the scouts come to watch, so he's offered an apprenticeship not with Fulham or Brentford or even West Ham but with the mighty Arsenal.[10] But it's still not over, even then, because if you look at any First Division youth team of five years ago, you won't recognize most of the names, because most of them have disappeared.[11]

(Footnotes mine, not Hornby's, of course.)

After battling through the youth and second-team ranks at Arsenal, Caesar got his chance in the usual way. A coach or two was fired, a player or two ahead of him on the pecking order got injured or benched for a game

---

6. This seems doubly so for a player like Boozer, not gifted with prototypical size or athleticism for a high-level interior player, nor the range of versatile ballhandling and playmaking skills which might make up for those deficiencies. Six-eight, below-the-rim power forwards don't become All-Stars without a high degree of Want It More.

7. Now the Premier League.

8. A rough British analogue of a top AAU program.

9. Or in the basketball context "Compton Magic."

10. At the time of Hornby's writing, this would be the equivalent of being recruited not by a midmajor or even lower-tier team from a power conference, but by a blue blood program like North Carolina or Kentucky.

11. NBA Summer League rosters allow for a great deal of "Hey, remember him?" college stars who couldn't quite manage the jump to the NBA.

or two. As Hornby writes, "Suddenly it's all on for him." He's had some success, and is recognized as an up-and-coming star:

> Now at this point, Gus could be forgiven for letting his guard down a little. He's young, he's got talent, he's committed to the life he's picked, and at least some of the self-doubt that plagues everyone with long-shot dreams must have vanished by now. At this stage you have to rely on the judgment of others…and when those others include two Arsenal managers and an England coach then you reckon there probably isn't much to worry about.
>
> But it turns out they are all wrong.

Now, tell me that doesn't sound exactly like every highly touted draft bust since forever.

But the notion that Caesar got just to the precipice of actual stardom and all the drive which pushed him that far simply vanished? Faintly ridiculous. As Hornby concludes, "To get where he did, Gus Caesar clearly had more talent than nearly everyone of his generation (the rest of us can only dream of having his kind of skill) and it still wasn't quite enough."

Occam's Razor suggests that those who run into failure in the playoffs don't reach the edge of their "character," whatever that means, but rather they just ran out of talent.[12]

Climbing the Pyramid

Suppose for a moment that the 30 NBA teams are starting the 30 "best" small forwards. The 16 teams which make the playoffs won't always include the top 16 best small forwards, but most will be there.

Now consider the team with the 10th-best small forward in the league. This is a position of strength over 82 games. Their 3-man is in the top third of the league! Suddenly, the playoffs start, and this strength immediately disappears. Once the 14 lottery teams are removed, 10th-best is toward the

---

12. One of the great sports quotes of recent memory comes from then-Rockets swingman Corey Brewer, who, when asked by his coach how he had missed a layup after a great move to get there, responded, "Coach, I did my thing. But then when I got to the rim, I ran out of talent."

middle of those remaining, perhaps even slightly lower. That position of strength is now closer to average and perhaps even a weakness.

Suppose the team wins their first-round series, advancing to the final eight. The 10th-best small forward might not yet be an absolute liability, but he's holding on by a thread. Advance to the Conference or NBA Finals and the hill becomes steeper, the boulder of superior opposing talent rolling downhill even faster.

So, from a pure quality of competition standpoint, it's a tougher environment. Not a lot of replacement-level opponents to fatten up a stat line in the postseason. The shrinking group of teams in each round of the playoffs all but assures that players, teams, and coaches are judged on a separate scale than for the regular season.

But this increase in difficulty level doesn't affect all players or skillsets equally. Baseball researchers have identified a characteristic which explains a lot of what was previously seen as a "clutch gene." Two players who perform identically against the entire range of opponents but look very different against the toughest and weakest tranches of opposition.

For example, two players could hit .300 overall, but one has splits of .305, .300, and .295 against the bottom, middle, and top third of opposing pitchers, while another is closer to .325, .300, and .275.[13] Since playoff rosters tend to be heavily weighted toward top-end players, the first guy is likely to perform better in a postseason setting than the second. So perhaps "clutch" is a real thing if defined as "performing well against top opposition." Postseason suitability could be more about the contours of a player's skill rather than an expression of moral fortitude or sport-specific genetic advantage.

The nature of basketball makes empirical replication of those baseball studies difficult. In many cases the advantages or disadvantages of a basketball matchup better resembles rock-paper-scissors than a more transitive environment where A beating B and B beating C compels that A will likely beat C. Still, it is not hard to imagine certain sorts of skills drop off more swiftly against higher-level opposition.

---

13. This is a completely made up example for purpose of illustration.

With the prevalence of better defenses and especially better interior defenses in the postseason, Boozer's archetype of below-the-rim interior scorer is likely a good candidate for this kind of decline.

Using a combination proportion of shots taken in the restricted area[14] and dunks rate[15] as proxies for this type produces a group that looks about right, especially if we allow that more versatile playmakers such as Green or Lamar Odom don't count as members.

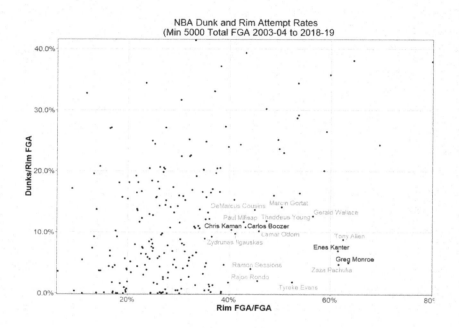

Boozer. Greg Monroe, Enes Kanter, Chris Kaman. If we lower the minimum attempts threshold, other similar players such as Craig "The Rhino" Smith and Kenny Thomas start to pop up as well.

On the flip side, Horry was a low-usage player whose value was his defensive versatility and ability to space the floor from the power forward

---

14. For reliance on interior scoring.
15. With infrequent dunkers qualifying as "below the rim."

spot. In the playoffs the league has trended toward preferring that skillset from 4s and 5s, often at the expense of interior scoring ability.[16]

Horry's teams certainly acted as if he was well suited to the playoffs. In 14 of his 16 seasons, including the first 13 of his career, Horry played more minutes per game in the playoffs than in the regular season. On four occasions, this increase was larger than five minutes per game. In 2002, the last year of the Lakers' Shaq-Kobe three-peat, Horry played 10.3 more minutes per game than in the regular season. This is notable because the Lakers' starting power forward for most of that season, Samaki Walker, was healthy and appeared in all 19 playoff games. Horry did not get the big bump in minutes out of necessity; he took those minutes away from Walker. Walker was mostly an interior below-the-rim player, if we're looking for patterns here.

Horry's increased playoff workload is notable for its consistency over the course of his career. It is a testament to his "16-game" worthiness that until he aged out as a regular season contributor, he was *always* a part of the playoff rotation. As depth decreases in importance, it tends to be the bench players who get squeezed out, but something about Horry meant it was always someone else feeling the pinch.

Rubber Bands and Blowouts

The increased reliance on a team's top players and thus decreased impact of depth leads to another difference between regular and postseason play: the disappearance of the "rubber band effect." This is a phenomenon[17] whereby trailing teams play better and leading teams worse once a sizable

---

16. Setting aside the coextensive trend of larger ballhandlers occupying the titular 4 spot in playoff games. Examples such as lineups featuring behemoths like LeBron or Giannis Antetokounmpo alongside three shooters and perhaps one traditional big abound. Even though the ball is in the hands of a "big," the practical effect is the same in terms of having a third off-ball player primarily on the perimeter.

17. Similar effects have been identified in multiple sports. For example, NFL quarterbacks often rack up huge yardage numbers in the latter stages of already-decided games against "prevent" defenses. This effect is so pervasive in sports with few scoring events, such as soccer and hockey, that "score effects" are an essential part of measuring performance. A top soccer team should be given more credit for a given level of attacking control of the game if they took a 2–0 lead after five minutes than if they had been stuck at nil-all against an inferior side for 85 minutes before scoring twice near the end for the same 2–0 win. The degree to which teams become more aggressive when behind, egged on by the turtle-like conservative tendencies of leading teams, is that strong.

lead is established. Essentially the larger the lead, the more the rubber band holding the two teams together stretches, exerting more pressure inward and causing leads to tend to slip.

Nathan Walker, a researcher at Stats Perform,[18] has found the magnitude of the force pulling teams together grows stronger more or less linearly with scoring margin. Regardless of why it happens, this effect puts something of a handbrake on a game getting too far out of hand. However, the force pulling teams together and keeping games close is far weaker in postseason than regular season play until the score margin is well into the teens.

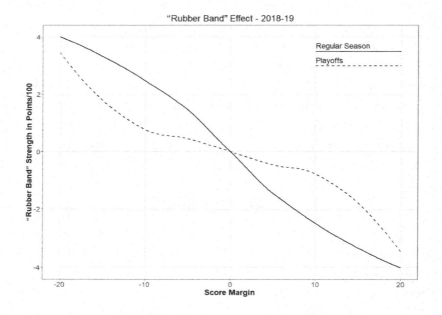

There are probably several factors working in concert to produce this change.

One theory for the existence of the effect in general is that referees tend to be kinder, unconsciously, to trailing teams. Obviously, differing standards for earning free throws would be of great benefit to the team getting a more generous whistle. This is certainly plausible, but hard to prove. Even

---

18. Nate, a long-suffering Charlotte Hornets fan, frequently posts his work on Twitter @bbstats.

a demonstrable difference in free-throw rates based on game state wouldn't be dispositive.

Teams with big leads ease off the gas. One effect of taking the foot off the pedal is longer, slower offensive possessions. Which means more late-clock jumpers and fewer early drives attacking the basket. Free-throw rates are highly correlated with shot distribution, so a stagnant and jump-shooty offense is going to struggle to get to the line even without referee bias being a consideration.

Another sign of a team "letting up" with a big lead is an alteration of the lineup of players in the game. However, the extra import of every playoff game and the disaster of letting even one big lead slip away in a short series means coaches err far more on the side of "playing my guys" longer. Just to be sure.

Even as the potential damage from blowing a lead in a single game rises, the cost to extending the minutes and increasing the workload of top rotation pieces decline drastically. While players' exertions have been monitored and (supposedly) carefully managed over 82 games, there is far less "tomorrow" to be prepared for in the postseason, especially if one starts giving away games already "won" by subbing too early.

Oddly, the heightened competitiveness of the playoffs doesn't seem to lead to more competitive *games*. Blowouts are surprisingly more frequent in the playoffs than during the regular season. Between the 2003–04 and 2019–20 seasons, 14.3% of regular season games were decided by 20 points or more. In the playoffs, just under 17% of games have had final margins that large. Even in the NBA Finals, there have been more 20-point laughers (15.5%)[19] than during regular seasons.

Optimizing and Exploiting

When discussing differences between regular season and playoff competition, the dearth of in-season practice time in the NBA has to be mentioned. The calendar is a grind, as much a mental challenge as a physical one. To

---

19. Interestingly, blowouts are more prevalent in the second round and Conference Finals than in the first round, when severe mismatches might be expected in the 1-8 and 2-7 matchups. For whatever reason, this hasn't been the case.

ease both burdens, full practices tend to be few and far between later in seasons.

This shouldn't be confused with players and coaches taking days off. Coaches still obsessively watch film. Players get in the weight room, receive treatment from the training and medical staff, and do on-court work to keep their skills sharp and maintain conditioning. As the season wears on, teams replace full group practices with "individual" days. Players will meet with coaches singly or in small groups of varying size, do their time in the training room, get fed by the dietician,[20] and get on the court for their "daily vitamins."[21]

On these days, players at the bottom end or out of the rotation play "church league"—structured pickup games—with assistant coaches, video coordinators, and occasionally members of the front office pressed into service as the basketball equivalent of wrestling jobbers.[22]

The above still represents a full workday for everyone involved. But what it doesn't have is "practice" in a form recognizable to those who played at lower levels or are thinking of depictions in films or TV shows. There might be quick run-throughs of offensive and defensive principles as refreshers, but no in-depth teaching or installation of a bunch of new plays. Full scrimmages are somewhat unusual later in seasons, and "everybody on the baseline" punitive sprints are rightly seen by professional players as some

---

20. One of the most unsung units within an organization are the chefs and dieticians who have to balance the caloric and nutritional needs of high-performance athletes with a highly variable schedule and the need to make everything taste amazing so that players will get the benefits of this work by actually eating the meals provided. Access to this culinary talent is also one of the foremost perks of working for a team and is one of the things I miss the most!

21. A practice popularized by the Spurs and spread across the league with disciples of Gregg Popovich getting a number of head coaching jobs of their own over the years, "vitamins" refer to an evolving and player-specific set of drills meant to enhance skills and simulate portions of game action relevant to a player's role on the team.

22. The anonymous individuals who show up in the ring to get pummeled by the actual stars to "enhance" their characters. Luckily for me, we had an ex-player in the front office who got the church league call-up so I never had to. Not that former NBA player and LSU star Ronald Dupree is a jobber; the coaching staff joked about offering him a 10-day after he carried his team to more than one church league "championship."

Mickey Mouse junior-high shit that causes local media to ask the dreaded question, "Has the coach lost the team?"[23]

As a result of the limited practice time, opponent-specific adjustments are strongly curtailed for all but the most malleable of teams. In the regular season at least.

Rather than describe how playoff prep is different, let me lay out two different weeks of action from my last year with Milwaukee, 2018–19:[24]

- On March 10, 2019, the Bucks played in San Antonio. Either that night or the next morning, the team flew to New Orleans. Regardless of time of arrival there was almost certainly no practice on March 11, though perhaps some players got some shots up and maybe there was a brief film session or walkthrough in the team hotel.

- On March 12, there was a game against the Pelicans. There was probably a brief shootaround in the morning, more to get guys loose than to do any real detail work for the Pelicans, who already were marking time until the end of the season. Anthony Davis played just under 22 minutes for New Orleans as he and the organization knew they were headed for divorce in the off-season.

- With two days before the next game, also on the road, the team may have flown home or gone straight to Miami. We did it either way, depending on circumstances. In that case, given the team was already in New Orleans and the top seed in the conference largely locked up, my intuition is that the team flew directly to South Florida rather than back to Milwaukee. Miami being Miami, the team likely had the day off on March 13 and golf was played. Practice would have been possible the following day but it was likely more of the sort of individual day described above.

---

23. Very frequently a precursor to losing the team more permanently and going back to a nice cushy announcing gig.

24. I'm going largely from memory here. Though an NBA team's season-long travel schedule is meticulously planned in advance and distributed by early October and I probably have my copy lying around somewhere, it is confidential. If nothing else, I'm sure team security, led by the wonderful and slightly terrifying former Secret Service Presidential Detail agent Adam Stockwell, would prefer I not divulge any exact routines.

- After playing the Heat on March 15, the team would have flown back to Milwaukee, had a light day on March 16, perhaps even an off day after returning from a lengthy road trip. Then the team played Philadelphia in a nationally televised contest on March 17.

Four games in four cities in eight days against four different opponents with at most one real practice in there. By contrast, here was the schedule for the final week of the regular season into the first game of the playoffs:

- On April 7, we played Atlanta at home. The Hawks weren't good, and we won easily despite none of our projected playoff rotation playing more than 25 minutes.

- We concluded the regular season on April 10 against Oklahoma City. We had long since clinched home court advantage throughout the playoffs and rested basically everybody, with our third-string point guard Tim Frazier playing the full 48 a few weeks after he played *all 53 minutes* in another game where we rested a bunch of guys that ended up going to overtime.

- Though the playoff schedule had yet to be set, we knew we would open at home on either April 13 or 14. The "race" for the eighth seed was unusually complicated as we entered the last few days of the season with five teams[25] alive for that spot.

- Once matchups were set and we knew we'd get the Pistons starting on April 14, that left three full days for Detroit-specific prep[26] as well as additional full practice days on top of the few we had available knowing players were going to rest against the Hawks and especially Thunder.

---

25. Brooklyn and Orlando, who finished sixth and seventh, respectively; Miami and Charlotte, who just missed the playoffs; and our eventual opponents from Detroit.

26. From a worker bee standpoint, this scenario was Armageddon, as the video coordinators and analytics groups needed to have full film edits and statistical dossiers for all five possible opponents ready to go. The computer geeks had this a lot easier than the film room, as you can run similar statistical analysis on multiple teams at once reasonably easily. You can't scout multiple teams simultaneously. Coffee runs were made, Red Bull was consumed, and we killed a lot of trees making notebooks, 80% of which never saw the light of day, or at least a coach's office.

Of course, it wasn't just the time to prepare for the first game of the series. After each game, there was time to analyze the previous game and adjust to the next. Now, the Pistons were not an especially stern challenge. Their best player, Blake Griffin, was absent for the first few games of the series and hobbled for the rest following a late-season knee injury. But beating them in four games was nice because it kept our guys rested and gave us plenty of time to prep for the next series.

The increased lead time and multiple games against the same opponent allow for some unusually direct real world application of game theoretic concepts. To be incredibly reductive, there are two basic approaches an individual or team can take in terms of strategy. On the one hand there is what is known as game theory optimal (GTO) play, which aims to maximize expectation against the range of possible opponents. On the other end of the spectrum is fully exploitive play, meant to perform best against a specific opponent.

Over the course of an NBA regular season, teams tend toward GTO strategies. Some coaches and teams adjust for opponent game-to-game more than others, but the very structure of an NBA season puts a somewhat rigid upper bound on how deep and specific those adjustments can be. While of course coaches want to win every game, systems and game plans are implemented to maximize total wins over 82 rather than the chances of winning any given night.

The approach taken to prepare for one specific matchup is completely different. These are the exploitive strategies, the series-wide adjustments and tactics for which the playoffs are famous. Individual matchups, tendencies, strengths, and weaknesses of opponents come into stark relief. On stage at the 2019 Sloan Sports Analytics Conference, Golden State general manager Bob Myers described preparing for an opponent this way: "In the playoffs his first move is gone…whatever they know he does well is gone."

Perhaps the most succinct way to describe the two styles is that in the regular season, GTO setting, you are playing against yourself. Execute your own stuff well night in and night out and things will take care of themselves. In the playoffs, the enemy is the opponent in the current series. It is not enough to have the best move; a team or player must be prepared for the opponent's best move as well.

The wrinkle which puts additional strain on individual talent is the series format itself. Myers was likely being a little flippant when he suggested "your first move is gone." If it were that simple, the first moves of the best players would not be the first moves of the best players. The best players have enough gas on the old fastball that even if the opponent knows it's coming, they can't do much with it. Alternatively, they have a wide enough repertoire to make sitting on that "first move" untenable; the countermoves to that first move will pick an opponent apart.

So rather than "one neat trick" to neutralize an All-Star, teams will devise Plans A, B, C, and so on. As the series progresses, they will be tested, modified, mixed, and matched to try to find the right combination to force players deeper into their bags.

For all but the very best players, one of the approaches will work, at least to a degree. Which, as Myers put it, is "why you need to check as many boxes as possible" to succeed in the playoffs. These extra demands of the exploitive multi-game environment which characterizes the postseason also explains the added importance of elite talent to top teams, as discussed in Chapter 7. While a First Team All-NBA player might be worth twice as many regular season wins per season as a third-teamer, they are worth about *three times as much* in terms of championship equity. Checking those many boxes is a big reason why.

But we already knew that superstar talent is hugely important. "Just go get the best players" isn't helpful advice for assembling a playoff winner. So how do we find the Horrys and avoid the Boozers of the world? On the latter, examining playoff matchups faced by Boozer in his prime is instructive. Aside from 2012, when Derrick Rose's ACL tear in Game 1 of the first round led to Boozer's Bulls being upset by the 76ers, Boozer himself was at a sizable disadvantage in each series his teams lost.

The opposing power forwards were Tim Duncan (2007), the combination of Pau Gasol and Lamar Odom (2008–2010), and Chris Bosh (2011 and 2013). Given the size and defensive chops of that list, it is perhaps no surprise that Boozer's below-the-rim junk-balling was ineffective as a primary offensive weapon, while he was either too small, too slow, or both to credibly guard those players on the other end.

Meanwhile, the opposing 4 was nearly always "better" than Horry. During that 2002 title run, he faced, in order, Rasheed Wallace, Duncan, Chris Webber, and Kenyon Martin. First, we should note that's four very different challenges, illustrating the importance of versatility. Second, Horry could plausibly guard each of them, at least for spells, and as importantly his ability to space the floor meant he could be enough of a threat on offense to draw attention, even if he couldn't be counted on to score one-on-one against any of those opponents. Isolation scoring was never Horry's game in the first place, so it wouldn't have been missed.

The last point brings up another key element: the importance of role. Horry's role allowed him to be effective even when at a talent disadvantage. Even if and as he got outplayed, he was relied upon not to win a matchup, but to keep it competitive. By comparison, Boozer was no lower than third in usage rate on any of those 2007–13 teams, so by taking him away, opponents turned a counted-upon strength into a weakness.

If there is one lesson to take, then, it is this: 16-game players have to be able to do what they do best against the best. Unfortunately, by the time it is discovered a player can't, it is often too late, both for themselves and their team.

Chapter 12

The Practice of NBA Analytics

"Big data isn't about bits, it's about talent."
—Entrepreneur Douglas Merrill

Much of the misconception about how basketball analytics works is a misunderstanding of how basketball *analysts* work and what they work on. This chapter is meant as a tour through what an analytics or research department might look like and do. While what follows is based heavily on my own experiences, it also incorporates those of current and former analytics professionals from teams around the league. Interpret these descriptions accordingly, as something akin to "league average."

Roles

The first thing to know about the job of basketball analytics is that there is no one job. The field is several distinct, sometimes overlapping specialties which get lumped together under the analytics umbrella.

A team dipping its toes into the world of data for the first time often reveals itself in their initial job listings. Facing this "cold start" problem, the team will demand an applicant qualified to work at an expert level in many if not all of these areas. In the tech world, this would be referred to as a "unicorn hunt," for good reason—it's seeking a candidate which doesn't exist. This phase is usually outgrown quickly. As the org gains a better understanding of what it truly needs to incorporate data into their basketball operations, job requirements become more realistic.

Even limiting the discussion to basketball ops,[1] "analytics" is not one job description, but many. The lines of distinction between roles can be fluid, and job titles less than instructive. Still, there are broad categories which tend to recur:

- **The One Stop Shop:** This isn't really a role within a modern analytics department. Rather, in the early days of adoption within the league (and still the case in a dwindling number of organizations), one person was responsible for everything.

  Set up databases? Check.

  Source, acquire, and integrate data feeds? Triple check.

  Build a draft model? Check.

  Create dashboards and persistent reference applications? Still check.

  Run the day-to-day reports for coaches, scouts, and other front office staff? Also check.

  Be a resource to help others in the organization understand what any of it means? You bet, check.

  Operate as an informal IT service when someone has computer issues, or the projector doesn't work in the main meeting room? Even this, check.

  Thankfully, we've largely moved on from those days, with the essential tasks listed above broken out into separate and better-defined roles, while the non-essential ones allowed to disappear.

- **Data Engineering:** There is more information out there than we know what to do with. A key step toward gleaning insights from that data is making it accessible. The "data engineer" role is responsible

---

1. Most if not all top-level sports teams are really two separate organizations. The business side, which handles marketing, ticket sales, partnerships, community relations, legal, HR, and so on, is completely separate from, in the case of the NBA, basketball ops, which encompasses not just players and coaches but "front office" execs, medical and training staff, equipment managers, administrative, and travel planning. Business operations' groups have their own use for analytics, but those roles have little or nothing to do with the task of selecting players.

for creating and maintaining that accessibility. Whether stored in a local database or made available via a cloud API, this has become a much more vital task in the era of tracking data and near-real time collection of biometric data.

Nothing about this job is sexy; former Utah Jazz analyst Cory Jez describes data engineering as "the offensive line of data analysis." The work product created by the engineer won't be seen by the consumers and end users of analytics, at least not directly. But the ability to perform every other function of an analytics group rests on the reliable, consistent, and timely collection, cleaning, and maintenance of the data itself.

- **Statistical Technique and Research:** Much of the first wave of "advanced" sports analytics was essentially econometric in nature. Relationships between factors and the weights of various inputs were often determined by various forms of regression analysis. As "machine learning" or artificial intelligence technologies have become more widespread, deeper understanding of mathematical and statistical concepts becomes more necessary. The introduction of tracking data has only turbocharged the growth in the demand in this area.

  Whether to directly examine raw tracking data, or create complex predictive models combining an array of data sources, this role requires considerable skill in terms of statistical theory and techniques. It's not enough to be proficient in building these models or performing the relevant calculations. Selecting the right tools, and importantly avoiding the *wrong* tools, for each task and properly interpreting the results requires a high degree of sophistication.

- **Programming, Design, and Development:** While the analytics *group* might not always be available to answer questions, proper use of technology can bring a wide suite of information to the fingertips of the entirety of basketball ops. Creating and maintaining these websites or mobile apps requires a different skillset than those in the above two groups, though the data feeds and statistical processes will flow into these applications. At times, building internal dashboards and the like has been an additional job responsibility of the data engineers or statistical researchers, but increasingly teams have hired specifically for this sort of technologist role.[2]

On top of programming and app development skill, there has been an increase in the attention paid to the aesthetic realm. Whether those hired for their graphical skills are styled as front-end developers, data visualizers, or web designers, putting a good wrapper on a statistical product can be as or more important than the quality of the technique or analytical logic used to produce that product. A common refrain from colleagues after their team has hired a designer is how much more success they have had "selling" their product within the org. On more than one occasion I've heard a variation of "Yeah, our director of scouting told us, 'Your stuff has gotten really good the last few months' when literally the only thing which has changed is our new designer hire made everything prettier."

- **Analysis:** Correlation is relatively easy to find. Proving causation and extracting valid and actionable predictions from those correlations is hard. The "analyst," for lack of a better term, takes the data assembled by engineers and works in concert with the statistical modelers or researchers to properly contextualize the issues studied, and then interprets the results in more familiar terms and language for "basketball people" throughout the organization. This is a communications role as much or more than it is a data role, with that communication taking many forms, whether verbal, written, or visual.

  A growing subset of this category are individuals tasked with coaching analytics. The numbers became more difficult to track in 2020–21 with limitations on travel parties, but in 2019–20 around a dozen teams had a dedicated analytics staffer traveling with the team to provide statistical support to the coaching staff.[3]

  While technical chops are useful in this role (whether attached to the coaching/travel staff or not), there is a wide range of ability across

---

2. This practice is already widespread in baseball, where many teams have two separate departments, sometimes divided between "analysis" and "research and development" titles.

3. In 2020–21, at least four teams (Toronto, Utah, Orlando, and Dean Oliver himself in Washington) had someone with a dedicated analytics background with an assistant coach title.

the profession. Though coding and mathematical skill are important components of this work, a high degree of knowledge of basketball-qua-basketball is a prerequisite for performing this function well. In many ways, this is the main point of contact between an analytics group and the more established groups in a front office. Being "bilingual" in both basketball and data is "strongly preferred," as a job listing might say.

While I may joke about the relative importance of each role—each one is *the* most important function in an analytics group—they all matter. A particular group might be stronger in one or more of these areas than others, but even without a designated specialist, each area is necessary for a team to get as much as possible out of a research department.

The Calendar

A frequent question asked of a team-side analyst by an outsider is, "So what does your average day look like?"

There is no such thing as a normal day in the NBA. But there is a general rhythm to the year that at least informs what the day might look like. This is true across a basketball operations department, and perhaps the easiest way to clarify how analytics is practiced within a front office is to describe that calendar and how an analytics group fits within this schedule.[4]

Late August to Early September: As there is no "start" of a circle, this is as good an arbitrary point of entry as any. In the normal calendar, this is the unofficial beginning of the "pre" preseason. Everyone (*everyone*) has gone on vacations following the completion of the summer free agency period in July and throughout August, but now that's done.

Players are returning to the team facility to work out with coaches or trainers and play semi-structured pickup. Coaches are making final decisions about schemes to be implemented for the upcoming season while finalizing the training camp calendar. Front office staff is setting broad scouting

---

4. Writing this in the midst of the 2020–21 season and referring to a "normal calendar" feels almost aspirational, but what I'll describe is illustrative of how the league operated in the months and years leading into March 2020 and to which I suspect it will largely return soon.

agendas, conducting initial leaguewide roster analyses, and perhaps even producing an *extremely* preliminary board for the following June's draft.

From an analytics perspective, this period is all about deliverables. What does the coaching staff want to see in pre- and postgame reports in terms of both content and timing? Are there other, more longitudinal data points or indicators—10-game snapshots, for example—they want to receive on an ongoing basis? What are the deadlines for the results of draft models and player projections? From a player personnel and front office perspective, what stats and indicators are being tracked as a matter of course, and how will that information be made available or delivered?

A lot of work is done now to make sure it does not need to be done under the time pressure and generally elevated agitation level of a professional season. If there is one lesson I learned, it is this: automation is your friend. The games come thick and fast enough that simply not having to spend much time on "everyday" stuff every day is a *massive* time savings.

Automation is also a great way to make friends for life with the video room,[5] who are also responsible for tons of pregame prep and postgame analysis themselves. It might seem trivial, but allowing a video coordinator to assemble a "last five games" summary of the rotation patterns of an upcoming opponent at the click of a button rather than having to comb through those five games allows them precious time to do other important things like eat lunch sitting down. Or sleep.

This is just about the only time all season there is a confluence of time to work on systems development along with the availability and attentiveness of the end "consumers." As such this also represents the most likely time of the season to discuss, educate, and influence.

Those interactions are vital. Those less familiar or conversant with the level of detail available have trouble articulating the question they want answered. Coaches without solid background knowledge of the state of NBA metrics tend to ask for very specific statistics, rather than pose basketball questions. Preseason is a great opportunity to play the "what is it

---

5. Shoutout to the VR-5; Zach, Blaine, Ryan, Schuyler, and Wes. You guys are the best.

you *really* want to know?" card to best deliver the material most useful, as opposed to that which they already know how to ask for.

Everyone is still undefeated in the preseason, making it the ideal time to have these sorts of semantic, philosophical, or even pedantic conversations. This in turn can increase the appetite for additional statistical insights. As Second Spectrum CEO Rajiv Maheswaran told me: "Once you solve peoples' problems, they will just come back and ask you for more and more and more." Strengthening the communicative tissue between areas of an organization is always a good thing, and there is no better time—perhaps even no *other* time—to do so than during this pre-preseason period.

Similar discussions happen with front office and player personnel decision-makers. In many cases these conversations cover the same analysis as requested by coaches, but with the necessarily different focus of the front office group, it might require some repackaging.

While it is too early for results from an updated draft model, this period is also an excellent time to help the amateur scouting department out by identifying some lesser-known prospects who may have "popped" in the previous season's model. A few recent examples of players pinged in one of my models in seasons prior to their draft year include Ja Morant, John Konchar, and Xavier Tillman.[6]

Early October: Preseason.

Preliminary versions of reports are circulated. Comments are received. Form and content are iterated. Data feeds are checked, rechecked, and checked once again, knowing that as soon as real games start, *something* won't work quite as expected.

As teams around the league make their final roster decisions and exhibition games give some hints as to the rotations coaches will employ, win and playoff probability projections get dialed in as well as possible.

Late October through November: The season starts.

Fingers are crossed that all, or at least most, of the automated data feeds required for regular reporting work as intended. Coaches, scouts, and front office decision-makers remember that one thing they wanted and forgot to

---

6. It is with good reason the Memphis Grizzlies are the current darlings of "NBA Draft Twitter."

ask for earlier. Usually these are minor data pulls, easily accommodated. Occasionally they are more involved and there begins a delicate game of expectation management and perhaps-too-fast-for-comfort development work. Which is as terrifying as it sounds.

Thanksgiving through Christmas: Remember holidays?

Thanksgiving tends to be an off day. The league doesn't schedule games. Even if the team is in-market it is usually a light workday for the players and coaches. Most of the front office takes the day off completely, unless on the road for a scouting assignment, hopefully near family so they can get a day or two of in-season R&R. There won't be much room for down time after this until the All-Star break.

From an analysis perspective, this is a quiet time, more about maintaining existing processes. There is some prep work to be done for the trade deadline and the start of in-depth draft scouting meetings. If there is a sense that certain players might be realistic targets for trades, there is time to do deeper analysis with specific examination of how their skills might fit (or not) the existing team construction.

Mostly though, this time of year is just watching a lot of basketball. While keeping tabs on the whole league, the primary focus is on identifying areas of strength or need on one's own team as early in the season as possible. Whatever version of a "trade machine" is in use in the office gets quite a workout as people come up with endless "what if they traded us all their good players for the guys we don't want anymore?" ideas.

December through Beginning of February: Trade talk season and The Board.

The NBA operates on deadlines. For the most part, trades cluster around certain dates: the draft, the start of free agency, December 15,[7] and especially the trade deadline. Without hard stop dates, far fewer trades would end up getting done. FOMO is real, and the possibility of a better deal being out there somewhere would make actual agreements too hard to reach.

But there is a deadline, allowing teams to work backward from that date. The Board comes out. In some cases, it's an actual whiteboard, blackboard,

---

7. The first day players who signed new contracts in the preceding off-season can be traded in the normal NBA calendar.

magnet board, or even smartboard. In others it's metaphorical, though presumably someone has a spreadsheet with all the potential deals marked.

That's what The Board is. A list of all the "live" deals and deal concepts a team is considering.

The Board is a product of seemingly never-ending rounds of phone calls, texts, emails, and pregame conversations between executives trying to gauge the interest to deal away or acquire various players or to trade intelligence about what other teams around the league are doing.

There have been enough accidental "Board" leaks that teams can be a bit paranoid about information security. After the 2017 incident in which the agent for Orlando Magic signee Patricio Garino posted a photo of the Argentinian to social media with about half of the Magic's Board visible and legible in the background, this seemed less like paranoia and more just good safety sense. In Milwaukee, we either erased the physical board at the end of each day or used rolling whiteboards which were locked in a storage closet. The last thing we wanted was for anyone, *especially* one of our own players, to accidentally stumble across the list of concepts. It's easy enough to intellectualize the fact that most Boarded ideas might as well be doodles for all the likelihood they have of coming to pass…until it's your own name in one of the doodles.

During this period, a trade concept might get a firm "no" in response, but almost never a "yes." More frequently it is, "We'll put it on The Board and talk it over with our group."

From an analytics standpoint, The Board is incredibly useful, as it shrinks the universe of available players from over 400 to perhaps 50, a decent chunk of which are only on The Board as salary ballast for a larger deal. The smaller the pool of players, the deeper and more player-specific the dive can be.

The evaluation is not only for overall ability, but for what the player would bring to the current roster. Would he start or be the sixth man? Where is he on the development/aging curve? Given contract status, under what circumstances will he under- or overperform his remaining contract or be available for retention at a "good" number?

Since The Board lists not just possible targets but actual deal concepts, it is possible to examine the other side of the ledger in terms of what the team would lose with the outgoing players.

Early February: Trade season.

To stay on top of all the scenarios thrown out by The Board, the analytics group is incredibly busy up until deadline day. Deadline day itself goes one of two ways.

If the team has already made its moves, there is still due diligence to complete, ground balls to run out. But nothing tends to come of it as those calls are completed—at which point everyone gathers in the conference room, breaks out the snacks, and stares at their phones until Woj, Shams, or Stein tell us who got traded where.

If the team is involved in live discussions, the day is far more frenetic. The "war room" is set up, with a bank of phones and lots of writing surfaces to spitball ideas to expand or modify a trade idea in order to get something done.

Most complex[8] deals which go down don't start out that way. More often, there is a relatively simple swap between two teams that just needs a little something extra. Maybe one team needs an extra second-round pick to balance the deal, or a third team is needed as a landing spot for one or more players for salary purposes.

Shrewd teams have a way of inserting themselves as the middleman in this spot, picking up something extra to help facilitate. Many of the machinations which occur in trying to get a deal over the finish line are about trying to find that third party who will help make it all happen without too much of a finder's fee.

This is the point at which if the statistical analysis isn't already done and ready at the press of a button or turn of a page, it's probably too late. If you're doing new analysis at this point, you're way behind, and analytics are going to be brushed aside in the decision-making process. This isn't a desirable situation, but it can happen even if there is a smooth process in place. Though most deals which end up getting done have been kicked around

---

8. As soon as a third team gets involved, the details can start to get wacky.

between the parties for a long while, some do come together quickly at the last minute; you just hope that there has been enough foresight and planning to be able to offer a cogent opinion at a moment's notice.

All-Star Break: Exhale.

Perhaps there is time to write a midseason report. But mostly, this is down time. A perk for this time of year is the Sloan Sports Analytics Conference, held in Boston. Since one of the founders of SSAC is Daryl Morey, the conference is scheduled to come after the deadline, and it is the closest thing the basketball analytics community has to an annual meeting. Though most of the "meeting" parts are usually after hours with beverages in hand.

March: The dog days.

With the trade deadline passed, there aren't many personnel moves left to make. Perhaps a buyout candidate, or players to sign to rest-of-season minimums to fill out the roster. Teams without title hopes use this period to try out promising young players signed to team-friendly deals, making low-cost bets around the margins, hoping for but not expecting big returns.

The draft model is built, but with March Madness still to be played, any results will be the penultimate run of the model.

Mostly, it's waiting for the playoffs. Playoff prep can get started to an extent, but that work is so opponent-specific and the range of opponents so broad up until the last few weeks of the season, that this is more deciding on the form that various reports will take rather than starting the analysis.

End of Season into the Playoffs: For a team anticipating a deep playoff run, this is the busiest time of year, with playoff prep and the meat of the predraft process stacked on top of each other. Playoff prep is discussed more fully in Chapter 11, while the draft process is covered in Chapter 13, but suffice it to say that doing both at once is a lot. As a father of two, perhaps the best comparison I can make is that while minding one process or the other—playoff or draft prep—is taxing, the difficulty increases exponentially when watching both at the same time.

End of June to Early July: Draft week and free agency. Even for teams which play in the NBA Finals, there is at least a week or so to make final preparations for draft night.

The war room from the trade deadline comes back out. A final draft board is produced with players both ranked and tiered. The latter is an essential strategic tool to identify spots where trading up or down might be advisable. If a team is about to be on the clock at pick 21, while 12 players from their top remaining tier of prospects are still on the board, an offer to trade back to 29 is well worth considering. They can still select a player of similar ability to whoever they might draft at 21, while also picking up an extra asset or two for their trouble.

In addition to the draft itself, execs are working the phones to try to line up possible deals for players who go undrafted. These might be two-way contracts, "Exhibit 10s,"[9] or Summer League deals. The depth of prep both from the analytics and broader scouting staffs shines through on these prospects. In 2019 it was easy for everyone to have informed opinions on Zion Williamson and Ja Morant, but prioritizing and signing a player like Lu Dort or Naz Reid as an undrafted free agent can prove to be a huge win for an organization.

Since there are no more games being played aside from a few remaining from overseas leagues, the final run of draft models is executed. While teams use multiple models for different types of predictions, for ease of communication there is usually "The Model." The risks of presenting multiple models at once include confusion; releasing only one model prevents cherry-picking the result most favorable to a preferred selection.

Once the draft is concluded, there is only a brief time to regroup before free agency begins.

In some respects, this is backward. Teams have more and often much riskier decisions to make in the free agency period than they do in the draft. While the first few picks in the draft draw sizable salaries,[10] it isn't possible to make a $100 million mistake in the draft quite like it is in free agency. Anyone who has ever made the leap from draft-style to auction-style fantasy sports knows how much more complicated the latter is given the need to not just identify to right targets, but accurately gauge the market.

---

9. A type of contract which has a small guarantee but includes an invite to training camp.

10. Anthony Edwards, the first overall pick in the 2020 draft, will get paid just over $44 million over his first four years in the league as required by the collectively bargained rookie salary scale.

Thankfully, the parameters of free agency are largely set shortly after the end of the regular season when the draft lottery makes the final determinations about the order of the draft, which in turn impacts the salary flexibility available to teams. Further, the evaluation of free agent targets is similar enough to trade deadline work to allow for the incorporation and reuse of many of the same tools and metrics from that period.

However, there is still a great deal to be done identifying team needs both in terms of positions and skillsets. Long-range forecasting will shape the team's budget for acquisitions not just for the upcoming season but also several years down the road. Failure to plan ahead can often put a team in a bind, and today's panicked trade or bad signing is often the result of yesterday's lack of foresight. Avoiding contractual pitfalls is thus of great import.

The front office group will game out multiple scenarios, as ending up having to pay a little more than expected on the first signing in free agency can drastically alter the pool of players available in other slots. Properly valuing players is essential, as discussed in greater detail in Chapter 7.

At no point does anyone have any contact with either the free agents themselves or their representation prior to the official start of the free agency period. That would be against NBA rules, which are always followed completely, scrupulously, and to the letter. However, the prep work on all sides is so remarkably efficient that it's not at all unusual to see complicated long-term deals agreed to in mere minutes once the negotiations can start.[11]

As the free agency period commences, the role of the analytics staff becomes more reactive, as the work is already done, but sometimes decision-makers need refreshers on valuations and preferences between multiple options, and quickly, as the market moves rapidly.

Summer League: Vegas baby, Vegas.

If the Sloan Conference is the unofficial annual meeting for analytics workers, Las Vegas Summer League is the semi-official meeting for the entire league and industry. From a work standpoint, LVSL is a great place for those without a lot of experience to get scouting reps in a relatively low-consequence environment. Up to 10 games per day are played across

---

11. Some or all of this paragraph is a lie.

two gyms, with the players being a mix of just drafted rookies getting their first taste of professional basketball, second- and third-year players assessing their progress over the last year, undrafted rookies trying to get signed either by an NBA or overseas team, and veterans who have been on the fringe of the league.

For the analytics group this is mostly something of a working vacation, taking in some frenetically bad basketball, networking with colleagues around the league, and generally enjoying the Vegas experience.

True Off-Season: By late July, the burner is turned to a low simmer. By and large, free agents and draft picks have been signed. Trades have been executed. The Vegas heat has been survived. With nothing pressing on the docket it's a perfect time to get to that back-of-the-mind project, update the codebase, or finally do that study of offensive rebounding that's been on the to-do wish list since…AHAHAHAHHAHAHAHA.

Just kidding. Along with everyone else in the organization, the analytics group is wiped out and needs a *real* vacation. Depending on the size of the group, some of those longer-term projects will get done. But especially coming off the draft/free agency double-dip, the candle has been burned at both ends and in the middle. Rest and relaxation isn't a luxury, it's a necessity.

PTO is taken, batteries are hopefully recharged, and suddenly August is becoming September and it's back to square one.

And that's a season in the life of an analytics department in the NBA. As should be apparent, the charge that analytics are ruining basketball simply can't be true; when would we find the time?

Chapter 13

Trying to Do the Impossible Well: The Many Pitfalls of the NBA Draft

"I don't think CEOs encounter many problems where they have intuitive expertise. They haven't had the opportunity to acquire it."
—**Psychologist Daniel Kahneman**

For NBA front offices, the busiest season is a period when no games are being played. Over a stretch of two weeks every summer, every team has the best chance to remake and rebuild a roster that they will see all year. This span encompassing the draft and free agency period is the final exam for personnel evaluators; when the report cards show up, "draft" and "free agency" will be two of the projects carrying the most weight in final grades.

It can be easy to lose sight of this amid the whirlwind of player movement, but these exams cover two very different subjects. While both involve evaluating basketball talent, one is part of the math and science curriculum, while the other is in applied arts.

Plugging an established player into the world of player value metrics and salary cap projections can be approached at least somewhat scientifically. There is not only a track record and hard data of performance under NBA conditions, but so much of the natural maturation process which occurs

205

through one's late teens and early 20s has already come to pass; individuals being considered haven't just become the players they largely will be, but the *people* as well.

By contrast, the draft is the domain of the delicate art of divining the future of a group, seemingly younger every year, of new hopefuls. Not only is this cohort still very much in development, both as basketball players and human beings, but the data needed to judge what they *were* as players, let alone what they will become, is thin, error-ridden, and subject to a far wider range of contextual factors than anything seen in the NBA proper.

It is an intensely difficult endeavor, filled with more failure than success. The rewards of that success can alter the trajectory of a franchise for years to come. And the worst part is you might not know which until three or four years down the line. The *really* worst part is that, even then, you won't know why it worked or why it didn't.

Even with a perfect process and decision-making somehow free of bias, a lot can and likely will go wrong. That perfection of process is itself hard to achieve with a number of tempting but ultimately incorrect paths to choose from at every turn.

Before getting into how and why drafting is so hard and the selection process can go wrong, we have to briefly discuss why they are so important to begin with. In some ways, the draft receives outsized attention. A team makes more decisions than that, and those choices entail far bigger downside risks in free agency and trades than in the draft.

Small wins are great; Chapter 10 is all about little things that can add up to swing a game here or there. But a team has to win *huge* to reach championship level. As we saw in Chapter 7, the few players at the very top of the NBA pyramid do the most to determine ultimate success. For most teams, the draft is the best shot at that jackpot.

As with any form of gambling, any wager carries with it the chance that it will be a loser. The goal is to keep the long odds against you from getting even longer. And then hope everything works out so you can pretend you knew it would all along.

The Math Problem

On the eve of the 2019 draft, Tom Haberstroh, writing at NBCSports.com, asked, "Are we getting worse at the draft?" By Haberstroh's calculations, the relationship between draft order and NBA production was weaker in the 2014–18 drafts than it had been for any of the three previous five-year windows, and by a decent margin.

This rough patch of talent prognostication wasn't for lack of effort, as Haberstroh recognized: "[L]ottery teams prepare countless reports, stay up ungodly hours, and talk to hundreds of people to help identify the next star. Teams have more data than ever…And yet, the draft seems as much of a crapshoot as ever and lottery teams continue to miss on stars."

While I'm not sure Haberstroh was asking the correct question, he was right on the money on one point: a high pick does not a superstar guarantee. Despite the copious time and effort spent on making these selections, there is little to be done about the underlying math problem. Much as there aren't enough max players to go around for 30 teams, there might be only a single superstar to emerge from every second or third draft class.

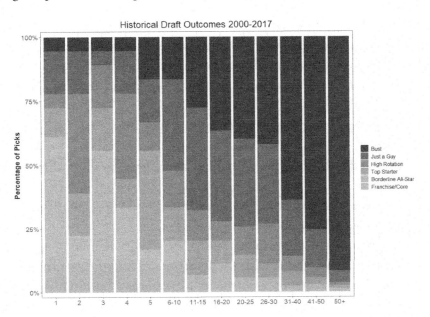

It's not only that there's an insufficient number of stars in the draft. Fewer than half who are picked in the average year will stick in the league in a meaningful way.

But enough will stick that the draft continues to sell hope and sell it well. Every pick *could* be a star. All-Stars have come from every part of the draft in the modern, two-round era. Beyond that, just finding someone who can play at an NBA level is a win.

Jake Loos, former head of analytics for the Phoenix Suns, notes, "There's an incredible amount of value in drafting a player who can contribute to an NBA team, because half of players can't, at least in the first round. In the second round it's obviously a lot more [that fail]. Being able to ensure that you're at least getting a player who can contribute to winning, you're doing better than the rest of the league if you can do that consistently."

Against this backdrop, I would reframe Haberstroh's inquiry: How well should we reasonably expect to draft?

Trust a Process

Much like fans, decision-makers tend to simultaneously overvalue the impact each class of players will make while underrating the sheer difficulty involved in predicting who will be the players that do so. On some level, this is a survival mechanism. As we'll see in the rest of this chapter, you have to do the work. But if the reward for all that work is a chance to flip a fair coin as opposed to one that's rigged against you, what's the point? A touch of swaggering overconfidence might be just enough to guide one through the process.

Unless it derails you entirely. Drafting is an exercise in sifting through an enormous amount of information about dozens of players collected by different groups with distinct fields of expertise delivered in units of measure incompatible with one another.

The temptation to wing it and "go with your gut" is enormous, especially when imbued with the confidence-bordering-on-hubris just mentioned. There is enough randomness involved that drafting by intuition might work, at least for a time. But you'll never know why, nor will there be any warning when the well of luck is about to run dry.

The psychologist Daniel Kahneman suggests three necessary preconditions for reliably successful intuitive decision-making: regularity in the environment, lots and lots of practice, and immediate and accurate feedback.[1]

I ask you, do any of those conditions apply to the NBA draft?

The degree of variance between productivity and draft order at minimum strongly suggests some irregularity in the environment. Each draft class is different, as is the situation of the team drafting each year. The traits which should be valued are in constant flux as the overall league style of play changes.

How might the careers of old-fashioned big men like Enes Kanter, Tristan Thompson, and Jonas Valančiūnas[2] have differed had they been drafted a few years earlier? Alternatively, how much lower would they have been selected had they been in the 2014 or 2015 draft classes, after the trends that devalued their archetype of player had taken firmer root?

It's not only trying to hit a moving target. It's doing so in stiff, shifting winds while standing on a swaying platform. Good luck dialing that range in with only a few chances to try.

At the conclusion of the 2020 off-season, the average NBA head decision-maker had overseen 6.4 drafts. Even that modest figure overstates the level of experience. The five with the longest tenures (Gregg Popovich,[3] Pat Riley, Danny Ainge, Donnie Nelson,[4] and Sam Presti) account for over half of the total,[5] with the shot-callers in place at the other 25 franchises at the time of that draft averaging 3.6, including the 2020 edition. Even though

---

1. You may recall the similar definition of a "kind" learning environment from Chapter 5. This is largely the same idea.

2. The trio was drafted third, fourth, and fifth, respectively, in 2011. As seen in Chapter 8, the 2011–12 season represents something of an inflection point after which the three-point revolution accelerated towards its current crescendo.

3. Pop is a perfect example of another difficulty in assessing ability in drafting: in many organizations, who is ultimately making the decision is somewhat opaque from the outside. If instead of Popovich, the general manager Brian Wright counts as the current "drafter" for the Spurs, the overall average drops almost a full year across the league, which only serves to emphasize the point.

4. Ainge and Nelson left the Celtics and Mavericks, respectively, in June 2021, further reducing the collective experience of the league as a whole.

5. Averaging 20.2 drafts per exec.

much of the current crop of top execs are on their second or third stop in that role, it's not a whole lot of practice at making a pick or three a year.

Finally, *useful* feedback on draft selections is neither timely nor always accurate. While day-after pick grades are fun,[6] the success or failure of a draftee isn't readily apparent until three to five years into their careers, when extensions/second contracts kick in and players enter their athletic primes. By the time the feedback is delivered, half of those on the receiving end might have new addresses.

As far as accuracy of that feedback, recall lesson one from Chapter 1: shit happens. Did Philadelphia make a better gamble on Joel Embiid's health than did Portland on Greg Oden's?[7] Or did Portland just happen to roll snake eyes?

The difficulty in post facto evaluation of a draft pick goes well beyond injury luck. "Donovan Mitchell turned out the way he did because we lost Gordon Hayward in free agency,"[8] says former Jazz head of analytics Cory Jez.[9] "If Gordon stays, we don't know anything about Donovan at that point. Coach [Quin Snyder] uses him differently. The system is different. Usage changes dramatically. He turned out the way he did for an incalculable number of reasons."

It's the same story up and down the draft. With a few exceptions on context-creating superstars, every player's outcome should be viewed as a function of their talent, the situation to which they are drafted, and topped with a big dollop of luck, good or bad.

---

6. And definitely get those clicks.

7. Leave aside for the moment that Oden was selected first in a "two player draft" ahead of Kevin Durant, while Embiid was taken third in a "three player draft" after Andrew Wiggins and Jabari Parker. How skillful of the Sams, Presti and Hinkie, to have those selecting ahead of them choosing what turned out to be the wrong doors!

8. Mitchell was selected with the 13th pick in the 2017 draft on June 22. Hayward announced his intention to sign with the Boston Celtics as a free agent on July 4 of that year. While the possibility of Hayward leaving was likely factored into Utah's decision to trade up for the pick they used to select Mitchell, it was considered far from certain that he would do so.

9. Jez now runs the research and analytics group for Austin FC of MLS. For what should be obvious reasons, everyone quoted in this chapter is a *former* NBA scout or team analyst, but their thoughts and observations completely mirror those of individuals still in the draft trenches with whom I speak and have spoken on the topic.

To paraphrase Kahneman, very few GMs have intuitive expertise in drafting, as they haven't had the necessary experience. Because nobody does. In such a situation, Kahneman advises creating a decision-making process if for no other reason than to slow down intuition, allowing the brain's other reasoning tools to kick in.

A key part of that process is determining which pieces of information to keep and which to discard as irrelevant. There are so many possible ways the attention can be drawn to the extraneous. Separating the wheat from the chaff is made harder by the fact that those same irrelevancies which can confound the selection process arise as part of required information gathering right alongside the more relevant data. And none of that data holds a sign saying, "I'm the part worth paying attention to."

The Trouble with Tools

Tools can be seductive. They can unlock superstar potential, but just as easily they can blind an observer to less visible deficiencies that will keep a prospect from reaching that potential. Or rather, maybe the potential was merely an illusion created by the tools to begin with.

What I mean by tools consists of both measurables—height, weight, wingspan, vertical leap—and physical skills such as jump shot mechanics, handle, and touch around the rim. These are the building blocks of a basketball player. But the draft isn't the search for the best tools; without the connective tissue that allows a player to select the right tool and use it properly in the moment, these gifts can be wasted.

But tools are necessary, and the reason they can be overvalued is because they are so vital. The G-League and top European divisions are littered with NCAA stars who were "not quite." Not quite big enough. Or quick enough. Or strong enough.

While those deficiencies can sometimes be overcome—players such as Joe Ingles and Kyle Anderson lack the quickness and vertical explosiveness typical of NBA perimeter creators, but have made up for those deficits to a large degree via their size, skill, and feel—the margin for error drops. If Ingles were merely a very good rather than elite shooter or Anderson were only able to slow the game to three-quarter speed instead of half-speed, they would be in the "not quite" bin as well.

"I think sometimes you can look at a guy and watch him play and you see all that he *could* be, you know?" says former Bucks scout Adebayo "BJ" Domingo.[10] "Instead of paying attention to the whole picture, you get a little bit too focused: 'He's making some of these types of mistakes but look what he could be if he corrects it.' Sometimes you can get tricked by the way a guy *looks* on the court." Among the more common illusions Domingo mentions include pretty jump shots that don't seem to go in, or the tool which has become so obsessively tracked that it has become a meme: wingspan.

Wingspan and length have become prospect buzzwords. Unfortunately, they have also become shorthand for "perceived defensive potential." "It's completely dependent on whether or not the player can use it," says Spencer Pearlman,[11] an analyst for Loos' Sports Info Systems Hoops consultancy group. "Some wing could have a 7'2" wingspan, but if they're not using it to get deflections or to help on digs, get steals, or block shots, if they're not using the length, then they might as well have a negative wingspan."[12]

Tools can be so beguiling because they are so salient. If something sticks out as memorable, it can easily be overvalued. The physical dimensions of a player are always on display. It doesn't matter if it's a traveling scout seeing the player in person, film study, or a statistical dossier, things such as height, bulk, wingspan, standing reach, or hand size are going to be inescapable.

Movement skills are another area where this kind of "visual measurable" could play an outsized role in player evaluation. Leaping ability tends to

10. Domingo is now Assistant Director, Men's National Team for USA Basketball, with a focus on Team USA's juniors teams. My time in Milwaukee overlapped with BJ's. He would like you to know he has admitted he was wrong to doubt me about Luka Dončić and De'Aaron Fox.

11. Pearlman has also consulted on prospect evaluation for NBA teams and player representation agencies.

12. In scouting conversations, wingspan is often referred to in terms of plus or very occasionally minus. A player who stands 6'3" with a 6'10" wingspan will be described as having "+7 wingspan" while the unfortunate 6'6" player with 6'5" wingspan will be "-1." Lack of plus wingspan is generally seen as an impediment to a player's defensive potential, though there are exceptions. For example, at the 2011 Draft Combine, Jimmy Butler measured at 6'7¾" in shoes with a 6'7½" wingspan and he seems to have worked out just fine defensively.

stand out. As Jez says, "Sometimes you see a guy dunk once in a layup line, and you've kind of got it."

But Jez also cautions, "If one guy who can jump out of the gym has 100 dunks in a 30-game college season and another has 30 with the same athletic profile, one of them is doing something different. Maybe it's the team, maybe the player, but there's something there that you need to figure out."

Much like wingspan, if a player can't harness their vertical into impact, they might as well not have it. In fact, for players who have struggled to make an impact, elite athletic measurables could be a negative. How well is a player who is just average *despite* an overwhelming physical edge in a collegiate setting likely to do once that advantage is diminished or eliminated?

Working Out

An area where the salience of measurables can mix with another deadly deadly evaluative sin—valuing the most recent information to the exclusion of previous data—is in predraft workouts.

NBA rules allow teams to have up to six draft prospects on the floor at any given time for a workout. It is rare for all six guys in a workout to be "real" prospects, though if you expand "prospects" to include players under consideration for G-League or Summer League spots, more might qualify.

More often, a workout is scheduled around getting two players who are under genuine consideration into the gym. The others present are mostly there to provide competition—sometimes chosen as a favor to an agent by getting one of their lesser clients some exposure—for those "featured" invitees.

Any team worth its salt prepares reference materials on èvery player in a workout to either inform or remind observers about each player's background, statistical profile, and, perhaps most importantly, a head shot and pronunciation guide to the player's name. During my time in Milwaukee, this dossier included the output of our draft modeling and other statistical evaluations of each player as a precis on our analysis of and projections for that player.

On more than one occasion, a "non-featured" player might appear on paper to have been a limited, off-ball wing in college. They had decent-to-good three-point and free-throw percentages, but their low usage, high proportion of assists on their made shots, and underwhelming rebounding and "stocks"[13] totals precluded them from being considered real prospects.

Then the guy would show up at the workout and *look* every inch of an NBA wing—a well-built 6'5" with plus wingspan and excellent leaping ability. He would throw down thunderous dunks, turning whichever video coordinator was that day's designated obstacle into a crash test dummy (using pads which could have come from a football blocking sled). They would crush strength and power tests and explode up and down the floor in timed sprints. They would even have a few "wow" moments in the competitive 3-on-3 portions of a workout. Off the sample of that hour, they looked amazing.

Thankfully, there would still be time to review the player prior to the draft. A quick look at the film would reveal and remind why they had such pedestrian stats. In actual game action, none of those tools which had shone in the workout translated, perhaps because they had no sense of what to do. They lacked the ability to make the myriad conscious and unconscious decisions an individual is faced with on every possession. They couldn't *play*.

Feel

Playing basketball well is not only about having the right tools in the chest, but about selecting the right one, quickly, and using it properly. Nearly as important for most players is knowledge of which tools *aren't* available, and not calling upon them.[14] Executing these voluminous micro-decisions well is described in many ways, with "high basketball IQ" and "great instincts" being two of the more common.[15] I prefer to term it "feel for the game" or simply feel.

---

13. Steals plus blocks, two stats which have been shown to be reasonably predictive of NBA success, especially so with steals.

14. Though on balance a guy who tries to do too much is probably easier to slow down than a guy who doesn't do enough is to "rev up," in my observational experience.

15. To a large degree those two terms for the same concept have become racialized—a white player will be described as possessing that IQ, being a real coach-on-the-floor type, whereas the Black player will "have great natural instincts." This isn't a new phenomenon and is well past the point of cliché.

Players with great feel end up in the right spots and get to those spots earlier than others. They make the best decisions with *and* without the ball. Sometimes they can verbalize why they made a certain choice or executed a certain move, other times it is simply their experience taking over,[16] allowing muscle memory to kick in for execution.

Paying attention to surface measurables reveals next to nothing about the presence or absence of feel in a prospect.

Lack of feel can cause warning lights to flash in the scouting context. Domingo says, "My basketball scouting pet peeve is guys who don't recognize the simple play. For example, you're attacking the basket, you've done your job of drawing that second defender or even a third defender, and you don't understand that in that moment, it's time to move it. Talking about translating to the NBA, you want guys who have a certain level of understanding."

Among scouts and analysts there is some consensus that one of the best ways to evaluate a prospect's feel or understanding is off-ball defense. According to Loos, "On most half court possessions, each player on the court has a decision to make on that [defensive] side of the ball. Typically, it's a pretty simple decision: 'Be at the nail.'[17] Knowing what type of pick-and-roll coverage to engage in, stuff that can be coached. But the beauty of basketball is that it changes every possession, and there are going to be unique choices that a player has to make on the fly, where you can't necessarily have coached it."

---

16. Recalling Kahneman's discussion of where intuitive decision-making tends to work, whereas a GM/CEO will likely never have gotten enough reps to reliably reach good decisions intuitively, players have gotten those reps in a wide variety of game situations to the point where these intuitive decisions can be of high quality. For the players with great feel, that is.

17. The "nail" is a vital reference point for modern defensive schemes. It is the spot at the middle of the free-throw line and represents something of the center of focus for perimeter defense. According to longtime skills and development coach Doug Eberhardt, "If you head to your local high school or recreation center gym, walk to the free-throw line, center yourself, and look down, you'll see a small indentation mark or hole on the line's paint. That little hole or mark was once the home of a galvanized piece of metal. A real physical nail, straight from your local hardware store. That nail was used to anchor a string, which in turn helped the builders of the court measure dimensions (key, free-throw, three-point, etc.) and paint the various lines." (https://www.sbnation.com/2013/12/19/5227374/nba-defense-breakdown-nail-spurs-pacers)

In those random situations, players who can quickly read and react will stand out. That ability to react gives them a chance to operate at NBA speed.

Identifying this high-value, low-salience characteristic is quite difficult. It requires close, directed attention and is nearly impossible when an observer is trying to watch everything at once.

From a draft process standpoint, this is an area where statistical analysis can add value. According to Jez, among the most important questions about that process itself is, "How can we use our time most effectively? That may be using the statistical part to eliminate players as much as we use it to find needles in haystacks." Reducing the size of that haystack gives those doing the qualitative evaluation the time to give that directed attention.

Draft models don't just rule players out. They also can say "yes, maybe?" with varying degrees of confidence. Though the relationship can certainly break down,[18] the statistical record might capture feel, at least partially. "When I first started [draft] modeling, I was just trying to predict ceilings. What I slowly learned is one way that modeling could be super helpful is identifying, 'Hey, these players are the people who are the best at basketball today,'" says Loos, with the implication that if we're in the prediction game, being good at basketball today isn't a bad start for being good tomorrow as well.

Of course, a player's collegiate production is not *just* a measure of feel, but rather the confluence of feel, skill, role, and no small amount of luck. Which is why the best process involves a strong mix of quantitative *and* qualitative analysis. As Jez notes, "Both things can be done well or poorly. Ideally, they're both done well and done in tandem."

Background Ambiguity

"Sometimes [the NBA] is the first time guys really hit basketball adversity, in terms of having to sit, not being able to start, not being able to play every game," says Domingo. How players will handle this adversity is part of the broader question of adjustment into the league. "You never know how a guy's going to respond to the lifestyle in the league. Guys can come in very

---

18. Such as in the case of Russell Westbrook's triple-doubles, discussed in Chapter 4.

motivated and all that, but there are always a few young guys who hear their name called [on draft night], they sign that first contract, and then they kind of relax."

While *knowing* with precision which players will and won't make the adjustment well is a fool's errand, chipping away at that uncertainty is a vital task in prospect evaluation. The "background and intel" investigation on potential draftees is considerable. And it is an area where analytics struggles.

"Off-court behavior, personality, intel. Those are key pieces to making any decision in terms of a draft pick. Trying to figure out, is this player going to be able to improve or have the best chance to come into a program and be a good member of the team? That's something that [statistical] modeling really struggles with assessing," says Loos.

One part of background work is the search for red flags. Does the player have past or ongoing legal troubles? Do they have a rep for partying? Were there disciplinary issues with his collegiate coaches?

Legal issues aside, this is an area where things get tricky. A "rep for partying" sounds a lot like hearsay. We talked earlier about salience; the star basketball player at a raging campus party might be pretty memorable, which can lead to a lot of "I heard" reports that turn out to mostly be a college kid acting like a college kid. Similarly, especially for players talented enough to be under draft consideration, friction with a college coach might be a two-way street. It is not unheard of for a coach to give not quite glowing references early in the intel process for a player he hopes will come back to school. If you think that sounds grimy, that's college basketball, folks!

While not strictly in the same vein as the search for character flags, medical evaluations can also stop an evaluation short. Even before they start their professional careers, players tend to have an extensive list of past injuries. Everything from rolled ankles or broken fingers to concussions and surgeries.

In the predraft process, this history will be meticulously cataloged, after which teams' training and medical staff will attempt to determine which player represents an elevated risk of future injury. Occasionally,[19] a medical

---

19. *Very* occasionally in my experience, as medical staffs tend to be very cautious about making "basketball decisions."

team will slap a "do not draft under any circumstances" warning on a player with a particularly worrying history or degenerative condition. Mostly, it is an exercise in risk identification. Balancing this risk against the player's on-court potential is one of the most difficult aspects of the entire process.

To try and better understand how a player will make that adjustment Domingo mentioned, prospects will undergo psychological evaluation as well. Aside from rare cases,[20] this analysis is usually equivocal in much the same way as more traditional character and background information. This ambiguity represents one of the easiest ways to go wrong in the draft process.

By the time character and intel enter the discussion, scouts and decision-makers tend to have at least a preliminary opinion about a player. Which is unfortunate; people tend to be far more stubborn with their first impressions than they realize. But this "prevaluation" is necessary.

Gathering background is time-intensive and, to the extent it involves experts like psychologists or private investigators, expensive. Shrinking the universe of players to those relevant for selection allows proper coverage of that smaller group. To make that list, there already has to be *a* list, meaning rankings built from those partial evaluations.

Unfortunately, these first impressions mean evaluators have players they like but others not so much. The interpretation of equivocal information cannot help but be slanted by those preconceptions. Synthesizing the disparate forms of information requires construction of narrative, a story about the player upon which to drape that info.

What to make of a player who has been visibly remonstrative of teammates during games? It depends: are we telling a positive or negative story about them? If it's a good story, this is evidence of leadership and competitive spirit. For a less favored player, it just means he's an asshole and likely a bad culture guy.[21]

---

20. The worst psych report I can recall included the doctor admitting to being afraid of the prospect, in the room, while performing the evaluation. That player was not on our final draft board that season.

21. The reality is that both interpretations could easily be true, or at least predictive of the player once he lands on an NBA team. A common adage in the league is that about one in 10 players will be model teammates regardless of circumstances. On the other end of the spectrum, 10% will be clowns. The other 80% could go either way depending on the environment.

Confirmation bias such as this is most evident in the interpretation of qualitative information, but it can infect the quantitative realm as well. High turnovers could indicate the player is making reads his teammates can't and bodes well for his ability to adjust to the highest level...or he is careless and loose with the ball and doesn't read the game well. A player with pristine shooting form but poor percentages either went through a bad streak and will shoot it fine in the NBA or is a "shooter" that can't make shots.

Humans tend to need a narrative to understand complex situations, and it's far easier to fit facts to an existing mental narrative than to construct a new one as new facts come to light.

Comparative Anchors

A close relative of confirmation bias is the effect of anchoring.

Come draft time, the bane of the existence of an analytics staff is promulgating player comparisons for that season's list of draftable prospects. Comps are attempts to find the closest historical analog to a given player.

Comps have some superficial appeal. Referencing a more familiar player can focus the mental image of a prospect. However, there may not be a common practice more destructive to running a clean draft process. The problems are manifold, but they start from that same exoskeleton. Once a comp is introduced[22] it is all but impossible to see anything else. Worse than this mental substitution is that it tends to be the wrong version of the compared-to player.

If a statistical model noted similarities between Trae Young and Stephen Curry (as they all did), this is not a suggestion that Young's season at Oklahoma is comparable to Curry's MVP-level play in the NBA. Rather, for whatever reason[23] Young's performance that year with the Sooners resembled Curry's time at Davidson. The mental leap that is often unconsciously taken is that because Curry became *Curry*, the model is predicting Young

---

22. Whether via statistical proxy or similarities in size or movement patterns.

23. Largely shot profiles, especially with respect to the number of deep, off-the-dribble jumpers each player created for themselves.

will also become Curry. According to Jez, "It's this development fallacy: 'Because the player I comped him to developed...'"

Recognizing how much both context and the randomness of the universe feed into any one player's developmental path renders this "comparative projection" completely nonsensical. The relationship between Young's collegiate profile and Curry's professional achievement is too attenuated, one path among several thousand possibilities. But without great care, making that one mental leap too far without even realizing it can be hard to avoid.

The problems with comps don't end there. The limitations of the statistical data used to make those comparisons makes the comparisons even more abstract. The context in which a player's numbers were accumulated is needed to properly analogize between previous prospects. But that context is hard enough to determine with NBA data. For other leagues? "The issue lies with the actual data that we have available," laments Loos.

Perhaps most worrisome is the effect of another form of bias: survivorship. "You're not comping [a prospect] to all the other players who are in that same cluster who never made it, because you don't know they exist anymore," says Jez.

The choice of the group from which to draw comparisons is among the more difficult decisions in basketball analytics. Cast the net too wide, and a prospect's closest neighbors in multidimensional model space are likely to be so esoterically obscure—there have been *a lot* of college players—that the names will draw a series of "Who?" and "Is that the guy from Southwest Texas State or maybe it was Canisius?" questions even from experienced scouts with encyclopedic memories. Define the sample too narrowly and you start to feed into the very irrational exuberance and optimism about prospect futures that you're here to fight against; if you ignore all the ones that failed, every player like the one being discussed ended up succeeding.

And finally, since analytically based comps describe statistical production rather than visible play style, they become easy clubs with which to beat analysts and analytics in general. Asked if there is anything he hates more than creating comps in the first place, Jez sighs, "People critiquing my statistical player comps is the only thing."

Attachments

Because final grades of a draft pick take many years to arrive, the opportunities to blow it with a pick don't end with the selection. With all the labor that goes into preparing for the draft, it is understandable for there to be an emotional attachment to one's selection. But that attachment can easily curdle into stubbornness and an inability to take "yes" for an answer.

As demanded by the sheer math, most picks will fail or at least disappoint relative to expectations. Knowing when to move on is a critical skill. Drafting Andrew Wiggins first overall in 2014 was defensible. We could argue about whether it was a *mistake* based on what was knowable at the time or not,[24] but it hasn't worked out. But even if the pick was a mistake, it paled in comparison to signing him to a five-year contract extension worth over $145 million after his third year.

To that point, Wiggins had never had a season where he had a positive Estimated Plus/Minus, and while RAPM metrics where slightly kinder, they too viewed him as average or slightly above. But for Minnesota, Wiggins was "their guy," so they went to the mat to keep him as a walking embodiment of the sunk cost fallacy.

That contract was among the very worst in the league from the moment it was signed, representing such an albatross that the Wolves had to add a potentially very valuable pick swap option to send him to Golden State for another player whose predraft rep outshone their post-draft play in D'Angelo Russell.

On the other side of the ledger, it can be tempting to be overly wedded to modest successes. As Loos said, getting a rotation-level player at any point in the draft is great. Nothing screams success in player evaluation and draft strategy quite like nailing a pick late in the first round or getting a rotation-quality player in the second. Not only do these players provide

---

24. The top three prospects by consensus in that draft were Wiggins, Jabari Parker, and Joel Embiid. Suffice it to say there is no debate over which of the three has had the best pro career. Yet, Embiid missed the entirety of the first two seasons after he was drafted, so it's hard to fault any decision-maker who was squeamish about his injury risk.

massive production per contract dollar, but they are shining examples of organizational perspicacity.[25] As such, they tend to take on outsized value.

We certainly had to contend with this feeling in Milwaukee. In 2017, Malcolm Brogdon became the first and to this point only second-round pick to win Rookie of the Year. This couldn't help but play into future trade discussions. Though none of these discussions[26] ever got to the point of a final "should we or shouldn't we" decision,[27] I do wonder if we would have been tempted to turn down a good deal because of the success he represented.

There were times we were on the other side of that coin as well. In the NBA, trades that might work in concept often fall apart at the details stage. One side needs to get a little bit more or to give a little bit less than what is currently on the table. These trade "balancers" are often either second-round picks or useful but ultimately non-impact role players. Such a role player was far easier for teams to attach to a deal if they were a veteran who had bounced around, rather than a "find."

I won't name the team or player, but there was one occasion when a team declared a rookie who had already shown himself to be an NBA-level player "untouchable" in trade talks. Though this player lacked the athleticism and top-end skill to have much upside past being a high-performing backup—he has started fewer than a third of his career games played to this point—he was solid enough to be worth something in the deal.

Yet he was being included amongst the team's "core." They weren't just demanding an exorbitant price; they weren't even listening to offers. I imagine that untouchability might not have survived a truly ludicrous offer, such as multiple future first-round picks. But demanding a dollar for 15 cents is mostly a polite way of saying "no."

Here was a situation where the psychic benefit of the Halo of Awesome Drafting precluded actual value gains for the team. Unless the player has a real chance to become one of the top 125 or 150 players in the league, the

---

25. Or that they got a bit lucky. But mostly both.

26. As discussed in Chapter 12, trade discussions between NBA teams are constant and ongoing but tend to only coalesce into action around certain deadlines imposed by the league calendar, such as the in-season trade deadline or the draft itself.

27. At least not to my knowledge.

surplus value they provide as a rotation piece on a minimum-level contract won't survive past their rookie deal, at which point they become properly compensated, at which point they are nothing special. This isn't to say teams should engage in continuous pump-and-dump schemes with their draftees. But the goal isn't to win the draft, it's to win the title.

Sadly, it's far easier to talk about how *not* to draft than to lay out a roadmap for how to do it well. Perhaps the best we can hope for is doing less badly, by avoiding as many of the biases which can poison the process as possible. But ultimately, to paraphrase the stage musical *Avenue Q,* "Everybody's a little bit biased." Maybe just being less biased than the next team is enough to get by.

Chapter 14

Next?

"Fifteen hundred years ago, everybody 'knew' that the Earth was the center of the universe. Five hundred years ago, everybody 'knew' that the Earth was flat. And 15 minutes ago, you 'knew' that humans were alone on this planet. Imagine what you'll 'know' tomorrow."

—Agent K, *Men in Black*

Today's breakthrough is tomorrow's optimized process is the day after's standard practice. Concepts such as per possession efficiency, pace of play, and rate-based stats went from being viewed with skepticism 10 or 15 years ago to an everyday part of the conversation among even the most traditional-minded coach or executive. The cutting edge today will be baseline conventional wisdom tomorrow.

In the race to stay ahead, what comes next? If I knew for certain, I wouldn't be telling you. At least not until I had cashed in on the knowledge in some way. But I have some guesses.

Though it's equally likely that the Next Big Thing is an innovation we can't even conceive of just yet, there are several potential avenues which extend upon the current cutting edge or address some of the hard questions we haven't been able get a handle on so far.

Measuring Decision-Making

There is plenty to still be mined from existing data sources. Player tracking data is new enough that the exploration that has been done so far is merely scratching the surface. Even without further improvements in data collection—things like limb placement, player facing, and body pose are all being actively researched and would add further granularity—I would estimate only around 5% of the insight derivable from tracking data has been accessed.

While these improvements touch on many areas, the most impactful will likely be shrinking the distance between a player's "feel"—that combination of perception, quick situational evaluation, and ability to successfully perform the desired physical action—and the stats which are produced by virtue of a player having good feel. The statistical record can indicate a player's level of feel via either traditional counting stats or more implicit measures such as RAPM, but direct measurement is still a long way off.

Further study of tracking data might bring us a step or two closer to that whole ball of feel. As of right now, a player's scoring efficiency has to be viewed to some degree as the output of a black box process combining context, physical talent, decision-making, and variance. Narrowing in on the first two aspects could unlock the ability to study the counterfactual situations, which in turn could help predict how well a player is likely to perform in a different system or role than their current context.

Some of this work is already being done in other sports. For the NFL's inaugural "Big Data Bowl" analytics competition, several entrants' submissions were attempts to quantify and evaluate the passing choices made by quarterbacks, including both the timing and target of the pass. One project which explored this area came from the team of Sameer Deshpande and Katherine Evans.[1] The NFL's website describes their project, "Expected hypothetical completion probability," thusly:

---

1. When we spoke, Deshpande was a post-doctoral statistical researcher at MIT who has since moved on to a similar role at the University of Wisconsin. At the time of their Big Data Bowl submission, Evans was a data scientist at Google subsidiary Verily, but was hired as Director of Strategic Research by the Toronto Raptors soon after. In June 2021 she was named Vice President of Research and Information Systems by the parent company of the Washington Wizards and Mystics.

Deshpande and Evans tracked receiver catch probability across entire pass routes. Their approach allows for an estimation of the receiver's performance regardless of when and where the pass was thrown.

With those theoretical probabilities calculated, "The idea is if he [the quarterback] had thrown it somewhere else, would it have been successful?" says Deshpande. "Let's try to figure out what might have happened had you made a different decision."

Comparing the choice made by a QB to the range of possibilities available provides a starting point for how well they read defenses. There are some clear parallels to how this research might be applied to basketball. In Deshpande's words:

> Let's assess the decision actually made in the context of a pick-and-roll. Given that a defender went over the screen, we can also ask the question, 'Let's assume that he didn't go over the screen…' Instead of just throwing up our hands and saying we have no idea what could have happened, what we're trying to do is try to forecast what might have happened, what are the range of possibilities for what could have happened?
>
> After that range of possibilities is defined, we can then ask, did the player make the right choice, or was there a better option available in the moment? How often does a given player choose the best or from among the positive options, and how does that compare to other players?

Measuring this read-and-react decision-making is a vitally important part of scouting a point guard prospect, as discussed in Chapter 13. Being able to identify and evaluate decision points would allow for both more of a detailed view of a given prospect as well as more useful comparisons between prospects. Similar analysis could be performed for any number of game situations, from shot/pass/drive decisions to defensive rotations.

Perhaps most intriguingly, better measurement of offensive decision-making could help better illuminate *defense*. If we need to count things
that didn't happen, knowing what could have happened but didn't would
provide incredible insight. Visibility into when a defense forcing or induc-
ing the offense into bad decisions or leaving them with unpalatable choices
would be a huge leap in the statistical understanding of the *how* of defensive
impact, instead of being stuck on measuring aggregate defensive contributions as we are today.

Audio

Speaking of defense, whenever I'm asked what the most useful data not
currently collected is, my answer is audio. For a defense to work well, all
five players must be working together as a unit. While a well-drilled team
simply adhering to the principles and rules of their defensive scheme will
be cohesive to a degree, verbal communication—both from the coaching
staff to players as well as between players on the floor—is a necessity for the
team to truly move "on a string." Even at lower levels, talking on defense is
imperative, as anyone who has been crushed by a blind side ball screen that
a teammate neglected to call out can attest.

At the NBA level, early and clear "calls" allow defenders to execute the
schemed responses to offensive actions, and to do so without taking the
time and mental energy necessary to independently assess the situation
before acting.

This is not merely calling out screens. Proper pick-and-roll defense is a
pair working as one. Whether the player guarding the ball should aggres-
sively chase over the top of a screen, slide under, prepare to switch, or force
the ball away from the pick depends almost entirely on what his partner is
doing. Early talk makes execution much easier.

Similar signaling happens all over the floor on defense, as players communicate responsibilities and identify threats to each other as the offensive
attack moves and shifts.

We know this is important. But who does it well? Who is loud and
clear? Does a young center—typically the quarterback in many defensive
schemes—get the calls right, but also have a tendency to be late? Audio with

identification of individual players' voices could help illuminate who is and is not contributing in this way.

Sports Science Integration

NBA teams have a huge blind spot when it comes to monitoring player health and wellness. Tech companies have developed increasingly sophisticated scanning and diagnostic devices and wearable tracking devices that help measure athletic exertion. But the league does not allow these wearables during game competition. For all that can be known about how strenuously a player works in practice, measures of workload during game play remains somewhat fuzzy.

Some measure of "athletic load," as the sports scientists call it, is derivable from game tracking data. Marrying that data with the more exact measurements possible in a practice setting is a challenge.

The implications of more precise and integrated measurement of workload are manifold. Obviously, injury prevention, management, and recovery are the top line items. If every team operates with a budget of around $120 million in salary, a team with a big chunk of that budget on the bench in street clothes is surely at a massive disadvantage.

More than that, technological improvements in this area would allow for better assessments of the risks and rewards for extending the minutes of top players in a given game or series of games. Much of the advance in sports science has been focused on the risk side of the equation. At higher levels of fatigue or stress, certain types of injuries become more prevalent. There is a degree of intuitive understanding that extreme caution is more warranted in some situations than in others—consider how a team is likely to deal with a sprained ankle in a preseason game compared to Game 7 of the NBA Finals—but the difficulty in assessing fatigue under game conditions brings with it uncertainties.

We accept as a given that players will perform worse not just from an athletic but a *basketball* standpoint as they fatigue. However, we lack an understanding of either when or under what conditions this decline will occur, and as importantly the degree of the decline and which areas of play will be most affected. Further, and to my mind more intriguingly, there is no a priori reason to suspect these declines will be similar across players.

In a hypothetical situation where a player entered a "fatigue state" after 36 minutes of game action,[2] the decision as to whether to allot minutes in such a way as the player will exceed 36 minutes will depend not just on the stakes of the game, but how well the player copes with fatigue. A star player who is 95% of his best self even dog tired is a better candidate to get huge minutes in important games than one who drops off to 60% effectiveness. The one who better deals with fatigue is at least buying something for the increased injury risk of extended minutes. The other is chancing not just injury but also ineffectiveness.

Computer Vision

A major obstacle to implementation of tracking data in non-NBA settings is the cost and complexity of installing the needed cameras and other equipment. An in-arena install of tracking cameras and associated hardware is at minimum a high-five-figures investment.

While a few college programs have either installed tracking systems at their own expense or share an arena with an NBA team and thus have access to a previous install, that still leaves hundreds of gyms, stadiums, and fieldhouses without the ability of capturing tracking in-arena. Neutral-site games, often featuring matchups of top teams with multiple high-level

---

2. Minutes are at best a *very* rough proxy for athletic exertion and thus fatigue, but are familiar enough to be used in a hypothetical. The determination of what constitutes fatigue would almost certainly be far more involved and specific than simply referring to a stopwatch. For this reason, "minute restrictions" applied to players coming back from injuries are more estimates, likely conservative ones, than hard and fast rules. There has yet to be a situation where a player spontaneously combusts upon exceeding their training-staff-allotted playing time limits.

prospects, will almost certainly not bear the expense of even a temporary install and will be a similar blind spot.[3]

The point being, waiting for SportVU or Second Spectrum to spread throughout NCAA Division I, let alone overseas leagues, AAU play, and other grassroots competitions, isn't going to produce results any time soon. However, there *is* video from most of these games, and research is ongoing on how to create a version of tracking data from broadcast or other film.

Recent advances in computer vision technology might signal the imminent availability of "player tracking-lite." A paper presented at the 2021 Sloan Sports Analytics Conference[4] described some of the challenges with pulling useful tracking info from a broadcast feed using Stats, INC.'s AutoStats system:

> It is worth emphasizing the key difference between an in-venue solution like SportVU and a broadcast-based solution we highlight here which enables such data to be generated are down to two key breakthroughs: a) calibration of a moving camera…and b) body-pose detection…which enables player re-identification… [W]e employ this data capture method to generate tracking data across over 650,000 college basketball possessions, which is over 300 million broadcast frames. However, generating the raw tracking data is not enough. To provide both descriptive analysis as well as a useful feature representation for our prediction task we next have to map the tracking data to a semantic layer (i.e., events).

---

3. In most NBA seasons, there will be a few games with no tracking data available. For a handful of games each year, something will be amiss with the system itself, but more frequent are the games in non-standard venues, such as when teams play in Europe or "throwback" arenas. Early in the 2017–18 season, the Bucks played a game at The MECCA—the team's old stadium which now hosts University of Wisconsin–Milwaukee home games. Trying to re-create even a sliver of tracking-derived stats from video of that game took around 20 man-hours to produce a fraction of the info, much of which was off by an order of magnitude from what would be automatically collated in a gym with tracking cameras running. While the data collected was borderline useless, it was a useful demonstration of just how much information the tracking dataset contains.

4. Patton et al: "Predicting NBA Talent from Enormous Amounts of College Basketball Tracking Data."

That is to say, much like with Second Spectrum, the moving dots are not themselves especially useful without first identifying the same "basketball words in the data" we discussed all the way back in Chapter 2.

The level of precision available from broadcast feeds is substantially lower than that of a direct-capture solution, so not every bit of tracking-based analysis will be replicable via broadcast-derived data, at least not at first. But even without the fine-grain details, closing the information gap to a degree will allow improved analysis of a player's ability to perform NBA-like actions in NBA-like situations while appearing in other competitions. This in turn could reduce at least some of the noisiness that make predraft predictions such tricky business.

Even more exciting a possibility is the same sort of direct (or at least more direct) measurement of decision-making and basketball feel among draft prospects along similar lines to identifying those traits in NBA players as discussed above. Visibility into which players might have truly elite feel could make identifying the next Nikola Jokić or Draymond Green and separating those rarities from the bulk of productive but athletically limited prospects who don't have the same kind of upside.

Player Development

In baseball, the first wave of the analytics movement—the so-called Moneyball era—used statistical analysis and technique to better find more impactful players. The Billy Beane story was about the need to make the Oakland A's more efficient to keep up with teams that could simply outspend them. While that work continues, the subsequent innovations have been as much or more about *building* better players. By combining a prospect's existing talents with the thorough application of technology and analysis, the goal is to refine that ability into something more impactful.[5] Not so much find better players, but *make* them.

Basketball is still very much in its own Moneyball era, as talent identification can and will continue to get much sharper. However, this doesn't mean the league should wait before entering a similar Analytics 2.0 era.

---

5. *The MVP Machine* from Ben Lindberg and Travis Sawchik is an excellent discussion of the topic.

Several organizations[6] have gained and maintained competitive advantages by being better at either identifying players on the margins, developing fringe prospects into effective role-fillers, or both.

Advances in this area won't be one big thing, rather a combination of smaller things in terms of recognizing which players have the requisite "feel" to improve a great deal as well as improving techniques for training feel alongside what is already largely expert training on pure physical skill development.

People Analytics

No area is more fertile ground for deep exploration than the broad range of topics which could be collected under the heading of "people analytics." We know context is a vital element of player production and development. Situation and system fit is a necessity for most players in terms of the opportunities they get during game action.

But the game is only two or three hours out of a day. With the length of an NBA season and the time members of a team spend in proximity to each other during that season, the interpersonal compatibility of teammates is an important aspect in successful navigation of that schedule. This is true no matter whether the team has championship aspirations or is in a rebuilding situation.

On-court success is almost certainly the biggest determinant of the general mood around a team. Winning is better than losing, and all the little annoyances one tends to have with co-workers are easier to let slide during an eight-game winning streak than during a 2–6 stretch. But having a team that gets along for the most part gives the group a little more cushion to deal with the rough patches without completely melting down.

Another avenue to examine would be better targeting not just skills but personalities most likely to help a team. Given the importance of the very top players to a team's success, insight into which other players or coaches will be good interpersonal fits with those stars would be immensely useful.

---

6. In recent years this group would include the Raptors, Thunder, Nuggets, Heat, and Spurs.

At minimum *avoiding* oil-and-water clashes could prevent a lot of heart-burn and seasons of unnecessary wheel-spinning.

It isn't difficult to imagine that personalities who would vibe with Tim Duncan would be a very different group—albeit with plenty of overlap—with those who could stand up to Michael Jordan's more verbally confrontational style.

The tools for navigating what have traditionally been seen as "human resources" tasks have been tried and tested over decades in many industries. While it stands to reason that the lessons of industrial psychology would require some modification to be applicable to as selective an endeavor as professional basketball, building and maintaining team cohesion is the focus of intense study and investment across many elite organizations. While those techniques would likely need some refinement and modification to address the peculiarities of the professional sporting world,[7] is life in the NBA really that much different than in other high-pressure, elite organizations such as Navy SEAL teams?

With all these avenues for study still unoccupied, there is no great reason to worry about the game becoming "solved." Every discovery along any of these paths will increase the universe of what is knowable little by little. But what will grow even more rapidly is the area of that universe which we know exists but can't yet see into. Every question answered leads to three more next steps.

To come full circle from where we started in Chapter 1, the goal isn't to reach some finish line, but to try to get and stay a step or two ahead of the next team. That is the very essence of competition, and the contest extends further past the floor than ever before.

---

7. Perhaps not least in terms of the restrictions on player movement between teams based on the league's salary cap and CBA, which has a way of limiting the range of options for management.

Afterword

"Prediction is very difficult, especially if it's about the future!"
—**Physicist Niels Bohr**

In my introductory note to the hardcover edition of this book, I mused, "I expect the play on the floor in the 2021–22 season to look more like the 2019-to-March-2020 version of the NBA than the 2020–21 version." It took until about the third week of the season for this prediction to be proven emphatically wrong.

I wasn't just wrong once, but repeatedly. And I didn't make the same mistake multiple times. Rather, I managed to fit in several different types of errors, which included:

- Not recognizing when the assumptions underlying established methods of analysis were no longer operative.
- Being overly skeptical of the likelihood of uncommon but not unheard of phenomena cropping up.
- Treating the league as a constant entity, rather than one which is always changing. The NBA continued to evolve, rendering a few previous understandings inoperable.

Also, certain players made me look silly. It was only Jimmy Butler's spectacular playoff run preventing the hard distinction I draw between Butler and DeMar DeRozan in Chapter 6 from aging like a wheel of brie on the counter overnight.[1]

This doesn't mean I was wrong about every or even most things. The trends and developments I wrote about a year ago didn't suddenly stop. Teams shot threes. The playoffs were different than the regular season. Drafting is still hard.[2]

But I also erred lots. And that's great!

As I wrote in Chapter 1, it's a lot easier to learn from failures than successes. Examining how one arrives at the wrong conclusions can help us be less wrong today than we were yesterday. Which is the goal; in coachspeak, "We got better today."

So what did I miss?[3]

Incorrect Assumptions

The lack of fans in the 2020 bubble and for much of the 2020–21 season altered several on-floor dynamics.[4] Insofar as I thought that dynamic would revert back to "normal" in 2021–22, I was mostly right.

Arenas were (mostly) back to full capacity. Shooting percentages returned to levels in line with historical norms. However, the pandemic still had far-reaching effects on the court, even more fundamental than a few points of accuracy on jump shots. Namely, COVID-19 affected who was even on the floor to take those shots during the 2021–22 season.

Absences due to COVID health and safety protocols and the introduction of short-term signees on "hardship" 10-day contracts made the environment from around late November through mid-January closer in many ways to what is usually seen in the dog days of March and (pre-playoffs) April than the early season sprint we are used to.

---

1. By which I mean eaten and then immediately puked back up by one of my cats.

2. Herb Jones seems poised to win the 2021 edition of the Draymond Green "We really like him, he was second on our board when we picked" trophy awarded to second-round success stories.

3. Shouts to Daveed Diggs.

4. Most notably by creating an *extremely* friendly shooting environment which likely contributed to the league smashing previous records for three-point proficiency in 2021–22.

The rapid cycle of players through rosters—605 players appeared in at least one NBA game[5]—was notable enough. But more than just being on rosters, these sudden signees were forced to play—and in some cases take on major minutes.

On Christmas Day, the Pistons called up Derrick Walton Jr. on a hardship 10-day from their G-League affiliate, the Motor City Cruise. Over the next week, he started all three games Detroit played, totaling 108 minutes, including just over 40 on New Year's Day. Then, his contract expired, the Pistons got some players back from H&S protocols, and Walton returned to the G-League for the rest of the season.

While this was the most extreme example, several other players whose most relevant attribute was the ability to get to the arena in time for tipoff[6] got significant clock.

The upshot was that for around a month, or about 15 to 20 games into the season, "non-rotation" players[7] were getting a significantly larger share of game minutes normal for equivalent portions of previous seasons—at the peak nearly double:

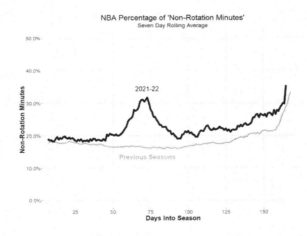

NBA Percentage of 'Non-Rotation Minutes'
Seven Day Rolling Average

---

5. Smashing the previous record of 540 set in 2017–18 and matched in 2020–21.

6. For example, on December 17, the Magic had five players test positive for COVID on the morning of a scheduled game against Miami. The Magic immediately signed four players from their G-League affiliate in nearby Lakeland, and those four combined to play 63 minutes that night in a narrow loss to the Heat in a situation which repeated across the league around that time.

7. Defined here as players who were neither in a team's top eight in minutes per game over at least 20 games played or top eight in total minutes over the season.

Every bit of a player's statistical output is to a degree a function of competitive context. For those two months, that context was so radically different that making year-to-year comparisons or evaluating in-season trends from the 2021–22 campaign should provoke a lot more finger-crossing and shoulder-shrugging than usual.

So, That Just Happened

The oddities weren't just about player availability–related alteration to rotations. Other weird stuff happened.

The regular season dominance of the Phoenix Suns resulted not in their return to the Finals but instead a mystifying collapse against a far-inferior-on-paper Dallas team which stormed back from a 0–2 series deficit and demolished Phoenix, *in Phoenix*, in Game 7.

This was not a situation where a team bows out of the playoffs early after suffering a key injury. The Mavs stole the series with their play on the floor. That they were able to do so against a team so seemingly superior, though, raises the question of whether the Suns' regular season performance may have oversold their strength.

Phoenix had its share of injuries and absences over the course of the season, but no team had better fortune in terms of keeping its own top players on the floor while facing opponents with stars missing during the aforementioned November-to-January period when rosters were in flux. That good fortune might have served to inflate both the Suns' record—itself buoyed by extreme success in winning close games—and their overall point differential.

The Suns not reaching the Finals was notable because of their regular season dominance, but the two teams that did meet in the championship round had strange seasons of their own, as the Warriors and Celtics each looked dominant for one half of the season and mediocre for the other.[8]

---

8. For the record, heading into the playoffs, I picked the Suns to face the Celtics in the Finals, while I wondered whether Golden State could make it past Denver in the first round. Oops.

For Golden State, the obvious break point between the two halves of its season was January 5, when back and calf injuries suffered by Draymond Green took him out of action. Through that day's games, the Warriors were 29–8, tied with Phoenix for the best record in the league.[9] The Dubs were only allowing 102.2 points/100 possessions, nearly two full points ahead of the Suns' 104.1 Defensive Rating.

Over the rest of the season, with Green essentially[10] missing the next two and a half months, Golden State's 24–21 record was 13th-best in the league, while their Net Rating was 14th. The Warriors still ranked sixth in defense, but were twice as far behind the league leaders—more on that in a second—than they were ahead of league average.

You can't necessarily point to one clear incident that turned Boston's season around in quite the same way, but on January 5 (when Green first got injured), the Celtics were tied with the Knicks for *10th place* in the Eastern Conference, with a record of 18–20.

To that point, their defense had been respectable, seventh in the league with a 107.3 DRTG. Seemingly out of the blue, the Celtics then became a point-prevention juggernaut. Boston won 33 of its last 44 games behind a historically dominant defense.[11] After beginning the calendar year down near the bottom of the standings, they even spent a day in first place in the East before finishing the regular season with the conference's second-best record.

In most cases, splitting a season sample into one that fits your preconceived notions of what a specific team is or should be is a great way to trick yourself into overexuberance about that team's playoff prospects. Normally, we'd say Boston was neither the early season 45-ish win team from 2021

---

9. While holding the tiebreak after taking two of the three December meetings between the squads.

10. He played the first seven seconds on January 9 before taking a foul and subbing out in order to be on the floor for Klay Thompson's return to the lineup after more than two seasons recovering first from the ACL tear suffered in the closing game of the 2019 Finals against Toronto and then a rupture of his Achilles tendon during a workout on the day of the 2020 draft.

11. Their defense improved to 105.3 points allowed/100 after January 5. However, league ORTG skyrocketed from 108.6 to 113.0 after that date. As a result, Boston's second half DRTG was 6.4 better relative to the rest of the league than it was over the opening months of the season. During this stretch, the gap between the Celtics and the second-best defense was as large as the gap between second and 15th.

nor the pantheon-level 68-win 2022 version. The Celtics won 51 games, with some high highs and low lows. And given their Jekyll-and-Hyde performance in the Finals—really throughout the playoffs—maybe that ultimately *was* who the Celtics were. But teams of that profile don't tend to *make* the Finals.

At least the Warriors had major lineup upheaval. Significant in-season changes can render the earlier portion of the year irrelevant for determining a team's playoff chances, whether for good or for ill. Two famous relatively recent examples of the former are the 1995 Rockets and the 2004 Pistons. Those squads were different enough after acquiring Clyde Drexler and Rasheed Wallace, respectively, that what came before didn't really matter.

Still, there were reasons to doubt we'd see the return of the early season Dubs. Stephen Curry missed the last 12 games of the regular season. While he showed flashes of his old brilliance, Klay Thompson was clearly having to adjust to the erosion of skills not just from the two serious injuries, but from the more than two years he spent between competitive games. Green was largely mediocre following his own late-season return to the lineup.

And yet, those doubts proved largely unfounded. The Warriors breezed to the Finals and eventually found the key to stifling Boston's offense— the Celtics ORTG was only 94.2/100 in their four losses compared to 126.0/100 in their pair of wins[12]—en route to a return-to-the-mountaintop title.

The Only Constant Is Change

For most of the last decade-plus, simply looking at where a team concentrated its shots, *even while knowing nothing more about those shots*, told us a lot about the prospects of that team's offense. Until the rest of the league

---

12. A narrative which annoyed me throughout the 2022 playoffs was the tendency to blame a series loss on the defensive failings of the loser, regardless of the underlying circumstances. In both the Eastern Conference and NBA Finals, the supposed inability of the Bucks and Celtics, respectively, to guard the opposition was scapegoated, when in reality it was those teams' *own* offensive failings that were more proximate causes of the defeat. The Finals presented an almost perfect illustration. Golden State's ORTG was 112.8, excluding garbage time. In the two games Boston won, Golden State managed 113.9/100, and in the Warriors' four wins it was substantially similar, at 112.3. I wouldn't say they defended the Warriors *perfectly*, but it was good enough to win if their offense had shown up a couple more times.

caught on, early adopters gained a genuine and sizable edge playing "rim and threes only" Moreyball. With the three now firmly established as a key weapon for every team,[13] the ability of a team to "math" its way to an efficiency advantage without regard to talent or scheme has all but vanished:

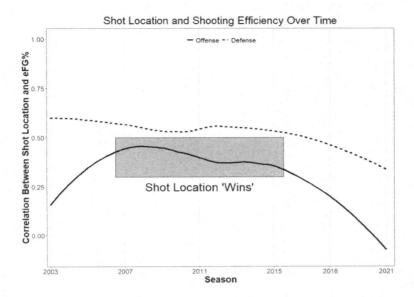

Shot Location and Shooting Efficiency Over Time

Quality offense is once again predicated on generating the looks that the players taking them can make at a high rate—or to put it another way, having offensive talent.[14] I'm glad for this development. While *trying* to solve basketball is fun, *actually doing so* would make the game far less enjoyable. If all it took to "solve" NBA offense was telling players, "Hey, shoot more threes," the proverbial dog would have caught the proverbial car.

---

13. In 2021–22, the Chicago Bulls were 30th in the league, attempting 29.3 3PA/100. This mark would have been tops in the league every season prior to 2009–10 and league average as recently as 2017–18.

14. That *defensive* shot location remains somewhat predictive of success is an interesting paradox which is explainable at least in part by the difference between the specifics of the shooters on a team's offense and their defense playing against the aggregate skill of the rest of the league. Forcing middies will be more effective against some teams than against others, but over 82 games against all 29 opponents, funneling shots into those areas will tend to be more effective more nights than not.

In a way, being wrong about these various things makes the entire endeavor worthwhile. Much as competition is more enjoyable *because* the outcome is in doubt, there always being more to learn is what keeps the study of the game fresh and rewarding. Long may that continue. I can't wait to learn what I'll be wrong about in 2022–23 and beyond.

S.P. July 2022

Appendix

Basketball Stats 101

"Any structure must have a strong foundation. The corner-stones anchor the foundation. For some reason the cornerstones that I chose to begin with I never changed."

—John Wooden

The primary value of sports statistics is to provide context. Context for measuring player achievement. Context for telling the story of a game, season, or era.

If all you knew was that a certain player had hit 38% of their career "to tie or lead" shots in the last 30 seconds of games, you would have a certain, likely negative, idea of that player's "clutchness." If I provided you with the proper context—league average accuracy on these attempts has been around 31% for nearly two decades—my guess is your mental opinion of that player just flipped from "choking bum" to "GOAT" or perhaps even "Dirk," as Nowitzki's 37.9% career accuracy on these game-saving or winning opportunities puts him among the all-time leaders among players with a significant number of attempts.

Context has changed over time. The rebounding numbers accumulated by Wilt Chamberlain (22.9 career RPG) and Bill Russell (22.5) seem almost mythical by today's standards. In the three-point era, only Dennis Rodman has averaged as many as 17 boards per game, a feat The Worm accomplished three times.

Context continues to change. In the 20 seasons between 1996–97 and 2015–16, players scored at least 20 points per game while playing in at least half of the possible games in a season 431 times, 21.55 per season. Between 2016–17 and 2019–20, there were 123 such player-seasons, 30.75 per season, an increase of nearly 50%. In the turbocharged 2020–21 season, *43 players managed this feat.*

The change in context can be dramatic. In 2012–13, only 11 players scored 20 per game. Dwyane Wade finished ninth in scoring at 21.2 PPG while making Third Team All-NBA. In 2019–20, Andrew Wiggins averaged 21.8 PPG, while John Collins managed 21.6 to finish 24th and 25th in scoring, respectively. Neither sniffed an All-NBA team that or, to this point, any other year.

The usefulness of describing someone as a "20-point scorer" couldn't outlast the changed league context. The confluence of factors from increased pace, pro-offense rule changes, and the rise in "heliocentric" roster construction—whereby teams revolve their offenses entirely around ball-dominant stars—lowered the barrier for entry into the 20-per-game club to the point where they started to just let anyone in.

The goal of basketball analytics is providing sufficient context to inform the narrative explaining such a change.

In Chapter 2 of the text, we discussed the importance of having sufficient statistical vocabulary for that narrative to be both accurate and comprehensible. This appendix is intended as a primer of sorts on the vocabulary made up of the metrics and numbers which form the building blocks of that vocabulary.

The Most Important Thing

What is the most important set of numbers in sports?

It's the scoreboard, silly. The point of the endeavor is the competition. *Finding a winner* is the raison d'être for the games. If playing to win the game is the religion, the scoreboard is the deity. Everything that matters flows from that simple running tally. It provides a near perfect heuristic to determine whether something "matters" in the context of a game; does it move the scoreboard?

At risk of belaboring the point, because it is that important, the scoreboard is the North Star for our navigation. Note that we are talking specifically about the *scoreboard*. Not points, and certainly not points scored by individual players. We learned about the difficulty in assigning the same credit to individuals for accumulating stats as we do the team in Chapter 3.

The Box Score Basics

With consumption of sports statistics having moved beyond newspapers into digital space, the name "box score" feels more than a little anachronistic. However, since it instantly conveys the meaning of "the stats I grew up with and have always used for my fantasy league," the name can stay.

Since there are going to be *lot* of different statistics discussed here, having a visual reference might be helpful. In fact, we're going to look at each set of stats through the lens of a specific player: Seth Curry. Because it's a great name.

Here are his career box score totals.

Seth Curry - Totals
(data via Basketball-Reference.com)

Season	Age	Tm	G	GS	MP	FG	FGA	FG%	3P	3PA	3P%	2P	2PA	2P%	eFG%	FT	FTA	FT%	ORB	DRB	TRB	AST	STL	BLK	TOV	PF
2013-14	23	TOT	2	0	13	1	3	0.333	1	1	1.000	0	2	0.000	0.500	0	0	NA	0	1	1	0	2	0	0	0
2014-15	24	PHO	2	0	8	0	3	0.000	0	1	0.000	0	2	0.000	0.000	0	0	NA	0	2	2	1	0	0	0	2
2015-16	25	SAC	44	9	692	102	224	0.455	50	111	0.450	52	113	0.460	0.567	45	54	0.833	9	51	60	87	22	3	36	41
2016-17	26	DAL	70	42	2029	338	703	0.481	137	322	0.425	201	381	0.528	0.578	85	100	0.850	25	154	179	189	79	7	92	126
2018-19	28	POR	74	2	1399	212	465	0.456	113	251	0.450	99	214	0.463	0.577	44	52	0.846	27	93	120	86	36	12	61	97
2019-20	29	DAL	64	25	1576	284	574	0.495	145	321	0.452	139	253	0.549	0.621	80	97	0.825	27	118	145	124	38	9	62	113
2020-21	30	PHI	57	57	1638	258	552	0.467	12	280	0.450	132	272	0.485	0.582	69	77	0.896	10	12	136	155	44	8	65	96
Career			313	135	7355	1195	2524	0.473	572	1287	0.444	23	1237	0.504	0.587	323	380	0.850	98	545	643	602	221	39	316	475

Note that in his first cup of coffee in the league in 2013–14, Curry appeared in exactly one game for both Memphis and Cleveland. We could (and many data sources do) split those out, but for the purposes of a quick runthrough, it isn't necessary.

The NBA box score has changed over the years. Steals and blocks didn't become official stats until 1973–74, also the first year offensive and defensive rebounds were recorded separately. After the three-pointer was introduced for the 1979–80 season, additional columns splitting out three-point makes and attempts from other field goals became necessary.

Even today, there are many iterations of the box score. In some formulations a "plus/minus" is included. Minutes played can be rounded off or listed to the second. The number of times a player had his own shot blocked might be listed, as might be the number of fouls the player has drawn as well as committed. But for purposes of this walkthrough, we'll group stats under the taxonomy of the most accessible repository for most basic and intermediate statistical information: Basketball-Reference.com.[1]

Seth Curry - Per Game
(data via Basketball-Reference.com)

Season	Age	Tm	G	GS	MP	FG	FGA	FG%	3P	3PA	3P%	2P	2PA	2P%	eFG%	FT	FTA	FT%	ORB	DRB	TRB	AST	STL	BLK	TOV	PF	PTS
2013-14	23	TOT	2	0	6.5	0.5	1.5	0.333	0.5	0.5	1.000	0.0	1.0	0.000	0.500	0.0	0.0	NA	0.0	0.5	0.5	0.0	1.0	0.0	0.0	0.0	1.5
2014-15	24	PHO	2	0	4.0	0.0	1.5	0.000	0.0	0.5	0.000	0.0	1.0	0.000	0.000	0.0	0.0	NA	0.0	1.0	1.0	0.5	0.0	0.0	0.0	1.0	0.0
2015-16	25	SAC	44	9	15.7	2.3	5.1	0.455	1.1	2.5	0.450	1.2	2.6	0.460	0.567	1.0	1.2	0.833	0.2	1.2	1.4	1.5	0.5	0.1	0.8	0.9	6.8
2016-17	26	DAL	70	42	29.0	4.8	10.0	0.481	2.0	4.6	0.425	2.9	5.4	0.528	0.578	1.2	1.4	0.850	0.4	2.2	2.6	2.7	1.1	0.1	1.3	1.8	12.8
2018-19	28	POR	74	2	18.9	2.9	6.3	0.456	1.5	3.4	0.450	1.3	2.9	0.463	0.577	0.6	0.7	0.846	0.4	1.3	1.6	0.9	0.5	0.2	0.8	1.3	7.9
2019-20	29	DAL	64	25	24.6	4.4	9.0	0.495	2.3	5.0	0.452	2.2	4.0	0.549	0.621	1.3	1.5	0.825	0.4	1.8	2.3	1.9	0.6	0.1	1.0	1.8	12.4
2020-21	30	PHI	57	57	29.6	4.5	9.7	0.467	2.2	4.9	0.450	2.3	4.8	0.485	0.582	1.2	1.4	0.890	0.2	2.2	2.4	2.7	0.8	0.1	1.1	1.7	12.5
Career			313	135	23.5	3.8	8.1	0.473	1.8	4.1	0.444	2.0	3.9	0.504	0.587	1.0	1.2	0.850	0.3	1.7	2.1	1.9	0.7	0.1	1.0	1.5	10.5

These stats are familiar enough to not need much explanation. However, this familiarity can often lead to overlooking importance nuance. **Minutes Played (MP)** is one stat worth further discussion.

In 2021, big minute totals are usually seen as a negative. Advances in exercise science and load management cause us to worry about long-term health implications of overuse. Moreover, certain lessons might have been learned almost too well. However, certain experienced observers automatically discount per game accumulation of those who get the most minutes; they don't become "better" just because their team has such a dearth of talent that he is forced to play huge minutes.

---

1. Thanks to Sean Forman and the folks at Basketball-Reference.com for allowing the use of their data in many of the following charts.

We might have overadjusted. As the aphorism goes, "The best ability is availability." While that maxim is more often meant to credit players who don't get injured or take games off for rest and load management, it applies within a game as well.

Longtime NFL fullback Leroy Hoard once summed up the difference between a player starring in his role and being a star thusly: "If you need a yard, I'll get you three. If you need five yards, I'll get you three." Per minute production is great, but a team still needs to fill 240 minutes per night. Often, a player with great per minute play can only perform at that rate *because* they are only asked for 20 minutes of high-intensity performance.

Floor time is an objective, purely descriptive stat. However, rotation decisions and subbing patterns are not naturally occurring phenomena. Rather, distribution of playing time is one of the most important choices facing a coach. The decisions made are a strong signal of the coach's opinion. Caring primarily about winning, coaches wish to have the players they think are best able to help them do so on the court as much as possible. You might not always get a straight answer directly asking who they think can play and who can't. But they will tell you. Just look at who is out on the floor.

Curry playing 29 minutes a night for the 2016–17 Mavericks after bouncing around the league's fringes for a few years illustrates the degree to which Dallas coach Rick Carlisle decided "Actually, this guy is quite good" and relied on him accordingly.

The Other Most Important Thing

There are many decisions to be made about how to measure events on a basketball court. It might seem too obvious to need restating, but the most important choice is selecting the proper unit of measurement. To make comparisons, things first have to be *comparable*. The question boils down to "per what?" There are a variety of options which fall into three groups: season totals, per game averages, and rate-based stats. Over the years, analysts have moved away from relying on totals and game averages toward a more rate-based approach.

Seth Curry - Per 36 Minutes
(data via Basketball-Reference.com)

Season	Age	Tm	G	GS	MP	FG	FGA	FG%	3P	3PA	3P%	2P	2PA	2P%	FT	FTA	FT%	ORB	DRB	TRB	AST	STL	BLK	TOV	PF	PTS
2013-14	23	TOT	2	0	13	2.8	8.3	0.333	2.8	2.8	1.000	0.0	5.5	0.000	0.0	0.0	NA	0.0	2.8	2.8	0.0	5.5	0.0	0.0	0.0	8.3
2014-15	24	PHO	2	0	8	0.0	13.5	0.000	0.0	4.5	0.000	0.0	9.0	0.000	0.0	0.0	NA	0.0	9.0	9.0	4.5	0.0	0.0	0.0	9.0	0.0
2015-16	25	SAC	44	9	692	5.3	11.7	0.455	2.6	5.8	0.450	2.7	5.9	0.460	2.3	2.8	0.833	0.5	2.7	3.1	3.5	1.1	0.2	1.9	2.1	15.6
2016-17	26	DAL	70	42	2029	6.0	12.5	0.481	2.4	5.7	0.425	3.6	6.8	0.528	1.5	1.8	0.850	0.4	2.7	3.2	3.4	1.4	0.1	1.6	2.2	15.9
2018-19	28	POR	74	2	1399	5.5	12.0	0.456	2.9	6.5	0.450	2.5	5.5	0.463	1.1	1.3	0.846	0.7	2.4	3.1	1.7	0.9	0.3	1.6	2.5	15.0
2019-20	29	DAL	64	25	1576	6.5	13.1	0.495	3.3	7.3	0.452	3.2	5.8	0.549	1.8	2.2	0.825	0.6	2.7	3.3	2.8	0.9	0.2	1.4	2.6	18.1
2020-21	30	PHI	57	57	138	5.7	12.1	0.467	2.8	6.2	0.450	2.9	6.0	0.485	1.5	1.7	0.896	0.2	2.8	3.0	3.4	1.0	0.2	1.4	2.1	15.6
Career			313	135	7355	5.8	12.4	0.473	2.8	6.3	0.444	3.0	6.1	0.504	1.6	1.9	0.850	0.5	2.7	3.1	2.9	1.1	0.2	1.5	2.3	16.1

If normal starter minutes are around 32 per night, how much sense does it make to directly compare them to a player who has 20% more opportunity to accumulate per night because their team's roster or coaching situation has pushed them up to 38 MPG?

Rate-based stats can be a useful way of tracking changes in player ability over time. Most notable about Curry's **Per 36** stats is the relative consistency of output as he changed roles and teams. Give him regular minutes, he's going to give you about 16 points, three rebounds, and three assists Per 36, while shooting extremely efficiently from multiple areas of the floor.

At the same time, being able to maintain those rates as he got more minutes can also be a sign of improvement, at least in the eyes of coaches. It is important to balance rates and totals, but there is no easy formula for doing so. This problem is what makes player evaluation at least as much art as science.

Seth Curry - Per 100 Possessions
(data via Basketball-Reference.com)

Season	Age	Tm	G	GS	MP	FG	FGA	FG%	3P	3PA	3P%	2P	2PA	2P%	FT	FTA	FT%	ORB	DRB	TRB	AST	STL	BLK	TOV	PF	PTS
2013-14	23	TOT	2	0	13	4.0	12.0	0.333	4.0	4.0	1.000	0.0	8.0	0.000	0.0	0.0	NA	0.0	4.0	4.0	0.0	8.0	0.0	0.0	0.0	12.0
2014-15	24	PHO	2	0	8	0.0	18.7	0.000	0.0	6.2	0.000	0.0	12.5	0.000	0.0	0.0	NA	0.0	12.5	12.5	6.2	0.0	0.0	0.0	12.5	0.0
2015-16	25	SAC	44	9	692	7.1	15.5	0.455	3.5	7.7	0.450	3.6	7.8	0.460	3.1	3.7	0.833	0.6	3.5	4.2	4.6	1.5	0.2	2.5	2.8	20.7
2016-17	26	DAL	70	42	2029	8.7	18.0	0.481	3.5	8.3	0.425	5.2	9.8	0.528	2.2	2.6	0.850	0.6	4.0	4.6	4.8	2.0	0.2	2.4	3.2	23.0
2018-19	28	POR	74	2	1399	7.3	16.1	0.456	3.9	8.7	0.450	3.4	7.4	0.463	1.5	1.8	0.846	0.9	3.2	4.2	2.3	1.2	0.4	2.1	3.4	20.1
2019-20	29	DAL	64	25	1576	8.7	17.6	0.495	4.4	9.8	0.452	4.3	7.8	0.549	2.5	3.0	0.825	0.8	3.6	4.4	3.8	1.2	0.3	1.9	3.5	24.3
2020-21	30	PHI	57	57	1638	7.6	16.3	0.467	3.7	8.2	0.450	3.9	8.0	0.485	2.0	2.3	0.896	0.3	3.7	4.0	4.0	1.3	0.2	1.9	3.5	20.9
Career			313	135	7355	8.0	16.9	0.473	3.8	8.6	0.444	4.2	8.3	0.504	2.2	2.5	0.850	0.7	3.7	4.3	4.0	1.5	0.3	2.1	2.8	22.2

Per Possession stats are extremely useful for team level evaluation. One famous example is the "Seven Seconds or Less" Phoenix Suns.

Beginning in 2004–05, led by Steve Nash, Phoenix was an offensive dynamo. They never quite broke through in the playoffs,[2] losing in the Western Conference Finals twice before the trade of Shawn Marion to the Heat during the 2008 off-season broke up their core.

According to popular belief, the Suns lost because they didn't play defense. Despite averaging 58 wins per season over this period, this was supposedly their fatal flaw. Only the Warriors allowed more points than the 103.5 per game poured in by Suns opponents. But Phoenix's games featured the third-most possessions of any team in the league over that period, so *of course* they gave up a few extra points. Accounting for those extra trips up and down the floor, Phoenix's **Defensive Rating** of 106.9 points allowed/100 possessions was perfectly average; overall efficiency for those seasons was 106.8/100.

The flipside of this coin is mistaking an artificial milestone such as "holding opponents under 100 points" for a valuable achievement. This is a perfect example of where chasing an indicator goes wrong, violating Goodhart's Law as discussed in Chapter 4. The easiest way to hold an opponent under 100 is not to play better defense; it is to play at a slower pace to reduce the number of possessions, which is a far better strategy for holding the score down for both teams than for outscoring the opponent. Only one of those goals is actually important.

While the Suns were supposedly not guarding anyone, Portland allowed 97.5 points per game, ranked 13th in the NBA. They did so largely by playing at the second-slowest pace in the league; so rather than their defense being slightly above average, their 109.4 points allowed/100 was 26th. Despite

---

2. With the benefit of hindsight, we can see that while the Suns had shortcomings, notably depth, they were somewhat unlucky to have never made the Finals; consider the injuries, such as Joe Johnson breaking his face after a fall on a dunk attempt in the 2005 playoffs, and other misfortunes, such as when Amar'e Stoudemire and Boris Diaw were suspended for the pivotal Game 5 of the 2007 series against San Antonio for straying too far from the bench area during the brouhaha which followed Robert Horry body-checking Nash into the scorer's table near the end of Game 4. While it is a results business, shit happens. And this confluence of shit happening to the Suns was taken to invalidate their entire approach, an attitude which probably set the league back a decade—until the Warriors combined a similar style, slightly more talented rosters, and the complete absence of the bad luck which plagued those Suns to win three titles in four years.

their "stingy" defense, Portland only went 121–207 during that era and missed the playoffs every year.

With Per 100 ratings firmly established as the standard, the notion of calling Portland the better defensive team over that period feels faintly ridiculous. But this has been a relatively recent development in our collective understanding.

For individual players, Per 100 is probably a few too many possessions—Per 75 would have the desired pace-normalizing effect while also keeping stats on a similar scale as Per 36. But Per 100 is computationally easy and works well enough at the team level, so no real harm done sticking with Per 100.

An offshoot of per possession is **Per Play**. Also known as **Per Chance**, this level of analysis is useful for examining things such as individual isolation scoring. Suppose Carmelo Anthony isos on the wing. He misses the ensuing jump shot, but his team grabs the rebound and scores on the putback. Should that bucket count for Anthony's isolation efficiency stats?

In certain situations, a player might bend the defense enough to where they deserve some credit for offensive rebounds off of their misses, but that's an exception rather than the rule. For the most part, as with the Melo iso, the play ends when his jumper goes in or doesn't, hence "per play."

The important distinction is that while a possession only ends when the opposition gets the ball or the period ends, a "scoring event" ends a play or chance. Possessions can have multiple "plays" in this way, but each play contains only one scoring opportunity. Aside from "play type" breakdowns—isolations, post-ups, pick-and-rolls, and so on—"per play" evaluation is uncommon. The extra steps required for "per play" calculation, as well as the degree to which "per play" and "per possession" are pretty similar, make "per play" a bit superfluous for most purposes. But it is important to recognize when per play accounting is being used and not to compare per play efficiency to per possession numbers, as the latter will be around 15-20% higher due to the effect of the extra chances provided by offensive rebounds.

Which level of stats—total, per game, or rate-based—to use depends on the question being asked. Rate-based analysis is slightly more common in practice, but there are plenty of situations where volume is the more important consideration.

Counting Buckets and Attempts

The total of a player's scoring attempts conveys a tremendous amount of information. **Field Goal Attempts (FGA)** are a huge clue as to who carried the offensive load in a game. Comparing point totals to shot attempts gives a quick look at how effective they were at doing so.

Three-Point Field Goal Attempts (3FGA or FG3A) have been a front-and-center topic in NBA discussion for years now, with the explosion in frequency of these attempts being the most obvious expression of the changed style of play. On the player level, the number of threes *attempted* can tell us as much about who is and is not a good outside shooter as does the percentage they convert. Much as with minutes, there is an element of choice in terms of who gets to shoot threes and how many. If a player is a willing shooter and has permission or encouragement from the coach to let it fly, he can probably shoot at least a little and is usually guarded as such.

A vital metric in the three-centric era is **Effective Field Goal Percentage (eFG%)**, which factors in the extra point awarded for made threes:

$$\text{eFG\%} = (\text{FGM} + 0.5 * \text{3FGM}) / \text{FGA}$$

This calculation occasionally throws people for a loop; a player who takes nothing but threes and makes all of them will have an impossible sounding 150% eFG%. However, the familiar FG% scale was easier to explain than switching to a **"Points Per Shot" (PPS)** scale.[3]

Related to eFG% is **True Shooting Percentage (TS%)**. True shooting adds in the value of free throws to produce a single scoring efficiency number. The equation for True Shooting is

$$\text{TS\%} = \text{PTS} / (\text{FGA} + 0.44 * \text{FTA}) / 2$$

TS% is actually an estimate; the number of free throws per scoring chance used can vary from player to player, with three-shot fouls, and-ones,

---

3. PPS is simply eFG% * 2; a 55.0% eFG% is equivalent to 1.1 PPS.

and technical free throws meaning that it is not simply two FTA for every scoring chance, but multiplying attempts by 0.44 produces an accurate enough result for most uses.

No discussion of basic box score stats would be complete without a discussion of The Four Factors of Winning. First popularized by Dean Oliver in his 2004 *Basketball on Paper*, the **Four Factors**—really eight factors, since they are calculated separately for offense and defense—account for a tremendous proportion of teams' success and failure.

The real genius of the Four Factors approach is they map perfectly to some of the principles which have formed the bedrock of basketball coaching and strategy for decades:

- **Effective Field Goal Percentage:** Take and make good shots while preventing the opponent from doing the same;
- **Turnover Rate:** Take care of the ball while pressuring the opponent into turnovers;
- **Rebounding Percentages:** Finish possessions with defensive rebounds but earn extra possessions by corralling your own misses; and
- **Free-Throw Rate:** Get to the foul line often but don't foul on defense.

Basketball Stats 201: Play-by-Play and Beyond

If the box score is a statement of accounts, the **Play-by-Play (PBP)** log of a game is the ledger from which the needed sums are calculated. Available for every game since the 1996–97 season and reliably accurate since at least the early 2000s, play-by-play logs unlock new tools and contextual comparisons.

First and foremost among the PBP-derived stats is **Plus/Minus (+/-)**, or how many points did the team score when a given player was on the floor compared to what they allowed over the same period without them.

The next step is asking the same questions *per possession*. This produces some foundational stats: **Offensive Rating (ORTG)**, **Defensive Rating (DRTG)**, and **Net Rating (NET)**, which can also be expressed as points scored, allowed, or scoring differential per 100 possessions. These have largely overtaken points scored and allowed per game as measures of a team's overall performance. I'll repeat for emphasis: *a team's* performance. But we'll get back to that in a moment.

Seth Curry - Advanced Stats
(data via Basketball-Reference.com)

Season	Age	Tm	G	MP	PER	TS%	3PAr	FTr	ORB%	DRB%	TRB%	AST%	STL%	BLK%	TOV%	USG%
2013-14	23	TOT	2	13	13.8	0.500	0.333	0.000	0.0	8.8	4.3	0.0	7.9	0.0	0.0	10.3
2014-15	24	PHO	2	8	-11.4	0.000	0.333	0.000	0.0	27.7	13.7	15.6	0.0	0.0	0.0	16.5
2015-16	25	SAC	44	692	13.8	0.603	0.496	0.241	1.4	7.9	4.7	14.2	1.5	0.4	12.7	17.4
2016-17	26	DAL	70	2029	15.5	0.601	0.458	0.142	1.4	9.3	5.1	16.0	2.0	0.3	11.0	19.5
2018-19	28	POR	74	1399	11.4	0.595	0.540	0.112	2.1	6.9	4.6	6.5	1.2	0.7	11.1	16.6
2019-20	29	DAL	64	1576	15.5	0.643	0.559	0.169	1.8	7.8	4.8	11.6	1.2	0.5	9.1	18.4
2020-21	30	PHI	57	138	12.9	0.607	0.507	0.139	0.7	8.3	4.0	13.0	1.3	0.4	10.0	17.1
Career			313	7355	13.9	0.610	0.510	0.151	1.5	8.2	4.8	12.5	1.5	0.5	10.5	18.0

Beyond ratings, many "advanced" stats found on both Basketball-Reference.com and NBA.com are derived from play-by-play data.

Rebound Percentages (ORB%, DRB%, and TRB%) require knowing the number of chances for which a player was on the floor.

For example,

DRB% = DRB / DRB Chances

with the number of chances equaling the sum of the player's defensive boards, those collected by his teammates while the player is on the floor, and opponent offensive rebounds during those minutes.

Obviously, this calculation requires knowing how many misses and player rebounds occurred while the player in question was in the game. The majority of the most common "advanced" stats require play-by-play to supply the proper denominator. **STL%,**[4] **BLK%,**[5] **Usage,**[6] and **AST%**[7] fall into this category.

---

4. **Steals / Opponent scoring chances**.

5. **Blocks / Opponent FGA**. A more useful though not as commonly tracked measure of shot blocking is **Two-Point Shots Blocked / Opponent 2FGA**.

6. **(FGA + TOV + .44 * FTA) / (Chances on court)**.

7. **AST/ Teammate FGM**.

Some stats often listed alongside these advanced metrics include **Effective Field Goal Percentage (eFG%)**, **True Shooting (TS%)**, and **Turnover Percentage (TOV%)**,[8] though these require only box score data calculate.

Since on-court data was available for players, a team's performance with that player *off* the court was available as well. The comparison is inventively known as **On/Off** data.

On/off comparisons can be a useful starting point, but much like plus/minus, can be overinterpreted quite easily. Suppose a team's regular rotation tends to include stints where one particular starter shares the floor with four reserves. The team's scoring margin could easily be "better" with that starter *off* the floor because of those stints where the lone starter tries to hold the fort with the bench unit.

Another common bit of confusion centered around on/off data is the difference between a team's NET rating with a player on the floor, and their **On/Off Net Differential**. The former tracks the degree to which the team outscores the opposition (or doesn't) with the player on the floor, while the latter is the difference between that margin and a similar margin when the player is *off* the floor. Both are sometimes referred to as "Net" carelessly, so it is important to determine which meaning is intended.

Feedback Loops

Play-by-play data isn't just about on/off performance and rate-based stats. Basketball is a continuously moving sport in which the effects of one event often carry into the next. Play-by-play allows for examination of these dynamics.

My high school junior varsity coach was a very large man with an even larger, bellowing voice. He was fond of a catchphrase. Most of these are hilarious to remember now, and usually were at the time, unless you were the target and had a very large man with a larger voice bellowing them at you.[9]

---

8. **TOV / (FGA + .44 * FTA)**.

9. I say this with the greatest of affection and want to make clear this was never done in a manner that should be construed as abusive. He was just very loud when he felt he needed to get his point across, and our gym had great acoustics which amplified him further. Rest in peace, Coach Weber.

One of his go-to lines would appear during a practice or scrimmage, whenever someone threw a lazy or hopeless pass which was intercepted and turned into a fast break. Our coach would blow his whistle and boom, "If you're going to throw that pass, THROW IT UP IN THE STANDS! At least we can get back on defense!" Nine players who had not just thrown the pick-six would stifle giggles, and we'd return to practice.

Regardless of the volume or humor of the delivery, he was absolutely correct. Throwing a pass that is stolen isn't just a bad offensive play, it compromises the defense on the ensuing possession. The following chart illustrates how different "possession starts" lead to different offensive outcomes from the 2019–20 season:

Offensive Efficiency by Play Start
(2019-20 NBA)

Start Type	% of Possessions	PPP
Steal	8.1%	1.26
DRB - Missed FG	32.1%	1.13
FGM	37.8%	1.10
FTM	9.4%	1.10
DRB - Missed FT	2.2%	1.09
Dead Ball/Out of Bounds	10.4%	1.08

The difference between throwing "that pass" and just chucking the ball into the cheap seats is almost two-tenths of a point, 18 points of DRTG. For context, the gap between the worst (Washington at 1.16 PPP) and best (Milwaukee at 1.03 PPP) defensive teams in the NBA in 2019–20 was around two-thirds that. That loss of 0.2 points is a big deal.

Fast Break Points or **Points in Transition** are determined via the time between change of possession and the scoring event in the play-by-play log. While these logs are sometimes imperfect,[10] transition play is defined as

---

10. See Chapter 5 for examples of some of the oddities which can compact or expand the set of plays included in "transition."

when the scoring event occurs less than eight seconds after the ball changes hands.

Points Off Turnovers is exactly what the names suggests. However, as the previous chart suggests, there are two types of turnovers; those where the ball ends up out of bounds and "live ball" turnovers, AKA steals. The offense gains much more of an advantage from the latter than from the former.

In contrast to dead ball turnovers, steals frequently lead to fast breaks. According to the website Cleaning the Glass,[11] nearly 64% of steals did so in 2019–20. This largely explains the elevated PPP of chances which begin with steals. Meanwhile, defenses tend to be quite stout after dead ball turnovers. Since TOs are just about evenly split between live and dead ball turnovers,[12] Points Off Turnovers is tracking an odd amalgam of the highest- and lowest-value possessions a team might receive. "Points Off Steals" would be a better measure, but we seem to be stuck with points off turnovers.

Controlling for play starts can help better identify team strengths and weaknesses.

In 2019–20, the Portland Trail Blazers snuck into the playoffs after beating Memphis in the first "play-in" game to qualify for the eighth seed in the Western Conference. Led by the explosive backcourt duo of Damian Lillard and CJ McCollum, Portland finished third in the league in offense[13] but were only 27th in defense, allowing just over four points more per 100 possessions than the average team.

However, their half court defense was relatively solid. The Blazers allowed only 1.3 points/100 chances more than average in non-fast break situations, 20th in the league. Unfortunately for Portland, they were poor at both "finishing" defensive possessions and preventing fast breaks. The Blazers ranked 26th in both putback chances allowed[14] and transition defense efficiency.

---

11. An essential reference for NBA stats, CTG is founded and run by Ben Falk. The former head of analytics for both Portland and Philadelphia, Ben is one of the more thoughtful proponents of analytics in the public sphere.

12. In 2019–20, around 52.6% of turnovers were live ball steals.

13. In non-garbage time minutes, per CTG.

14. Per missed shot.

In particular, Portland allowed opponents to turn steals into transition attempts over 70% of the time, the highest rate in the league. So rather than head into the off-season knowing only that they needed to improve defensively, the Blazers could identify specific areas of weakness to target more specifically.

Shots! Shots! Shots!

The most important new information added by play-by-play was the level of detail included on shot attempts. No topic in basketball analytics has been more thoroughly studied than shooting, and with good reason. Shooting efficiency as measured by eFG% accounts for around 40-45% of the variation in team offensive and defensive ratings, with the other three of the Four Factors splitting the other half-plus-a-bit of the pie.

"Shot selection" and "shot quality" are massively important concepts in basketball analysis. Teams and players can go through surprisingly long stretches of exceptionally hot or cold shooting, but the shots they take or allow represent an efficiency baseline which both speaks to offensive and defensive processes as well as provides a baseline against which to measure variations in performance. Shot location in only one component of the assessment of shot selection, but it is a good start.

Seth Curry - Shot Selection
(data via Basketball-Reference.com)

Season	Age	Tm	G	MP	FG%	Avg. Dist	%2FGA	%0-3 Ft.	%3-10 Ft.	%10-16 Ft.	%16ft.-3P	%3FGA	%Corner 3FGA
2013-14	23	TOT	2	13	0.333	8.0	0.667	0.000	0.667	0.000	0.000	0.333	0.000
2014-15	24	PHO	2	8	0.000	22.7	0.667	0.000	0.000	0.000	0.667	0.333	0.000
2015-16	25	SAC	44	692	0.455	17.7	0.504	0.089	0.147	0.071	0.196	0.496	0.243
2016-17	26	DAL	70	2029	0.481	17.3	0.542	0.129	0.127	0.088	0.198	0.458	0.217
2018-19	28	POR	74	1399	0.456	19.0	0.460	0.116	0.077	0.077	0.189	0.540	0.187
2019-20	29	DAL	64	1576	0.495	18.9	0.441	0.091	0.129	0.105	0.117	0.559	0.171
2020-21	30	PHI	57	1638	0.467	19.3	0.493	0.083	0.111	0.096	0.203	0.507	0.157
Career			313	7355	0.473	17.5	0.490	0.104	0.117	0.090	0.179	0.510	0.189

The first place a change in a player's role will often show is in their shot location or distance data. For example, when an interior player's offensive rebounding drops sharply, one of the first places to look to identify why is average shot distance. As a big becomes more of a "stretch" player, they spend more time farther from the basket, which in turn gives them fewer chances to hit the offensive boards.

The classic recent example is Kevin Love. An elite offensive rebounder early in his career, to become more of an offensive fulcrum, Love upped his three-point shooting and mid-post playmaking. This meant he was more frequently stationed at the elbows than in the low post. As he moved farther from the basket, so too did his mix of shot attempts right alongside his offensive rebounding:

Kevin Love Career Progression
(via Basketball-Reference.com)

Season	Avg. Shot Dist	ORB%
2008-09	7.2	15.1%
2009-10	9.5	14.5%
2010-11	10.4	13.7%
2011-12	12.3	11.6%
2012-13	12.7	11.5%
2013-14	14.3	8.5%
2014-15	14.8	6.5%
2015-16	15.2	7.0%
2016-17	15.2	8.9%
2017-18	14.9	7.0%
2018-19	16.7	5.9%
2019-20	18.3	3.3%

The other area of shot selection which can hint at role changes is the proportion of a player's three-point attempts which come from the corners. This was covered in more depth in Chapter 8, but players who take a lot of corner threes tend not to do too much else on offense.

For as much as shot location can illuminate, it has limits. Two players with similar shot profiles in terms of location might still be taking shots of wildly different difficulty. Play-by-play provides only so much of the necessary context, making it unwise to conclude too much about a player's shot-making[15] ability based on shooting percentages alone.

Seth Curry - Shooting Accuracy
(data via Basketball-Reference.com)

Season	Age	Tm	G	MP	FG%	2FG%	FG% 0-3 Ft.	FG% 3-10 Ft.	FG% 10-16 Ft.	FG% 16 Ft.-3P	3FG%	Corner 3FG%
2013-14	23	TOT	2	13	0.333	0.000	NA	0.000	NA	NA	1.000	NA
2014-15	24	PHO	2	8	0.000	0.000	NA	NA	NA	0.000	0.000	NA
2015-16	25	SAC	44	692	0.455	0.460	0.700	0.394	0.563	0.364	0.450	0.556
2016-17	26	DAL	70	2029	0.481	0.528	0.637	0.584	0.516	0.424	0.425	0.486
2018-19	28	POR	74	1399	0.456	0.463	0.593	0.417	0.500	0.386	0.450	0.489
2019-20	29	DAL	64	1576	0.495	0.549	0.712	0.446	0.550	0.537	0.452	0.436
2020-21	30	PHI	57	1638	0.467	0.485	0.630	0.426	0.509	0.446	0.450	0.646
Career			313	7355	0.473	0.504	0.646	0.471	0.524	0.431	0.444	0.510

In Curry's case, he made shots from all over the floor at an excellent to elite level over his career.[16]

Another use of shot location data is to identify candidates for regression. Hot starts early in a season are often a result of a player making medium- and long-distance twos at an unsustainably high rate, and it is generally a safe bet that those players will come back down to earth.

Lastly, there are some other play-by-play-derived data points which can help illustrate changes in player role or effectiveness:

Seth Curry - Misc. Shooting
(data via Basketball-Reference.com)

Season	Age	Tm	Lg	Pos	G	MP	FG%	Avg. Shot Dist.	%Assisted 2FGM	%Assited 3FGM	Dunks	%FGA - Dunks	Heaves	Made
2013-14	23	TOT	NBA	PG	2	13	0.333	8.0	NA	1.000	0	0.000	0	0
2014-15	24	PHO	NBA	PG	2	8	0.000	22.7	NA	NA	0	0.000	0	0
2015-16	25	SAC	NBA	PG	44	692	0.455	17.7	0.423	0.780	0	0.000	1	0
2016-17	26	DAL	NBA	PG	70	2029	0.481	17.3	0.229	0.745	0	0.000	1	0
2018-19	28	POR	NBA	SG	74	1399	0.456	19.0	0.455	0.832	1	0.002	0	0
2019-20	29	DAL	NBA	SG	64	1576	0.495	18.9	0.424	0.800	0	0.000	1	0
2020-21	30	PHI	NBA	SG	57	1638	0.467	19.3	0.591	0.857	0	0.000	1	0
Career			NBA	NA	313	7355	0.473	17.5	0.401	0.804	1	0.000	4	0

---

15. Shot-making is typically defined as the amount the player's efficiency exceeds or falls short of his shot quality.

16. A guard shooting above 50% on two-pointers is usually a good sign.

For the most part, unassisted shots are the province of the star. Frequently, a decline in a player's efficiency will be coupled with a similar decline in the proportion of their makes which were assisted. It's easier to cook if you don't have to set the table as well.

While not much of an issue for smaller jump shooters like Curry, changes in dunk rate can be indicator of declining athleticism, especially when combined with looking at the frequency with which a player has gotten their shot blocked. This is a relative measure, viewing a player's own year-on-year numbers rather than comparing players to each other.

Can we *finally* remove end of quarter shots from beyond half court from a player's stat line unless they go in? One can understand why players would like to preserve their percentages, since that might be relevant at contract negotiation. Watching players somehow manage to not get the heave off until *just* after the buzzer is one of the unsightlier nightly features in the league.

Lineups and Positions

Play-by-play also allows for stats to be examined at the lineup or "combo"—2-, 3-, or 4-man units—level. While this data can give some insight into the synergies between players which can either unlock or hinder the best abilities of a player, it should be used with a light touch.

Seth Curry - Play-by-Play Stats
(data via Basketball-Reference.com)

Season	Age	Tm	G	MP	PG%	SG%	SF%	PF%	C%	OnCourt	On-Off	Bad Pass TO	Lost Ball TO	Shooting Fouls	Offensive Fouls	Shooting Fouls Drawn	Off. Fls Drawn	Assist Points	And1s	Blkd FGA
2013-14	23	TOT	2	13	1.00	NA	NA	NA	NA	0.4	1.2	0	0	0	0	0	1	0	0	0
2014-15	24	PHO	2	8	1.00	NA	NA	NA	NA	-20.0	-19.0	0	0	1	0	0	0	3	0	0
2015-16	25	SAC	44	692	0.35	0.63	0.02	NA	NA	-2.7	0.1	21	6	15	4	18	2	153	1	12
2016-17	26	DAL	70	2029	0.58	0.42	NA	NA	NA	-1.2	4.1	51	19	50	6	37	6	442	14	28
2018-19	28	POR	74	1399	0.14	0.70	0.16	NA	NA	3.3	-0.9	35	10	40	4	18	11	161	4	15
2019-20	29	DAL	64	1576	NA	0.73	0.27	0.01	NA	3.8	-2.0	24	19	39	7	28	11	306	10	14
2020-21	30	PHI	57	1638	0.18	0.81	0.01	NA	NA	8.0	4.4	30	15	31	8	21	8	366	5	16
Career			313	7355	0.26	0.64	0.09	NA	NA	2.6	1.6	161	69	177	29	122	39	1431	34	85

While not an "official" stat, lineup data allows for estimates of the proportion of floor time each player spends at a given position. Position labels and designations have always been more fluid than commonly recognized,[17] but traditional 1-5 positional designations still correspond to some degree with offensive and defensive roles within a unit. Much of the reason Curry's career took a few years to really get going was his "tweener" status. He has point guard size but shooting guard game, and had to land in a spot where that didn't matter as much. His effectiveness playing alongside larger ballhandlers like Luka Dončić and Ben Simmons illustrate the degree to which the blurring of positional lines allows for wider varieties of players to succeed. For example, in 2019–20 Curry's lack of "point guard skills" mattered less when he shared the floor with Dončić, one of the most ball-dominant players in the league, more often than not.

As an unofficial stat, positional estimates might vary wildly based on the method used by a given resource. The previous chart shows Basketball-Reference.com's estimations, while Cleaning the Glass makes different position assignment choices. The nice thing about the wide availability of sources is that if you don't like how one site arranges players in a lineup, you can come up with your own system; I typically only use public position data for the quickest analysis, preferring my own system when I dive deeper.

As noted above, lineup data is among the more powerful analytical resources available, while also being the most frequently abused and misused tools.

It is tempting to look at the ratings for a given lineup or combo and draw conclusions about effectiveness. This data is often not sturdy enough to bear the weight placed upon it. First, there is a "degree of difficulty" element. Does a lineup typically get to play against second units, or do they draw the tougher assignment against starters? Wherever a group falls between those two poles strongly influences their offensive, defensive, and net ratings.

---

17. The basketball historian Curtis Harris opines, "While the idea of a 'power forward' goes back to the early/mid-1950s with players like Vern Mikkelsen and Bob Pettit, the term wasn't regularly used until the late 1960s or early 1970s. From what I can tell it's not really until the mid-1970s that a terminological distinction is made between shooting guards and point guards, though again the idea preceded the terms. You might have had 'lead' or 'playmaking' guards in earlier eras like Bob Cousy or Oscar Robertson. Even into the late 1970s, most teams didn't invest in a 'point guard' the way we think of the position now. The Celtics had the trio of Jo Jo White, John Havlicek, and Charlie Scott bringing the ball up the court in the mid-1970s, while the 1967 76ers had Wali Jones and Hal Greer essentially split ballhandling duties. They were both just guards."

A far more important caveat is sample size. In 2019–20, 13,782 different five-player units saw time in the regular season. The average lineup saw just under 7:26 of game action for the entire season. The *median* lineup was used for 2:50. As a rule of thumb, player stats start to become trustworthy once they have played 250 or so minutes, around 500 possessions. Of those 13,782 lineups, just 22 (0.16%) reached that minimum threshold. Most lineups simply don't play enough to have much confidence that their ratings are more signal than short sample noise.

The same holds true of 2-, 3-, and 4-man units. Though more of these combos get to reasonable minute totals, the players not included in the group adds to the degree of difficulty problem by the variation in possible teammates. A three-player Dallas combo who almost always appears along-side Dončić will likely look better than one which does so rarely. It's a sliding scale—the fewer players being examined, the more groups reach reasonable minimums of playing time, but the more context is left unexplained by the blanks needing to be filled in for a given lineup, and vice versa.

Lineup and on/off data also form the basis for a whole suite of top-down "single-number" metrics, which have grown rapidly in popularity in recent years: the **Adjusted Plus/Minus (APM)** family of stats. For the purposes of this primer, know that these systems were developed to address the combination credit assignment between players and small sample sizes for most lineups discussed above. The origins and proper uses of these metrics were discussed at length in Chapter 6.

Level Three: Tracking Data

Though tracking data is the deepest repository of information currently available to analyze NBA play, the primer on this category of information will be the shortest. The reason for this brevity is exactly the same thing which makes tracking so powerful. The ability to see the game in such small increments means the building blocks are so small, the possible variations are limitless. Going from other forms of data is much like the increase in intricacy and complexity going from Duplo to Legos, but if there were another level or two smaller than Legos. The combinations are limited more by the imagination and skill of the analyst than by the available data.

So while it wouldn't be practicable to exhaustively list the existing or potential applications of tracking, to illustrate the kinds of questions tracking data can address, I have summarized some of the more well-explored areas. A number of stats and metrics in these categories are publicly available on NBA.com. Even the relatively limited sample publicly visible[18] has greatly expanded the ability of an outside observer to understand the game's inner workings.

Shooting

As mentioned above, the information available on every shot is far richer than even what can be gleaned from play-by-play. Some of the characteristics tracking has revealed include more precise court locations, the level of defensive pressure, pre-shot movement by the shooter, and the number of dribbles taken before the attempts, among many others. This in turn allows for a far more robust understanding of shot quality.

Passing and Ballhandling

No longer are assists the only real measure of a player's passing acumen. Tracking how often a player passes to shots that *aren't* made partially isolates playmaking skill from teammate shot-making. Meanwhile, tracking individual possession times and the frequency and location of touches allows for better description of players' offensive roles.

Rebounding

As described in Chapter 3, one rebound is not equally as valuable as any other. Tracking can help identify those who juice up their totals by collecting more than their share of the "free rebounds" which occur when an offensive team eschews chasing a miss for getting back on defense. Deeper analysis can assist in determining why a team consistently struggles to protect their own defensive glass. Are they in poor position when a shot is taken? Do they

---

18. I estimate that publicly available tracking-derived metrics account for no more than 5% of the potential use cases.

get outworked while the shot is in flight? Or do they simply get outfought and outmuscled when the ball is up for grabs coming off the rim?

Defense

Defense remains hard to describe, but as such is the area where tracking has the most potential for improving understanding. Even as that research progresses, certain areas of defense are now much more easily quantifiable. Most notably, even publicly available data does a good job measuring how well individual big men defend.

Even while *quantifying* defense remains difficult, tracking also produces a great deal of new *qualitative* data, such as identifying how often individual players have defended various situations and the tactical schemes they have employed to do so, and combines that with summation of the outcomes of those defensive plays if not the player's individual effectiveness in producing those outcomes.

"Actions"

Prior to tracking data, so much of what happened before a shot was attempted was nearly invisible to the statistical eye. Even the introduction of "play type" data from manually charted games only captured a small range of proceedings. For example, in event tagging by Synergy Sports—the most prevalent provider of charted plays—only chance-ending events are recorded. If a defensive team successfully shuts down two consecutive pick-and-rolls before the opposition sticks a tough jumper from a late-shot-clock isolation, only that isolation would get recorded and the results collated, while the excellent defense, and thus defenders involved, for the majority of that possession would get no credit or recognition. Through tracking data, nearly every component part of an offensive set can be broken out and examined in turn.

These categories are just scratching the surface as the ability of tracking data to provide proper context for comparison and analysis is so vast. Many of the insights throughout this book were only possible because of tracking data, and the leading minds of the industry are constantly pushing the boundaries of what can be known.

Acknowledgments

For all the worry about gatekeeping, culture clashes, and poor communication, the biggest hurdle the "analytics movement" has had to overcome has been one of mindset. Specifically, the distinction is between those who are comfortable with the degree to which randomness and uncertainty impacts most things in life, and those for whom...not so much. It is only natural in a highly competitive environment such as professional sports to want to see every bit of one's success as earned.

But we know better.

Looking backward at the path that led to this book reveals the absurd number of "sliding doors" moments which got us here. The number of people without whom this wouldn't have been possible is slightly overwhelming.

First of all are my parents, Peter and Patricia. I had a love of sports from an early age, largely inspired by my dad's lifelong obsession with the Boston Red Sox. Being on the phone with him as the 2004 World Series ended remains one of my most cherished memories. But it wasn't just the love of sports; it was the opportunity to play a wide range of them. Growing up, I tried soccer, baseball, swimming, and hockey. I didn't play organized basketball until high school, but despite—or, perhaps, because of—the many years of 4:30 AM wakeups for early morning ice time, there was little resistance when I informed them I enjoyed basketball more.

Speaking of enjoying basketball, for those who aren't familiar with Alaskan summers, daylight hours last late into the evening and sometimes the early morning. I've always appreciated my neighbors, Jan and the very sweet-shooting Michael Freeman, for putting up with my use of their driveway hoop for those extended hours.

At the same time, intellectualism, discovery, and discussion were far more valued by my parents than anything athletic. They still speak ruefully about the mistake they made in allowing me to take a class in formal logic in my early teens. It turns out that correctly identifying "Because I said so" as an appeal to authority doesn't negate the instruction to clean one's room. (Not for lack of trying on my part.) But as part of this process, they allowed and even enabled my growing obsession with the numbers of sports. *The Bill James Baseball Abstracts*, the highly amusing *Rotisserie League Baseball* (and later basketball) annuals, *Street & Smith's* guides. They didn't love video games, but I was allowed to play enough *RBI Baseball* to collect seasons' worth of hand-charted stats. Along with the father of my best friend at the time (probably more him than me, in retrospect), I created my first player rating system when I was around 12 years old to find out how the '86 Celtics would have fared against the '72 Lakers in the perfect simulation of *TV Sports Basketball*. It was not actually a very good simulation, but translating the player and team stats we had into Shooting-Passing-Defense-Rebounding-Quickness-Jumping, the six attributes available in the game, was a hell of a gateway drug.

For the mindset and basic intellectual tools to weigh and measure things, while also keeping in mind what *wasn't* being captured or measured, I'm thankful to the Department of Economics at Carleton College, especially Mark Kanazawa, for turning the light on; Michael Hemaseth, who I think still asks my then-roommate if I've finished my senior comps project yet; and H. Scott Bierman (now President of Beloit College), who not only literally wrote the book on game theory but was both the purest shooter and most incisive trash talker in the campus noonball games.

To Carleton's longtime men's basketball coach, Guy Kalland, for letting a skinny chucker with questionable commitment to defense hang around the team despite never having heard of me before I got to campus. I may not have played much in games, but I learned so much about how to actually play basketball and how to watch and analyze it after the fact.

To my teammates and friends from the world of Carleton hoops—especially Josh, Chris, Matt S, Matt T, Jordan, Andy, Eric, Ryan, Jim, Mike, Steve, and Scotty—for their lifelong friendship.

To the Carleton ultimate community: CUT remains a cornerstone of my life to this day, and I learned more about high-level competition there than in a lifetime of playing competitive sports up to that point. I have to single out my co-members of the Class of '99: Josh (again), Clay, Gus, Tomas, and Al. I still think we would have taken any CUT team before or since and you can't convince me otherwise. I also learned most of what I know about coaching because of the players on the 2002–04 teams who thought it was a good idea to put me in that role.

In the arena of basketball fandom and growth of understanding, I have to thank Dave Clark, Alex Rucker, and Keith Boyarsky for proving it is possible to discuss things intelligently on the Internet. Alex and Keith also demonstrated that it was possible to go from being just a dude on a message board to earning a spot in a front office. Without their practical example, I don't think I would have done the work which got me that opportunity.

On the writing side, I don't think I could keep my analytics cred without singling out Michael Lewis. Yes, yes, *Moneyball.* But also for conclusively demonstrating, not just in that book but even more so in his other writings, that even the densest and most technical of topics can be riveting reads if the story is well told.

On the complete other end of the spectrum, without Bethlehem Shoals (AKA Nathaniel Friedman) and the Free Darko collective, I don't know that I would have felt the freedom to think about basketball differently than the mainstream discourse. The "liberated fandom" aesthetic of Free Darko couldn't be more different than mine, but it wasn't the viewpoint per se as much as it was the permission *to have a viewpoint* about the game, how it worked, and what it meant.

Most writers suffer from crippling self-doubt; "Is this any good, and why the hell should anyone else care about about what I have to say?" Perhaps it doesn't speak well of me, but external validation was important-bordering-on-necessary for this to become A Thing for me. It meant the world to me that prominent voices like Chris Herring, Kevin Arnovitz, and Zach

Lowe gave me that encouragement early in the journey. Special thanks to Chris who, I know doesn't remember this, but took the time to compliment one of my earliest public metrics in a discussion on Twitter.

Thanks to Tim Bontemps for dropping everything to write the foreword for this book, as well as for his constant friendship during this wild journey through the NBA world.

As it moved from a hobby to a profession, thanks to Ian Levy and Matt Moore for creating the platform of Nylon Calculus, and also for not picking *The Midrange Theory* as the website's name. Having that in the back pocket certainly made picking the title for this book easier. Thanks to Neil Greenberg for giving me my first regular paid gig at the *Washington Post's* "Fancy Stats" blog, and thanks to Patrick Hruby for all the editing which made the stories I published at Vice Sports the tightest, best work I've done, certainly before and likely since.

In terms of the stupefying opportunity of working in the NBA, I wasn't privy to the discussions which led the Milwaukee Bucks to hire me, but in some measure and in alphabetical order, I have to thank Michael Clutterbuck, John Hammond, Alex Lasry, and Justin Zanik. It's still a little unbelievable to me that basketball is not just an obsession but a profession, so thanks, guys.

From my time at the Bucks, I have to thank not just Clutterbuck, but Faizan Subhani, Ashley Brio, and Mason Yahr for teaching me a lot about actually doing a data science. I'm continually indebted to Drew Franklin and Ronald Dupree, who did and do more than anyone to remind me about the people side of this game and business. I also have to shout out the 2018–19 film room, AKA "The VR-5," for the hours of collaboration, discussion, and comradeship. Zach Peterson, Blaine Mueller, Schuyler Rimmer, Ryan Frazier, and Wes Bohn, that was a special group. Congrats to Blaine and Schuy and everyone else at the Bucks for the chip.

I'm continually indebted to Drew Franklin, who did and does more than anyone to remind me about the people side of this game and business.

Getting back into the public writing and analysis space, thanks to Kevin Pelton, Ben Taylor, and Ben Falk for being lively discussion partners and inspirations for ideas. Thanks to Nate Duncan, Danny Leroux, and Dan

Feldman for the constant discussion and putting up with my "someone is wrong on the Internet" rants more times than I can count.

In writing this book, thanks to Eric Nehm, Mike Prada, Sean Highkin, Derek James, Jordan White, Amin Vafa, Kirk Henderson, Jared Dubin, Curtis Harris, and Matt Moore for all the feedback and help turning my stream of discursive consciousness into at least a semi-coherent narrative. Thanks to Randy Sherman and Mike Beuoy for pitching in on some of the graphics; to Andrew Patton, Kostya Medvedovsky, and Nathan Walker for help with coding and data issues; and to Ryan Davis and Darryl Blackport for the service they provide the analytics community with NBAShotCharts. com and PBPStats.com. Special thanks for Owen Phillips for coming up with a theme for the tables and teaching me the GT package so I could figure out how to use them.

Thanks to Dan Rosenbaum, Joe Sill, and Justin Jacobs for helping keep me from getting out over my skis when discussing technical aspects of adjusted plus/minus models, where, on my own, I know just enough to get myself in a lot of trouble.

Thanks to first Brian Kopp at STATS, Inc./SportVU and Rajiv Maheswaran, Mike D'Auria, and Matt Redfield of Second Spectrum for all the looks behind the tracking data curtain over the years. Cheers to Evan Wasch, Sydney Sarachek, Charlie Rohlf, Patrick Harrel, and Hao Meng at the NBA league office for letting me stay informed about how the league is advancing in the analytics. Also, apologies to Evan for the jokes on Twitter.

Shout out to Cory Jez, quote machine and good friend.

Thanks to my unofficial agent and Milwaukee goodwill ambassador C.J. Krawczyk and my actual agent, Steven Malk of Writer's House, for helping this project come together.

Special thanks to C.J. and the rest of the Bucks superfan crew—Andy M., Andy S., Jimmy Jumbotron, and wrestling Andy (Mondo Lucha forever)—for welcoming me into the community and making Milwaukee feel like home almost instantly.

Love to all the analysts and researchers working around the league, some of whom talked to me for this project, all of whom have formed a supportive community. I won't name most of them to protect the guilty, but I will single out Katherine Evans, Nick Restifo, Aaron Blackshear, and Layne Vashro for being friends, confidants, and occasional post-publication fact-checkers.

Thanks to the folks at The Athletic, especially Alex Mather and Adam Hansmann for giving me the platform to allow people to be interested enough in what I have to say for this project to be possible. Even more thanks to all my editors at The Athletic—Tyler Batiste, Bobby Clay, Or Moyal, Rob Peterson, and Khalid Salaam—for helping teach me how to write again. I'm eternally indebted to Sergio Gonzalez, the best, most nurturing and encouraging boss one could ever hope to have. Collectively, they made it possible for me to have the space to write this while also keeping the regular content train on the tracks as that process was happening.

Thanks to Alison Lukan, Michael Lopez, Chris Watkins, and Rochelle Lindsay for always reminding me that analytics isn't just about wins and losses, but people and voices as well.

To Dave DuFour and Mo Dakhil for gabbing with me every week and then allowing our conversations to be recorded and heard by other people. Maybe someday Mo will accept that the Elam Ending is actually good.

Thanks to the folks at Triumph Books, especially Josh Williams for convincing me I should write a book and Adam Motin for shepherding me through the process.

Finally, to my children, Reilly and Bruce, for mostly understanding. And especially to my best friend, Maia, who is the real writer in the family.

I'm not sure there are enough words to express the gratitude for Maia's sacrifice in letting me chase the sports pipe dream, and for seeing that some of this was going to happen long before I did. This was never really our plan, but you rolled with it better than anyone would have any right to expect.

S.P. July 2021